Persian Architecture

Arthur Upham Pope

Persian Architecture

The Triumph of Form and Color

George Braziller, New York

Color Plates IV–VI, VIII–XV, XVII–XX, XXIII–XXVI, XXXI–XXXIII
Copyright © 1965 Hans C. and Sonia P. Seherr-Thoss

Copyright © 1965 GEORGE BRAZILLER, INC.
All rights reserved.
For information address the publisher
George Braziller, Inc.
Number One Park Avenue, New York 16, New York

Library of Congress Catalog Card Number: 65–10275

Printed in the United States of America

Contents

To Mildred and Robert Wood Bliss, champions of excellence

Preface

This book aims to present the architecture of Persia factually but primarily as a fine art; to trace its long history of varied but continuous development; to discuss the intrinsic value of its forms and color; and to establish its definite and permanent motivations in Persian environment, character, and religion. Its scope is to evoke a heightened appreciation of the meaning and effect of the monuments discussed.

The Islamic architecture of Persia is a relatively recent field for scholarship because the important monuments were mosques and shrines from which non-Muslims (even non-Shi'as) were rigidly excluded. As these religious buildings occupied long-sanctified sites, much early history was also concealed within them. Thanks to the bold decision of His Imperial Majesty, Reza Shah, contrary to theological proscriptions and popular misgivings, and acting on the recommendation of H. E. Hussein Ala, permission was given to enter the mosques and other sacred buildings of Persia. M. André Godard, as resident Chef du Service d'Antiquités, undertook an exhaustive series of detailed monographs that have provided valuable material for all subsequent studies. Eric Schroeder of the Iranian Institute of New York, Dr. Donald Wilber, Ernst Herzfeld and many others followed with special studies. In the study of pre-Islamic Persian civilizations, Dr. Roman Ghirshman has provided invaluable material. To all of these scholars and to the numerous others who worked with me in preparing the Survey of Persian Art, *I am greatly indebted. My own extensive travels in Persia, which continued until 1939, and the study made possible in the course of these expeditions, certainly form the basis of both my enthusiasm and scholarship.*

The problem of transliteration does not permit of a wholly satisfactory solution. In this volume the system developed by E. Denison Ross, used in the Survey of Persian Art, *has been followed. However, in those cases where names have recently become familiar to English-speaking readers under a different spelling, this familiar one has been adopted. For a detailed explanation of the system, see p. xix of the* Survey.

My obligations are many and too diffuse for full acknowledgment. I want to thank particularly H. H. Merdad Pahlabad, especially in arranging for a team of photographers, Dr. Assad Behroozan and Mr. Kermani, to obtain color transparencies in many parts of Persia. My gratitude is also due Mr. and Mrs. Hans Seherr-Thoss for a special trip through Persia and Afghanistan to obtain further views of high quality. To Mr. Robert Payne I am grateful for his invaluable criticism of an early draft of the manuscript. And above all I am indebted to Mrs. Daniel Robbins, the editor of this book, for her painstaking hard work, sympathetic understanding, useful suggestions, and angelic patience.

Arthur Upham Pope
Warren, Connecticut
June, 1964.

List of Color Plates

I

II

III

IV

V

VI

VII

VIII

Introduction: General Considerations

Architecture in Persia has a continuous history of more than 6,000 years, from at least 5000 B.C. to the present, with characteristic examples distributed over a vast area from Syria to North India and the borders of China, from the Caucasus to Zanzibar. Persian buildings vary from peasant huts, tea-houses and garden pavilions to some of the most beautiful and majestic structures the world has ever seen, not to mention some stately and audacious bridges. Throughout its long history the characteristic feature has been simple and noble forms richly embellished.

In meaning and purpose, monumental Persian architecture was primarily religious; at the beginning, magical and invocational in character. The guiding, formative motif was cosmic symbolism by which man was brought into communication and participation with the powers of Heaven. This theme, shared by virtually all Asia and persisting even into modern times, not only gave unity and continuity to the architecture of Persia but was a primary source of its emotional character as well.

Available building materials dictated major forms. Heavy clays, readily available at various places, encouraged the development of the most primitive of all building techniques, *pisé*—molded mud, compressed as solidly as possible and allowed to dry. This technique, used in Iran from ancient times, has never been completely abandoned. The abundance of heavy plastic earth, in conjunction with a tenacious lime mortar, also facilitated the development of brick. The earliest bricks, though only sun-dried, when faced provided a durable building material and were utilized in various important structural forms. To be sure, both stone and wood were sometimes used—in the great Achaemenid monuments and for basement courses and bridges—but even under the Parthians and Sasanians rubble masonry was more common. Such masonry as well as brick construction is more rapidly and easily worked. Brick construction lacks the sharp contours, the effects of hardness and weight normal to stone masonry, but on the other hand it permits large, well-defined masses whose broad plain surfaces invite ornamentation that would be inappropriate or even impossible on stone. Like materials, techniques also varied, ranging from the shabby and loosely built to such superb structures as the Mausoleum of Oljeitu, the north dome of the Masjid-i-Jami of Isfahan, and some ingenious and durable vaults.

For more than 3,000 years, certain design elements of Persian architecture persisted. The most striking were a marked feeling for scale and a discerning use of simple and massive forms, a rather amazing consistency of decorative preferences, the high-arched portal set within a recess, columns with bracket capitals, and recurrent types of plan and elevation. Through the ages, these elements recurred in completely different types of buildings constructed for various programs and under the patronage of a long succession of rulers.[1] Indeed, some of the earliest styles still survive. The columned porch, or *talar*, revealed in the rock-cut tombs near Persepolis, reappeared in Sasanian temples, and in late Islamic times it was used as the portico of a palace or mosque[2] and adapted even to the architecture of roadside tea-houses. Similarly, the dome on four arches, so characteristic of Sasanian times, is still to be found in many cemeteries and in the little Imamzada tombs scattered through the countryside. Even the vast ovoid arch of Ctesiphon was an archetype which may still recur in a twentieth century farm building.[3] The four-ivan court, anticipated in Parthian times, became a thoroughly established and dominant form even before the tenth century. The notion of earthly towers reaching up toward the sky to mingle with the divine towers of Heaven lasted through the nineteenth century,[4] while the interior court and pool, the angled entrance and extensive decoration are ancient but still common features.

Persian architecture maintained a continuity that, although frequently retarded or temporarily diverted by internal conflicts or foreign intrusion, nonetheless achieved a style that could hardly be mistaken for any other. This is true even though detail was varied as circumstances and need dictated. Scale was consistently understood and skillfully exploited even though the Persians, unlike the Greeks, seem to have made no general study of harmonious proportions. The result is that there are no trivial buildings; even garden pavilions have nobility and dignity, and the humblest caravanserais generally have charm. In expressiveness and communicability, most Persian buildings are lucid—even eloquent. The combination of intensity and simplicity of form provides immediacy, while ornament and, often, subtle proportions reward sustained observation.

Most structures are simple in mass and contour, conveying, from a distance, a spirit of repose and assurance. This mood is much appreciated by Persians, especially when it is com-

10

bined with the controlled excitement that is provided by vast areas of richly colored, intricate ornament which invite leisurely exploration. This combination of stimulation and repose is characteristic of the Persian aesthetic experience. The great friezes at Persepolis and the encrustation of superb faience, as at Mashhad, are infinitely fascinating and absorbing in detail. When viewed as a whole, however, their details are subdued and absorbed by the overall rhythm of their quiet dignity.

A sumptuous and intensely developed surface ornament was an essential, happily renewed with fresh invention in every period.[5] Architectural ornament was almost wholly abstract, excepting only a few figural murals and calligraphic inscriptions, and even these inscriptions are notable as pure design. Yet this ornament in its range of styles, use of materials, pattern types, expressiveness, impact and intellectual subtlety is quite extraordinary. Sometimes, of course, inventiveness flagged; repetition, over-subtlety and fatiguing detail mark such periods of temporary impoverishment. But, with few interruptions, fascinating decorative brick lays— plain or enameled—and carved and polychromed stucco in ever new forms continued from ancient times; enameled tile—plain, painted or mosaic—has been used since the twelfth century. These elements were not merely repeated, for there was resourceful development of them all until a general cultural recession in the eighteenth century.

In most periods, ornamentation utilized rich and varied color, attaining in Islamic times an intensity and harmony that have never been equaled. This passion for color was favored by the landscape. Much of Iran for many months of each year is bleak and dreary, only to become in the springtime suddenly radiant with flowers; mountainsides are vivid tapestries, meadows vast expanses of thick bloom, valleys deep pools of enamel-brilliant blossoms. The desert—sterile, hostile, awesome—intensified appreciation of the garden with its foliage, fountains, security, and abundance. This vision of *Paradaiza*[6] permeated all thinking, all arts, and even daily speech; floral abundance became a sacred symbol of life and happiness to be exploited on every occasion and in every way. It was thus natural to seek to preserve in more permanent form the transient beauty of the garden.[7]

In addition to the influence of climate, available material, religious purpose and peripheral cultures, the patron also played a decisive role in the development of architecture. Great monuments were regarded as both the prerogative and duty of the ruler.[8] Darius and Xerxes, Chosroes II, Ghazan Khan, Timur, Mahmud of Ghazna, Shah Abbas, all committed the nation's resources as well as their own talents to building. Prime ministers, too, were responsible for many fine monuments: to Nizam al-mulk, the great Seljuk vizier, and to his rival Taj al-mulk we owe great eleventh century sanctuaries at Isfahan and the famous madrassa at Baghdad, both men formulating reasoned statements on behalf of a robust and enduring architecture. Similarly, in the fourteenth century Rashid ad-din and his rival Taj ad-din Ali Shah created magnificent structures at Tabriz and Sultaniya.

For the caravanserais, bridges, bazaars, libraries, tombs and gardens, local rulers, merchants and philanthropists—not infrequently women—were liberal patrons. Their great buildings were personal monuments, demonstrations of power, personality, rivalries, taste and status. It is not surprising then to discover the important role played by tombs in Persian architecture, a role so vital that sometimes a ruler's first act on ascending the throne was to begin planning his imposing mausoleum, perhaps as a valid claim to immortality.

The landscape itself—huge snow-capped mountains, valleys large as provinces, wide shining plains—required constructions conceived and executed in terms of grandeur. In such a setting, where ordinary buildings would seem but trifles, a feeling for scale, boldly used, was indispensable. The overwhelming character of the natural world offered still further suggestion: the world of and beyond the sky was the primal reality to the early peoples of West Asia. From that realm came the life-sustaining rains and the fructifying power of the sun. The unfaltering regularity of the constellations proclaimed a planned universe of ordered movement and fixed points, marking time, measuring distance and direction, and was conducive to reflection and mathematical thinking. Man was always conscious of his dependence on the powers of that heaven and his chief end was to achieve contact with the ultimate powers, through reverence, obedience and participation. This engendered a constant and potent sense of urgency.

It was the permanent office of architecture, both physically and symbolically, to bridge the awesome gap between the material world and the heavens by means of structures that reached toward the sky. In later periods, the vault of heaven was reproduced by magnificent domes, permanently supplementing the magic ritual that sought always the gifts of fertility, abundance, and power. According to the earliest myth, preserved for us in Sumerian, the elemental act of creation was the emergence of the mountain from the primal waters. This implies a continuing effort upward: effective worship demanded a high place which, leaving the earth behind and below, attained by proximity communication with celestial powers. The mountain—towering, yet stable—promised access to the Above and "was the habitual setting in which the super-human is manifest."[9]

From the mountain emerges the sustaining force of life and in winter, when a threatening semi-death settles over the land, or in summer, when the vegetation wilts during the equally destructive power of heat, it is the mountain that holds promise of renewal. Within the mountain are conserved the vital forces of nature, and on its beneficent outpouring of water depends all of human life. When the earth is blighted by heat or drought and the gods of fertility have disappeared, it is natural to think that they have withdrawn into the mountain. These imprisoned powers must be released so that the earth may be renewed and life resumed.

This almost universal belief (particularly widespread in the Near East) expresses a basic physical fact: certain cultures are mountain-derived. Where rainfall is deficient, the mountain, gathering snow or moisture from clouds, becomes the great reservoir. If there is any security in these regions, the mountain provides it. This beneficence is not a single occurrence, but a renewable and variable blessing which man must invoke. The symbolic character of the mountain and its crucial role in the maintenance of fertility and life continue throughout the entire history of Persian architecture, sometimes in specific symbols, sometimes in more subtle forms, and commonly in the use of ornament clearly evocative of vegetation.

An important feature of this mountain concept necessarily involves the entrance. Clefts and deep ravines lead into its very heart, and it is through these openings that the god recedes or emerges at the vital moment of renewal. Hence, in early representations of the mountain,[10] this entrance is indicated by a double recessed panel symbolically marking the sacred spot where the forces of heaven are in contact with the earth. In the earliest temples or ziggurats, which in their form and meaning represent the mountain, this niche, this gate to the divine world, is represented by the great outer portals. They mark the first step in the transition from the outer world of fact to the inner world of godly power.

The sacred inner spot, which in the ziggurats marked the point where contact was made between heaven and earth, survived in the pavilions which stood before the throne halls of the Assyrian and Achaemenid temples. It reappeared in the Sasanian fire temples as the inner recess accessible only to the guardian priests, and was again used in the Islamic mihrabs—those recessed arches pointing to the holy city of Mecca—and in mosque portals,[11] which are essentially symbols that transcend the less important reality of the mere physical structure behind them.

From Zoroastrian times, the beautiful was integrally associated with light. It was an essential component of divine personality, identified with the mind and with the good, opposed in every way to the dark, evil and disorderly. Physical light in Persia—intense, palpable, creative—persuasively expounds the role conferred on it by religion. In Persian art, both lightness and clarity are sought and, conversely, the obscure and confused are abjured. Persian ornament of all periods, no matter how elaborate, reveals a basic organization that is rational and precise.

Considerations of practical utility and invocational symbolism were supplemented and controlled by the Persian love of beauty in all forms. This instinctive joy, despite eloquent pessimism, is revealed in a thousand years of superior poetry, in pottery which challenges that of China and Greece, in metalwork, and in an unequaled mastery of carpet weaving, not to mention miniature painting and other arts of the book, as well as supreme designs for carved stucco, calligraphy, and faience tile. Moreover, this love of beauty existed in all classes and we find the humblest tools executed with an often touching taste. That beauty itself was significant, that it was an essential to be cherished and conserved, that, in truth, beauty was an attribute of the Divine, were universally accepted principles confirmed by deeds.[12] "God hath planted beauty in our midst like a flag in the city," wrote the mystic poet Shabistari in the fourteenth century, and—according to Zoroastrian theory—Yima, the first man, "made the earth in fairness like unto the House of Song."[13]

I. From the Earliest Civilizations to the Fall of the Achaemenids

The name Iran means "Land of the Aryans" and derives from the tribes which settled on the Iranian plateau and either drove out or completely dominated the earlier inhabitants. The Iranian plateau is the site of early highland settlements which date back some 10,000 years. Evidently the earliest known populations of this prehistoric Persia were distributed in widely scattered small villages. Over a long period of time a common environment had exerted pressure toward similar responses and out of these responses developed parallel customs, beliefs and institutions. As these cultural units emerged from primitive stages of hunting and food-gathering, they became less self-sufficient, more interdependent. Relations with the more rapidly developing Mesopotamian plain, though warlike, gradually became more and more fruitful. The religious motives so vital to architecture may have originated on the plateau, then been transmitted to the lowlands where they matured and subsequently returned to the Iranians of the plateau.

Out of these processes, content developed and maturity evolved. Temporal priority, as well as artistic superiority, has been claimed for the Iranian plateau peoples of this time, whose farming hamlets—small houses with stone in the foundations, walls, and beaten floors— dating from 8000–6000 B.C., have been disclosed by expeditions of the University of Chicago directed by Professor Braidwood. Although these humble structures could hardly be classed as architecture, they were its necessary predecessors.[14]

The cultural priority of these plateau peoples is also indicated by the painted pottery, houses, and figurines developed at Sialk in the fifth millennium, and, still earlier, at Adab. By the fourth millennium, painted pottery was advanced in its ceramic technique which produced thin and hard objects, as well as in its aesthetic and imaginative decoration. The ornamentation

14

of these early vessels exhibits a well-defined theory of the natural processes: symbolic figures which are clear, specific and consistent, are invocations for water and fertility.[15] The qualities and superiorities shown in this prehistoric art—lucidity, elegance, fertile decorative imagination —persisted as permanent features in all Persian art.

The earliest known phases of building in Iran are, for the most part, in the western valleys or occasionally a little to the east of the Zagros Mountains. These were all early neolithic communities. Thus at Ali Kosh, in the Deh Suran Valley, which is considered a continuation of Iranian Khuzistan, are remains of large houses on a level datable *circa* 6200–5800 B.C. These were built of handmade bricks. The rooms were quite spacious (10 x 16 feet) and in several instances a carefully made cooking pit was sunk into the floor; for example, a circular pit about 3 feet in diameter, the sides sloping out towards the bottom, was lined with white mud bricks surfaced with clay. In some instances there were indications that the floors also had been clay surfaced. Both the building bricks, which are gray, and the special white bricks had been made from local mud cut into approximate rectangles and sun-dried.

Evidences of very early competent building and painted pottery discovered at Jarmo (*circa* 6500 B.C.) and Hasuna (*circa* 6000 B.C.), just over the mountains in northern Mesopotamia, at Tepe Gawra (*circa* 4500 B.C.), in sight of the Zagros Mountains in northeastern Mesopotamia, point toward a similarity of culture existing along the line of the mountain range. All were settled "from a mountainous land to the east," which could only have been Persia.

One of the most interesting structures known in that "mountainous land" itself was at Sialk, dating from the fifth millennium B.C. The oldest settlement there, from earlier in the fifth millennium, evidently consisted only of huts made of tree branches, though the inhabitants were practicing rudimentary garden culture and had domesticated oxen and sheep. Moreover, they produced for themselves three types of handmade pottery, all of which shows efforts toward artistic values, however rudimentary. One type has the surface blackened, another is red, and the third has rudimentary painting with lines and streaks of black.[16] It was in the next stage that building began, with handmade mud brick: an oval lump of earth shaped by hand and dried in the sun. Even at this stage, however, thought was given to improving structural technique, for on the edges of these bricks are hollows, made by a thumbprint, in order to hold an extra depth of the mud used as mortar. At this time also, rudimentary architectural decoration was introduced and the walls of rooms were painted red with iron oxide mixed in fruit juice. The modern brick— rectangular, flat-sided, made in a mold—appeared in the fourth millennium, and apparently was also an Iranian invention.

1. Ziggurat of Choga Zambil, *circa* 1250 B.C. Plan.
2. Ziggurat of Choga Zambil. Girshman reconstruction.
3. Ziggurat of Choga Zambil. Portal.

The temple at Tepe Gawra (northeastern Mesopotamia, *circa* 4000 B.C.) shows architectural feeling in the well-marked but rudimentary portal, and in the precise correspondence of the interior panels and external buttresses. Moreover, the primitive color of earlier buildings, typically solid red, is here expanded and enriched by reddish brown, purple and some scarlet.

The creation in Mesopotamia of great cities after the mid-third millennium marked an important advance in civilization. These urban centers displaced the earlier meager farming communities as sources of progress. They were great in both extent and population, with complex administration, legal codes, highly diversified functions and active trade with other communities. Such contacts were a source of both economic enrichment and cultural stimulation, and out of them developed both new intellectual efforts and artistic attainments which were transmitted to Iran.

Architecture shared in these advances. The outstanding achievements were the great ziggurats, elaborate palaces and temples, the latter well exemplified at Warka. Exterior walls were variegated by alternating salients and channels, while piers were enriched with colored ornament. This ornamentation was made in a curious mosaic technique: hard earthen cones with colored circular bases were pushed into the plaster while it was still wet and soft, the varicolored bases, flush with the wall surface making polychrome designs, notably chevron patterns. In some cases, as at Al Uqair, *circa* 3500 B.C., piers were fluted and interiors were painted not merely in solid colors but with murals of boldly treated animals.

As we have seen, there existed throughout the ancient Near East a tendency to admire and worship the mountain form. The huge ziggurats which relieved the flat monotony of the Mesopotamian plain were but ritual imitations of the familiar sacred mountains which ring the Iranian Plateau. Thus, even if the impressive development of these colossal structures was Mesopotamian (ziggurats already being built in Sumer by about 2200 B.C.), their inspiration and meaning was clearly Persian. The great ziggurat of Enlil in Ur was called the "bond between heaven and earth," and Ninhursag, the Great Mother Goddess who was the source of all life, was called the "Lady of the Mountains." The men who came down from eastern lands could not bring with them their mountains, so they made their own and by naming them "The Holy Hill" or "The Mountain of all Lands," they indicated a supernatural status not conditioned by time or place— or realism. Their ultimate purpose "to reach the sky" was expressed in the very meaning of the word ziggurat: literally "an up-reaching finial."[17] The ziggurat is such a frequently found monument that it seems possible that every city was dominated by its own.[18] If these mountain replicas were to be effective, they not only had to be massive and high but also to be infused with beauty and interest, thus reinforcing theology with man's innate need for ornamentation. Indeed, in the course of their development ziggurats came to include all feasible decorative treatments: cone mosaics, colored and glazed bricks.

The Elamites,[19] the original inhabitants of the Persian region which corresponds to present-day Khuzistan and whose first kingdom dates from the third millennium, provided the link

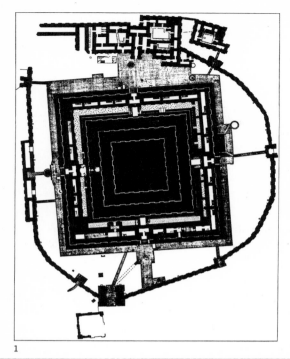

1

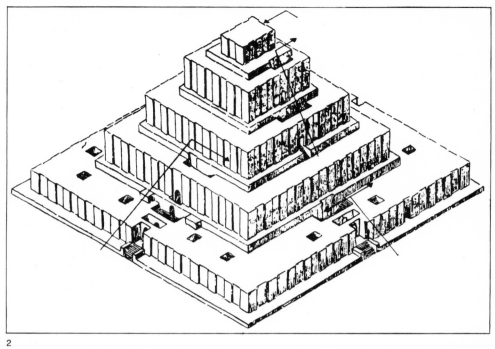

2

3

between Iran and Sumer. The Mesopotamian lowland intruded into the Persian territory, thus facilitating communication. A variety of excavations record frequent contact between the Elamites and their Sumerian neighbors to the west, to whom they were frequently subject. On occasion, however, they were strong enough to assert their independence and even to wreak destruction on their former masters, as in the destruction of Ur in 2025 B.C. Perhaps the greatest of all ziggurats is the Elamite structure of Choga Zambil. This earliest known Iranian monument of imposing dimensions and character rivals the pyramids of Egypt. It is an impressive witness to the passionate fervor accorded to the mountain form. Built at Dur Untashi, a city near Susa, by Untash-gal, King of Elam, about 1250 B.C., it was dedicated to the great god Inshushinak, whose name means "Lord of Susa"[20] and who was symbolized by the animal form of a bull.

Figs. 1-3   In a flat region close to the Mesopotamian plain, the ziggurat of Choga Zambil is an imposing artificial mountain—not merely heaped earth, but a planned complex which represents structural competence, immense effort sustained over a long period of time, great cost and a deep emotional commitment. In size it is huge: 165 feet high and 345 feet square at the base. It is the central feature in a sacred enclosure some 1,300 feet square, surrounded by two walls. Within this enclosure there were also included three temples with several courts paved with fired brick, sanctuaries and storage space. The storage chambers, in which were found important objects such as weapons and vases, had walls of crude brick on a bed of fired brick.

The ziggurat, which served as both temple and tomb, is composed of five separately built concentric towers of varying heights, the innermost and tallest of which was 115 feet square at its base and 160 feet high. Its four monumental portals, vaulted with tightly fitted brickwork, are 25 feet high. They lead into a complex of chambers, some over 50 feet long, tombs, tunnels, arches, stairways and drains. A temple crowned the flat top of the monument. The walls of the ziggurat, largely of sun-dried brick bonded with cement and bitumen, were extensively faced with glazed kiln-fired brick, blue and green in color and of a metallic shimmer. Inlaid ivory mosaics were also used and wooden doors were decorated with opaque glass mosaics which depicted prancing animals. Architectural details were rendered in glazed terra-cotta.[21]

More conventional architecture was developing everywhere. At Susa, the Elamite capital, three quite elaborate palaces[22] can be dated slightly prior to 1000 B.C., although the use of the site goes back to 4000 B.C. It is clear from the plan of one of these palaces that the same architect also designed the great palace of the Assyrian king, Esarhaddon. Elamite architecture was generally built of unfired brick, with red bricks used for revetment. By the twelfth century B.C. glazed bricks were used for decoration, blue and green at Choga Zambil and blue and yellow at Susa. The known Elamite architecture, in addition to the great ziggurat, includes temples built on huge platforms. The interior space was either a square or rectangular sanctuary, while the temples were sometimes more than one story high, covered with a wooden roof supported on brick columns. At Susa, some vaults of the Elamite apadana are 16 to 26 feet across. Although little detail remains of these Elamite buildings, the sophistication and taste achieved by this

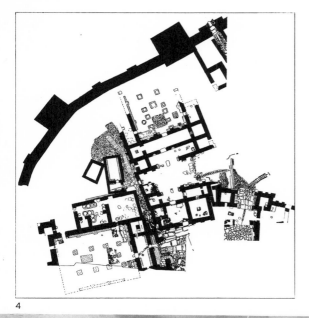

4

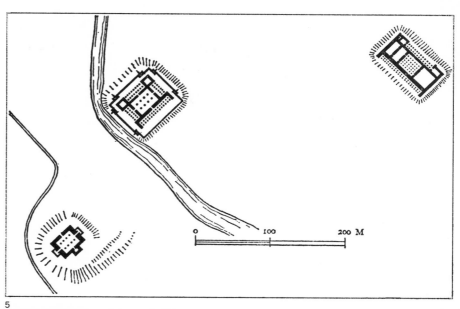

5

6

7

8

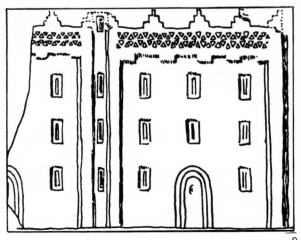

9

10

people is evidenced in sculpture which was by no means completely stylized; in fact, some superb examples show an amazing sensitivity to nature and individual expression.[23]

From about 800 B.C. a new world power was forming itself on the Iranian plateau and its mountainous western borders. In this region massive migrations took place, small nomadic groups moved about, and even the sharply individualized mountain tribes insulated by protective valleys, peoples living in fortified cities or in scattered villages, were at times temporarily united in the face of a common peril—aggression from Babylon and Assyria. It was from these diverse peoples that the Medes finally emerged as the dominant power, eventually winning their independence from Assyria and in 612 B.C. actually taking Nineveh. In the late seventh century, their king, Cyaxares, chose Ecbatana (modern Hamadan) as his capital.

By the ninth and eighth centuries, in northwestern Persia and eastern Anatolia, an interesting and influential stone and brick architecture developed. Assyrian pictorial carvings and inscriptions give us information of this highly developed culture and its architectural expression. Cities were protected by double, even triple, stone walls 12 feet thick and 40 feet high, which were further defended by ditches. The massiveness of these fortified walls can be seen here in the upper left of the plan of the ninth century fortress of Hasanlu. Irrigation was provided by canals, _{Fig. 4} some very large, strengthened by masonry. Gardens, groves and vineyards were abundant. Buildings, largely made of wood, seem to have been square, towerlike structures, with wooden columns which may have been tree trunks. Cyclopaean stone walls were topped with high towers that had a slight overhang, suggestive of machicolations. A town was often built against a hillside, sometimes against carved out solid rock, leveled where necessary and extended with terraces and masonry substructures. Aqueducts and stairways were constructed of huge stone blocks. Religious buildings, however, were conspicuously different, steeply gabled, with large columns forming a portico. A building of this type, as at Musasir, was "almost the exact picture _{Fig. 10} of a Greek temple long before there was anything like it in Greece."[24]

These buildings, with their alternating courses of black basalt and white limestone, multicolored pavements, lofty pillars of cypress, exposed beams plated with gold and other metals, must have been extremely handsome. It seems probable that lapis lazuli may also have been used as architectural embellishment, for the Assyrians recorded their capture of ten tons of that precious substance in one Medean town. A building depicted on an Urartean bronze from _{Fig. 9} Toprak Kale in the Van region, shows a wide decorative cornice that might well have contained color. Some forty Urartean fortresses that have been found within thirty-five miles of Lake Van are proof of the immense building activity of the region.

Migrant Persian tribes coming from the north and east settled in this northwestern district of Persia for some time and from these buildings of the ninth and eighth centuries B.C. they acquired architectural techniques and a sense of style. These important cultural acquisitions they carried with them to their final home in south Persia, where their influence was seen first as Masjid-i-Suleiman and then Persepolis and Susa.[25]

21

The Achaemenids

By 560 B.C., two powerful Aryan states, Media and Persia, were confederated, thus beginning the Persian Empire. This occurred when Cyrus the Great, the first Achaemenid, dethroned his grandfather Astyages, the reigning Mede. Because of two extraordinary men, Cyrus and later Darius I, the whole of Western Asia was conquered and organized into the world's first great empire—an empire which lasted for two hundred and thirty years. From the Nile to the Oxus, from the Aegean to the Ganges, a new epoch was initiated, an unaccustomed stability was assured; good government was imposed and a network of efficient communications encouraged commerce and produced immense wealth. The Achaemenid Royal Road from Susa to Sardis covered over 1,600 miles and, with one hundred and eleven stations for caravans, it enabled transportation of goods throughout the empire in less than ninety days; dispatches covered the route in a mere week. The routes from Susa to Persepolis and from Susa to Ecbatana were even paved!

The remarkable Achaemenid achievements were due not merely to courage, strength and enterprise, but also to superior intelligence: a capacity for large-scale planning and practical administrative ability. These capacities were reinforced, moreover, by humane sympathies, products of a noble faith that inspired racial, religious and cultural tolerance, in which a highly developed sense of justice played an important role. Doubtless the security offered by nearly two hundred years of relative peace—at least peace from major aggression—strengthened the support given to Cyrus and his successors by such a varied group of subject peoples.

Figs. 5-7 Cyrus and Darius must have contemplated their achievements with the deepest emotion, not just elation over battles won or the stimulus of power and wealth acquired, but an intense realization that most of the then known world had been brought under one rule. It had been organized into a new kind of state, one unprecedented in size, strength, economic resources and —most significant—imbued with a new character of spiritual and ethical values. Aware that nothing comparable had ever before been accomplished, they acknowledged in their inscriptions that they had been so empowered only by the grace of Ahura Mazda, the great God.

As the first expression of political power and divine sanction, about 550 B.C. Cyrus began construction of the complex of palaces and temples at Pasargadae, in the southern province of Fars. Construction was thus begun while Cyrus was still, in effect, a vassal of the Medes, but in an inscription on a tall stele he announced himself as "The King, an Achaemenid." This first imperial focus defined the Achaemenid architectural style and clearly reveals its sources. A huge artificial platform with enormous stone revetments and the use of tall slender stone or wooden columns recall northern practices. There were three palace buildings, each enclosed by its own large masonry wall. Its size tells the imperial story: the central room of the main audience hall or temple (political and religious functions were intermingled) covered an area 230 feet by 131 feet, and there were other rooms half as large. This main building was square and probably had an entrance on each side; the other buildings were rectangular. Black and white, strikingly combined, as well as rich polychromy (some of the wooden columns were painted blue, green, red,

22

and yellow) and impressive use of precious metal plating, all emphasized that this was a city apart, the focus of royal and sacred power. For the holy fire, there was a square tower, now ruined. This tower seems to have been very like the tower at Naqsh-i-Rustam, a similarity which emphasizes how ancient was the history of the fire-worshipping cult.[26] Fig. 8

It was here, at Pasargadae, in a gabled temple recalling early ziggurats and the temple at Musasir, that Cyrus the Great was buried. Around the structure were free-standing columns, perhaps representing the sacred grove, and a simple portal marking the entrance to the sacred area. Cyrus' temple-tomb crowns six stages which decrease in height as they progress upward: a miniature ziggurat, potent beyond any considerations of dimension. Evidently, even for the first great Achaemenid, the mountain and its symbolic form was as essential as in Mesopotamia. The tomb's dimensions are modest, compared with later Achaemenid structures, but its true scale can be sensed when one realizes that the lowest "step" or base course is in fact higher than a standing man. It was built before Cyrus' death in 529 B.C. and, although he died in battle far to the northeast, his body was brought back for burial in this previously prepared tomb. With the exception of this single enduring structure, Pasargadae is now largely in ruins, providing little hint of how it must once have appeared. Occupying a beautiful expanse of park-like meadow, it was in fact rather like a nomad camp, with its various elements widely scattered.[27] Fig. 11

The establishment at Pasargadae, imposing though it must have been in many respects, was not adequate as the capital city of a rapidly expanding empire nor as an expression of newly won imperial glory. Too open and too low to be easily defended, it was also inconveniently located away from main routes. Cyrus must have been aware of these factors and probably selected the Persepolis site before construction was actually undertaken there in about 518 B.C., for planning and preliminary work were extensive and difficult.[28] It is possible that the great political capital at Susa was also planned by Cyrus, for the great palace at Susa was built by Darius I just prior to construction of the Apadana at Persepolis. Because Persepolis was the religious capital, it indeed seems logical that a political center would have been conceived at the same time, although it is not specifically recorded that Cyrus had anything to do with either site.

Apart from such speculations, however, we know that by 521, Darius I, having succeeded Cambyses II, decided to build a great working capital at Susa, leaving Persepolis to be developed as a national shrine, as the spiritual focus of the nation rather than its administrative center.[29] Susa, the ancient capital of Elam, was a familiar site (although the palaces and temples of the Elamites had been ruined by the sack of the city by Ashurbanipal in the ninth century B.C.[30]) and was conveniently served by four rivers. It is difficult today to imagine how an imperial capital could have been maintained at Susa, where the heat for seven months of the year is almost insupportable. Dr. Ghirshman, who has spent a great deal of time at Susa in the course of many excavations, states that simply with the introduction of irrigation and the growing of crops permitted by this innovation, the incredible heat has been delayed each year for

11. Tomb of Cyrus the Great (died 529 B.C.), Pasargadae.
12a. Susa, addorsed bull capital. 12b. Susa, inverted lotus-bell column base.
13. Susa, 521 B.C. Plan: (A) So-called Tomb of Daniel, (B) Village, (C) Acropolis, (D) Tower,
(E) Apadana, (F) Palaces of Darius and Artaxerxes Mnemon.
14. Persepolis, *circa* 521–465 B.C. Plan: (A) Grand Stairway, (B) Gate of All Nations,
(C) Apadana of Xerxes, (D) Hall of a Hundred Columns, (E) Palace of Darius.

12a

12b

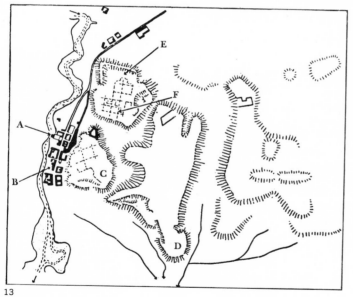

13

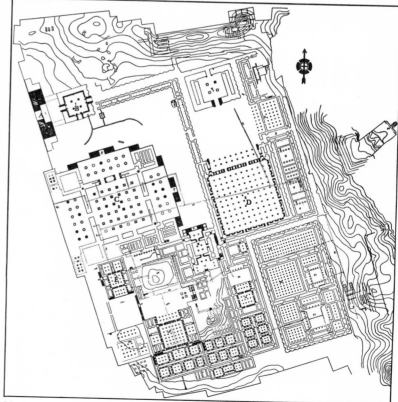

14

15

16

two or three weeks. Because the area was well forested in Achaemenid times, the climate was probably more tolerable than at present. If simply the growing of crops can delay the heat by a matter of weeks, it does not seem unreasonable to assume that huge forests might have had a still more tempering effect.

The handsome palace of Darius at Susa is built around a court (over an ancient Elamite cemetery). An inscription found there gives a remarkable account of the construction of this palace. Reading almost like a builder's contract, it is probably a valid guide to the techniques used for similar constructions at Persepolis and other Achaemenid sites. It reveals considerable technical knowledge and experience but where this was acquired is somewhat uncertain. The techniques resemble those of Urartu and northern Iran, a region where the Persians had settled for a while before coming south. In this inscription King Darius says:

"I constructed this palace. Its decoration was brought from afar. . . . The ground was ex-cavated till I came to the firm soil [bed rock] and a [drainage?] ditch was made. Thereupon gravel was thrown into it and packed down on one side some forty cubits in height, on the other up to some twenty cubits in height. The palace was erected on this gravel.

"The excavation and the fill and the sun-dried molded bricks were the work of people from Babylonia. The cedar timber was brought from a mountain called Lebanon. The people of Assyria brought it to Babylonia, and the people from Karka and Ionia brought it from Baby-lonia to Susa. The wood called 'yaka' was brought from Gandhara and Karmana; gold came from Sardes and Bactria and was wrought here. The precious lapis lazuli and carnelian were brought from Soghdiana, and the turquoise from Khwarazm. The silver and ebony came from Egypt. The decoration with which the walls were embellished was brought from Ionia, the ivory from Ethiopia, from India, and from Arachonia, but was wrought here. Stone, here wrought into columns, was from a town called Abiradu in Elam. The stone cutters and sculptors who made them here were Sardians and Ionians. Those who worked in gold were the Medes and the Egyptians. The wood carvers were Sardians and Egyptians. Those who made mosaic in ivory were the Babylonians and the Ionians. Those who decorated the walls were the Medes and the Egyptians.

"By the grace of Ahura Mazda I constructed a magnificent palace in Susa. May Ahura Mazda protect me and my . . . father and my country against injury."[31]

The first operation obviously was the clearing and building of a great foundation platform. This was 820 by 490 feet and contained a central court 116 by 118 feet, paved with brick rubble set in lime and polished with red ochre. This platform was surrounded by a high, strong wall of unfired brick flanked with projecting towers. Beyond this the river Shavur supplied enough water for a deep moat, which made the slightly elevated site almost impregnable.

The layout of Darius' huge and complex palace is rational and impressive. It has unity, coherence and apparent practicability. Its main feature was a large columnar, reception hall (375 x 180 feet) with columns 65 feet high set 27 feet apart. These were crowned with capitals composed of the forequarters of addorsed bulls and their shafts issue from an inverted lotus-bell

Figs. 12a, 12b, 13

27

17

18

base. Great width between the columns provided the light, elevated feeling so especially appreciated by the Persians and so unlike the ponderous gloom of Egyptian temples. This hall was the antecedent and model for the Apadana at Persepolis and was to be repeated again at Susa in the palace of Artaxerxes Mnemon (405–359 B.C.). Two main courts, each about 92 by 112 feet, provided space and light for part of the adjoining complex of halls, corridors, galleries, offices and—possibly—residential quarters. A large elevated terrace, 50 feet above the already raised platform, made it possible for the entire population to view ceremonies performed in the open air.

Walls were decorated with polychrome enameled brick panels (7 x 5 feet) in the Babylonian style, but the Persians endowed these stately and imposing animal forms, including a frieze of naturalistic pacing lions, with elegance and vitality. In addition to heraldic and mythical figures, there was a frieze of archers of the Royal Guard, the so-called "Ten Thousand Immortals," depicted with their sumptuous costumes of silk gauze studded with pierced gold bracteoles[32] worn over armor. Darius, like Cyrus, always gave a position of recognized honor to the army as the indispensable support of the state and its authority.

Today, Achaemenid Susa is but an instructive ruin, ravaged by its enemies, destroyed by Shapur II, and rebuilt by the Sasanians as the city of Nishapur. For centuries local inhabitants have followed a Sasanian precedent, using these older buildings virtually as quarries from which to draw materials for new structures. That Susa once contained the magnificent palace of Darius rivaling the splendor of Persepolis, that it was a powerful fort and a flourishing administrative city with a large civilian population, is scarcely evident.[33]

The Achaemenid empire was rapidly increasing in wealth and power. Even with the new royal center at Susa, and with the summer palaces at Ecbatana, Darius proceeded with the labor of creating a special ritual city: Persepolis. This city, as Darius probably conceived it, would not only glorify the divinely sanctioned dynasty, proclaiming the political and religious unity of the state but—even more important—it would also concentrate and heighten his empire's appeal to the powers of heaven for fertility and abundance, particularly at the great spring festival of the new year. Such a great center of terrestrial power, built as an earthly copy of the ancient mythic City of Heaven, would assure concord with the divine, providing an effective setting for invocation and worship, assuring safety and well-being for all the people of this vast empire. Accordingly, perhaps following plans initiated by Cyrus, Darius began the great constructions at Persepolis about 518–516 B.C. It was not quite completed when Alexander destroyed it in 330 B.C.

The unification of political and divine power in the identity of king and high priest, and the affirmation of their coincidence by means of a special architectural ensemble, are as old as Sumer, where Gudea's palace, temple and garden complex were the ultimate antecedents of this Achaemenid sacred city. The imaginary castle of Kangdiz, for instance, was traditionally described as having seven walls, built respectively of gold, silver, steel, bronze, iron, crystal, and lapis—a notion that goes back to Babylonian traditions in which the number seven (symbolic of the seven days that constitute a quarter of the moon) played a considerable part; this is further emphasized by the late cultic concentration on seven planets. Herodotus (I.99), describing Ecbatana, indicates that this scheme was reflected in the crenelations of the city walls which were painted seven colors, white, black, scarlet, blue, orange, silver and gold—the symbolic colors of the planets culminating in the metallic tinctures of the moon and the sun. All these were expressions of the ever-recurrent attempt to establish communication between the heavens and human life on earth. In a long history of symbolic ritual palace-complexes in the ancient Near East, Persepolis was the final and supreme example.

The usual view that Persepolis was primarily a group of impressive palaces built in the capital city of a great empire in order to express political might and to gratify royal pride is Western thinking: factual, literal, rationalistic. It fails to comprehend the constellations of assumptions, attitudes, hopes that had descended from the ancient Orient with its ingrained reliance on emotion and symbolism.[34] Persepolis does proclaim boastfully, in traditional manner,[35] the achievements and power of the Achaemenid kings, but it also emphasizes their divine investiture. It was the dynastic shrine but never, never the political capital: none of the thousands of documents found there are political and the location was quite unsuited for governing an empire. The great kings were in residence only rarely, and then only temporarily; Susa, Babylon, and Ecbatana, all more practically located, were the seats of government. Persepolis was, in fact, a sacred national shrine dedicated to a specific purpose: to serve as potent setting for the spring festival, Nawruz. By all the resources of symbolic representation, the Divine Powers were implored to grant fertility and abundance. Persepolis itself exhibits magnitude, power and wealth, with a commanding force sufficient to evoke those powers.

If the Achaemenid kings thus conceived Persepolis as a supreme invocation, the site would naturally be sacred and exclusive. This would explain why such a remarkable creation which should have been one of the wonders of the known world was unknown in other countries. For instance, the Bible has no word about Persepolis, although it is an important source of information on other imperial Persian constructions at Susa and Ecbatana.[36] No Babylonian, Assyrian or Phoenician document refers to it and Ctesias, author of a history of Persia who lived at the Persian court for twenty-four years, has left no mention of it. It was, of course, the most sacred spot in Persia, a veritable "holy of holies," with the exclusiveness normal to an Oriental religion. The invisible and precarious flow of magic powers is sensitive to contamination and might easily be dispelled by alien presences. Hence it was not to be shared with foreigners unless they were members of the empire. To share in its revelation would be their ultimate privilege.

In addition to its primary magical function, and apart from power, pride and boasting, Persepolis was the expression of a regime that was aware of an ethical and religious mission. Cyrus proclaimed that he sought peace for those who were always at war, and that order and justice

30

20

21

22

were primary aims; Darius declared: "I am one who loves righteousness and hates iniquity . . . It is not my will that the strong should oppress the weak . . . God's plan for the earth is not turmoil but peace, prosperity and good government."[37] These humane sentiments found expression in the nobility and sheer beauty of the buildings: more rational and gracious than the work of Assyrians or Hittites, more lucid and humane than that of the Egyptians. The beauty of Persepolis is not the accidental counterpart of mere size and costly display; it is the result of beauty being specifically recognized as sovereign value.[38]

The site of Persepolis, in the province of Fars—scene of the perils and initial victories of the Achaemenids—is backed up against a rugged mountain and commands a wide, mountain-ringed fertile plain. From the beginning, Persepolis was planned as a whole, a fact demonstrated by the complex subsurface systems for water supply and drainage that had been cut out of the solid rock before construction began and which were provided with outlets corresponding exactly to their subsequent use. A huge platform 900 by 1,500 feet, partly excavated, partly filled, was surrounded by a retaining wall which also served for defense. This wall, 40 to 60 feet high, was made of masonry blocks, some 50 feet long and weighing about 30 tons, which were set without mortar and bound with iron clamps; in some cases the joints are almost invisible. This wall was topped by another of unfired brick which was at least partially faced with polychromed tiles like those at Susa (brown, yellow, green and blue). Fig. 14

The approach itself announced a creation of impressive power: a majestic double stairway 22 feet wide, diverging and returning on itself. These stairs (A on plan), instead of being composed of separate slabs fastened together, were carved from enormous single blocks that sometimes even included a part of the side wall. From the modern point of view this may appear illogical, but certainly we cannot assume that builders who could erect such lofty columns, with their capitals weighing several tons, were inept. Two explanations are possible. The first is that such an amalgamation gave greater solidity to the structure than a composition of separate units would have. The second is that the builders did not envision the structure as a mechanical assemblage but rather as a sculptural whole. This method, making the unit a sculpture rather than a fabrication from various elements, was also used in doors and window frames, which were frequently carved from one solid block of stone. The grand stairway, of an inclination sufficiently gradual for horsemen, leads to the platform and immediately to a monumental pavilion (B on plan) guarded by colossal human-headed, winged bulls. This pavilion bears an inscription by Xerxes proclaiming that this is the "Gate of All Nations"—a declaration that all peoples pass there into the spiritual domain of the presiding powers. Indeed through this pavilion one entered a world of overwhelming splendor. The high wall excluded the familiar world without, reduced to irrelevance by revelation of sheer grandeur, glowing with color and gleaming with flashing metals. Fig. 15 Fig. 19

The irregular terrain was built into terraces of various levels (in a few cases the individual foundations were excavated rather than built up) so that each structure stood on its own terrace

33

23

24

reached by its own monumental stairway. Spaces between buildings formed courts, each with its own garden. Dominating the whole complex was the Apadana of Xerxes (C on plan), 250 feet square on the exterior, with a central room 195 feet square and porticos on three sides, each 65 feet deep. The whole was sustained by 36 slender columns, elegantly tapered without entasis, 7 feet thick, 60 feet high, with 36 to 48 concave flutes, and crowned by striking 10 foot capitals composed of richly polychromed addorsed bull forequarters. Lions and one hawk-nosed griffon were similarly treated in capitals, but were unfinished and apparently rejected.

Figs. 16-18

Figs. 20-22
Color Plate I

The interior of the Apadana was a forest of columns, among which the walls of sun-dried brick were almost concealed. Because orientation was difficult, it may have created a sense of un-reality, an unearthly vision of the sacred groves of heaven. As it was a reception hall large enough to hold 10,000 people,[39] it is quite probable that the processions circulated concentric-ally toward the king in the center, curtained off by sumptuous draperies which often lavishly adorned these huge structures, as we know from representations in contemporary carvings. The pavements were black and white; the beams of cedar, ebony and teak, were plated with gold and inlaid with ivory, precious metals, dull green serpentine and ruddy haematite. The deeply coffered ceiling was probably about 15 feet thick. Lovely heraldic animal figures wrought in gold were attached to the bronze and iron doors, and gold leaf was applied to some of the walls.[40] Specialized workers came from every province of the empire for Persepolis as well as Susa.

Across the court stood the so-called "Hall of a Hundred Columns" (D on plan). It was probably the rendezvous of the Imperial Guard for it was once directly connected with the en-trance gate and other military facilities.[41] Beyond the Apadana was the much smaller palace of Darius (E on plan), probably used as temporary quarters during special ceremonies. Here, as in the other palaces, the doorways were crowned with cornices bearing a reed-cavetto pattern, recalling Cambyses' conquest of Egypt; on the inner jambs of the doorways each relief is a mirror image of the relief it faces. Beyond this lie the palaces of Xerxes and Artaxerxes and other less important palaces and administrative buildings. Outside the walls lay the royal city and the sumptuous palaces and gardens of Cyrus and Darius,[42] for Persepolis itself was occupied by the Achaemenid monarch only for ceremonial, not living, purposes. Between the south end of the terrace and the mountain there was a series of buildings now all but obliterated, but still indicated by column bases.[43]

Fig. 23

The finish throughout the buildings of Persepolis was meticulous, as becomes a royal and sacred building. Some of the walls were polished to mirror brightness[44] and sculptural details often seem to have been executed with jeweller's tools: they are almost as sharp as if cut in metal.

The conception as well as the composition of the sculptural friezes confirms the solemn and humane character of the whole. There is nothing of the violence and agony of Assyrian sculp-ture; instead there is a lucid and suave simplicity, reserve and tranquillity appropriate to a great, vital moment and to an awareness of a transcendent Presence. Nonetheless, the Persepolis sculptures owe a good deal to Assyrian models and, in some features, to the earlier Hittite reliefs. But in theme, treatment, and mood the differences are profound and instructive. The theme in Assyrian reliefs is the glorification of the monarch, his sanctity, his ruthless and irresistible power, his superhuman achievement in war and his personal prowess in the hunt.[45]

Technically, the Assyrian friezes were conventional, long-established relief forms with the background cut away, leaving the figure isolated on a flat shallow surface that was then sharply incised rather than modeled. The range of subjects, in addition to gods and men, included all the special operations and horrors of war, such as sieges, destruction, victories and massacres, depicted with vivid detail and dramatic intensity. Included also was the setting: cities, rivers, mountains, marshes, vegetation, even gardens, although strictly subordinate to the figures. These panels—most often 5 by 7 feet but at the entrances sometimes 14 by 17—were placed where they could be seen, leisurely contemplated, and the story of Assyrian triumphs clearly and fully read. The formulae were relatively few but economical and forceful. Animals were individually drawn with startling realism born of acute and sympathetic observation. But the distribution of these panels as well as the composition of the scenes themselves were insufficiently organized, scattered without a proper feeling for the whole. Elements of the composition were often quite confused by overlapping and contradictory scale among the components. Their narrative sequence rarely established real unity and was nearly always cluttered with irrelevant details of harness, clothing or ornament. Not only was the dominant mood violent and savage (as a matter of propaganda and policy) but all was specific, factual and completely empirical. Actuality was conveyed with force, but the spectator—however stirred by the sight—remained passive. The work was done *for* him and not summarized, generalized, nor was it even deeply symbolic. He was left neither scope nor opportunity for imaginative supplementation.

Figs. 24-26   Like the Assyrian reliefs the Persepolis friezes are arranged in registers and of shallow relief, but they are of quite a different character. In the first place, they are consistently subordinate to the architecture which they ornament; they are to be seen *en passant,* not leisurely read. Furthermore, they simultaneously embellish and emphasize the structure. Organic to the total mass, limited to crucial areas like portals and foundation courses, their scale and movement is appropriate to the whole. The processions converge on a common point, and their symmetry—divided only by representations of the Tree of Life—provides a gentle rhythm. The Persepolis friezes are united by the forward movement of the procession, by the placement of each figure within the whole group. The spacing is planned, controlled, beautifully but quietly rhythmical; groupings are regularly marked by emphatic pine trees or by change of personages and costume. Changes of movement or character within each group subtly alleviate any effect of monotony (except for the long file of the Imperial Guard whose monotony is an evidence of collective and imperial power). The consistent verticals are suggestive of stable support —almost as if they were structural.

25

26

Moreover, Persepolis reliefs are sensitively modeled and their rounded surfaces indicate living substance. In the slanting light of early morning, some of these friezes almost come mysteriously alive.[46] The figures stand out against infinity, there is no background of any kind. The individual figures are fully separated, clearly outlined by graceful contours that give each one a separate and marked individuality. As the Assyrian sculptors strove constantly for exact factual detail, the Persians strove for maximum clarity, simplicity and repose. Their representations of animals, especially camels and sheep, have rarely been equaled.

All the figures are solemn but not forbidding, pervaded by a sense of their awareness of some divine presence. Costumes are simplified, sometimes quite plain, with the principal decoration being beautiful overlapping folds of drapery—a convention probably brought from Asia Minor. If the Assyrian sculptures were wholly empirical, those at Persepolis were abstract, suggestive, pointing beyond fact to meanings. A sense of form and order, a preference for the clear and well defined, so characteristic of the Persian mentality, is a relief from the excessive character of Assyrian carvings. In place of vehemence and arrogance, the Achaemenid designers created order, grace and proportion. One senses a norm, a standard which was missing in Assyrian work. Even when the monarch, shown on doorways of the Palace of Darius, slays a monster, he does it without excitement. This is no realistic encounter, ferocious and dangerous as in an Assyrian relief. Instead it is almost a pantomime, a record and a symbol of the good king overcoming evil. It is an idea rather than a replica of a violent event. Even the huge man-headed bulls that guarded the portals or crowned the columns, formidable and terrifying as they must have seemed, were somewhat humanized by the Persian sculptors. The stance of these monsters at the Gate of all Nations is firm and vital, with the huge wings sweeping upward in a fan-like curve, graceful yet alert. By comparison, similar guardians of the Assyrian palaces are heavy of body, relatively inert, the wings straight and graceless, the expression brutal.

The Persepolis frieze was meant to convey a double meaning. It was the tribute procession, a conventionalized picture of tribute-bearers bringing to Persepolis the wealth of the empire,[47] but even more significantly it was also a demonstration to heaven of the empire's hopes and needs. This pictorial inventory of valuable properties—blooded stock, fine horses, wines, sumptuous vessels of bronze and gold, tamed animals, furs, fabrics, a chariot and a throne—was a vivid demonstration of prosperity.

Such a procession has for thousands of years occurred at the Nawruz festival, which even today is still the greatest holiday of the year. It occurs at the critical moment of seasonal transition, the springtime renewal, when worship and supplication for the coming year should be most effective. In Achaemenid times representatives came from all over the empire, rejoicing in their hopes for the new year, expressing their common devotion to the monarch ("father" as he was actually called), and at the same time invoking the cooperation of both God and King, his surrogate, for the continuation of prosperity. The steady changing of the seasons could not be taken for granted. Life itself depended on it and any failure, through accident or neglect of ritual support, could bring disaster to the whole community, to the entire empire. On this day of mass appeal depended future harvests and on the efficacy of united worship depended all prospects. It was probably for just this great pageant that Persepolis was built and dedicated—by its majesty and grandeur deserving the attention of the powers above, providing a fitting site for the appeal meant to evoke a response beneficial to the empire.

Symbols everywhere confirm the invocational nature of the place. The columns, of which there are five hundred and fifty on the platform, represent the sacred grove,[48] an essential of Near Eastern iconography; their bases are inverted lotus forms, symbolic of perfection and life-giving power. The capitals of the Apadana porch columns represent the flowering palm with its corona of pendant fronds, while above, vertical Ionic volutes suggest floriation. All other Persepolis capitals terminate in addorsed animal protomes. The much worshipped bull was a major symbol of primal generative forces and here, by implication, it impregnates the supporting trees which are represented by columns. The same idea is affirmed also by the thousands of rosette ornaments, traditional sun symbols acknowledging the sun's necessary life-sustaining force. Even more significant, on the underside of the pivot stones of doors is carved a large open sunflower, placed face down in direct contact with the soil, evidently to transfer directly into the earth its germinating power.

The calm representation of Ahura Mazda emerges through the celestial winged disk against a clear space: a serene but intense figure bestowing benediction on his people. Elsewhere the human head of a great mythological animal is austere, inscrutable, all-powerful, though ultimately benign. A sphinx-like deity places a paw with an adoring gesture on a flowering palm, symbolizing the sacred moment of fertilization. One very vigorous figure, several times repeated, represents a ferocious lion devouring a young bull—another iconographic appeal for fertility: the lion (Leo) represents the summer heat which is necessary to check the heavy winter rains and floods caused by the bull (Taurus),[49] in every way the opposite of the summer sun. Heavy rains are temporarily welcome, but if persistent they are ruinous to crops. The bull's curving horns refer, as in many other cults and cultures, to the crescent moon with its night associations of dew and mitigated heat. Also important among evidences of the invocational powers of this complex is the row of stepped pyramids that crowns all parapets. They have been called "crenelations," or "pleasantly ornamental," or even named "battlements," although they certainly had no defensive value. Actually, they are the repeated symbol of the sacred mountain, used for many centuries on pottery, bronzes, tombs, altars, crowns, painted on doors, and even woven into textiles—everywhere that this sacred and potent form could express a hopeful appeal to the powers of the mountain.

Beyond the deep emotional appeal of these symbols and the assurance of hope and security through magic power—the motive and purpose of this great structure—Persepolis provides magnificence and architectural beauty that are independent of such special purposes. Indeed, it seems independent of time itself.

Figs. 27-29

Fig. 18

In regularity and symmetry, Persepolis represents an advance over the relative incoherence of early ritual ensembles. The main buildings are square, in contrast to the rectangular forms at Pasargadae.[50] A uniform axis is strictly maintained throughout and even the sculptured friezes are symmetrically repeated with fidelity. The firm regularity of the plan gives to the ensemble a dignity appropriate to its ceremonial character, confirming the emotional effect of individual structures. The great columns of the Apadana are widely separated (30 feet apart), and this gives a sensational and—for the period—unprecedented ratio of voids to solids,[51] providing a feeling of elevation and spirituality, inducing a sense of spatial freedom and a denial of materiality which contrasted sharply with the somewhat clumsy palaces and the solid and inert ziggurats of Mesopotamia or the dark and gloomy Egyptian temples. In those oppressive structures, one was overwhelmed, lost, confused; sheer mass was everything, human control denied. In the Apadana of Persepolis, ample and serene, the spirit is free, rational, humane and enlarged. Such is the power of form.

The walls of the buildings of Persepolis were of sun-dried brick, long since crumbled, with the imposing scale augmented by lavish color throughout. The effect, depending as it must have on tonal sequence and illumination, is not easily recovered. Some of the interior columns were plastered and painted blue, white, and red, while others were plated with metals. The sculptured friezes were also colored, and traces have been found of turquoise blue, almond green, orange, yellow, light scarlet, and violet. The timbers were covered with thick sheets of varied precious metals. In this region, as in Greece, the intense daylight would have softened and harmonized such varied tones.

In its true monumentality, larger than any Egyptian temple or medieval cathedral, Persepolis constituted an affirmation of power beyond man. Despite its tremendous size (an area covering 1,300,000 square feet) it was nevertheless unified and consistent, and this was achieved without sacrificing dramatic variety. Although the constructions and carvings at Persepolis were executed over a period of more than a hundred years, one sees very little development or difference in style. The major forms were traditional, restrained by myths whose magic could not be jeopardized by changing the formula, nor by personal preference or experiment. The highly trained designers and craftsmen who produced them must have worked to a strictly controlled plan.

Persepolis clearly represented the State: its art was in fact a state art which gave multiple races and nations assurance and pride as members of a great community. In short, as a monument it transcended individual life, conferring awareness of other dimensions—not merely of the past but of hope for things to come. It was the embodiment of a national consciousness and, as such, Alexander understood that he must destroy it.

Fig. 30

On the same plain as Persepolis, Darius I chose the site of his tomb, having it carved out of the solid rock face at Naqsh-i-Rustam. This tomb, clearly modeled on the buildings at Persepolis and Susa, similar to them in its portico, columns, capitals and other details, served as the

28

29

prototype for later Achaemenid tombs, which were cut into the same rocks. Later, during the Sasanian epoch, when leaders sought to trace their lineage back to the great Achaemenids, this same site of Naqsh-i-Rustam once again became a monument to Persian strength.

The Achaemenid achievement at Persepolis, in concept and purpose, in structural forms and in embellishment, in materials and labor had made use of essential contributions from Sumer, Babylon, Assyria, Urartu, Elam, Egypt and Ionia. At Persepolis, however, all these contributions and influences were completely fused; details, materials and techniques were amassed from all peoples of the enlarged empire, but the planning and execution was basically Persian. It should be remembered that Pasargadae, which had been constructed *before* the formation of the Achaemenid empire, is a smaller, less majestic version of Persepolis. The buildings of Pasargadae were basically the same in plan, conception, and method of construction as those of Persepolis, only scale and grandeur varied significantly. Persepolis, more elegant and more lucid than its antecedents, in its completed individuality is a purely Persian artistic creation.

Potent symbols, suggestive of unfathomable realities, create a sense of individual insufficiency and dependence; rational, orderly and finely finished they can provide deep and self-enlarging emotion. Persepolis proclaimed the vastness of the great empire far beyond an individual's experience or comprehension. Confronted by the overwhelming power and glory of it, the individual was both diminished and assured, thus attaining a psychological fusion with the object. This is the essence of the aesthetic experience—total realization and total participation in a transpersonal reality.

Diffusion

The faltering Achaemenid empire swiftly collapsed under the onslaught of Alexander. Achaemenid architecture, deprived of purpose, of leadership, and of lavish support, seemed to be already a fact of history, its gaunt and charred ruins but a funeral monument. With the imposition of new Hellenistic styles and unfamiliar modes, Persian building traditions languished; accumulated skills for construction in the grand manner were frustrated. But if Persia as an independent state then briefly ceased to exist, if her political life perished, the vitality of her architectural concepts and superb techniques did not.[52] India, which had enjoyed a sophisticated urban development from the third millennium, eagerly received the creative impulses and skills that came in from the Iranian plateau.

Although no dates can be assigned for the earliest relationship between India and the northwest, the first proven contacts occurred during the Sargonid period, about 2350 B.C.[53] Relations between India and Persia during the Achaemenid period, however, are specifically documented and to the native kingdoms of the Ganges valley "Persia transmitted, directly or indirectly, not merely the patterns of Empire but important new skills and utilities,"[54] including

the use of iron and metal coinage. By 518 B.C. Darius had conquered and occupied north-west India so that Sind and part of the Punjab—for two hundred years—constituted the twen-tieth satrapy of the Persian Empire, the largest, most populous and richest of all. The Indus river was then the boundary between Persia and India.

Friendly relations continued between India and Persia after the conquest by Alexander, and even after the Seleucids were defeated and expelled from India (*circa* 303 B.C.) by Chandra-gupta (321–296 B.C.) who, apparently, married Seleucus' daughter. Chandragupta copied the Achaemenid Royal Road system, modeled his military power on Persian tactics and weaponry, and echoed Persian court ceremonials. Generations of contact with the competent administration of the Achaemenids had supplied an instructive imperial organization which the Indian ruler evidently emulated. Persian designers, masons and engineers, as well as returning Indians, de-prived of opportunities in Persia were eager and well equipped to assist the Mauryan building program. Thus, Megasthenes, only forty or fifty years after the fall of Persepolis, reported that the Indian city Pataliputra outshone even Susa and Persepolis. One hall with eighty columns at Pataliputra and still another mentioned as having a thousand columns were obviously based on the Persian apadanas. Their great stone columns were the first in India and the buildings were set in a large park with trees and fountains, reminiscent of the Persian Paradise garden. Especially significant is the fact that the columns of these Indian buildings all show the Persian polish, a costly and very slow process, unknown in India before the Mauryan period. Further-more, one of the remaining stone capitals is carved in strict Achaemenid style.

Evidence of Persian models and styles in India during the reign of Asoka (264–227 B.C.) is even more varied and abundant. These include rock-cut edicts which follow a precedent known through Darius, the use of animal capitals as at Sarnath (245 B.C.), and the inverted lotus-bell capital which is the Achaemenid column base lifted to the top of the column. Other important Persian constructions which had a continuing impact in India were the rock-cut and cave tem-ples. These ranged from simple excavated chambers to elaborate temple interiors. In all Persian examples of this type of construction, the portal reproduced the familiar façade of a house. Similarly, the Lomas Rishi cave in Bahar reproduced the wooden entrance of a typical Indian house. On the interiors of these rock-cut chambers is also found the mirror-like Persian stone polish.

By degrees, this Achaemenid-inspired architecture was modified by local taste and craft habits until, within a few centuries, it was absorbed into Indian styles. In the process, India was substantially enriched and the great Achaemenid tradition grafted onto new roots.

II. Seleucids, Parthians, Sasanians: Reassertion of Persian Forms

The Seleucids

When Alexander left Persepolis in ruins, after shattering the Achaemenids, and imposed a new political regime, the spirit of Persian art was by no means totally extinguished. To a certain extent, of course, a marked stylistic disruption occurred and under the successors of Alexander Persia's design tradition became temporarily engulfed by Greek importations. After the death of Alexander in 323 B.C., it was Seleucus who, about 312 B.C., took up the reins of the empire. He was the only Macedonian who had retained his Persian wife, thus at least in a limited way individualizing Alexander's vision of a combined Greek and Persian civilization. Under Seleucus and his successors, Hellenic design became dominant but never completely absorbed. Cities were laid out according to geometric Greek plans, temples were built on Greek models and characteristic elements of Greek design were used for ornament. However, acceptance of strongly Hellenic forms seems to have occurred only in areas which had a heavy concentration of Greek and Macedonian personnel.

Although the ruins of some of these cities have been identified and partly studied,[55] few architectural monuments remain to testify that Seleucid splendor or imagination ever existed. The meager ruins visible today at Kangavar, thought to have been constructed about 200 B.C., show a temple that was quite Greek in character. Only its enormous dimensions, about 660 feet on a side, and its megalithic foundations which echo Achaemenid stone platforms constitute Persian elements. It was a columnar temple dedicated to Anahit, with Doric capitals topped with Corinthian abaci. Similarly, so little remains of the Seleucid temple at Khurra that it can scarcely be called a monument. Nevertheless, from the two columns still standing it is possible to see that this too was based on Hellenic design, but in terms of the Greek aesthetic

Figs. 31, 32

it consisted of Hellenic forms clumsily designed. The columns are too tall and slender for Greek proportions, more like the Achaemenid columns at Persepolis or the tall wooden columns which had provided the Achaemenid prototype; their capitals are poor, weak imitations of the Ionic style. Far more eloquent traces of the Seleucid period exist in sculpture and coins, but even these testify to a gradual dissolution of Hellenic forms in Persia, indicating a widespread lack of interest in their development or adaptation. Copies became paler and paler as their prototypes became more distant in both time and understanding.

The Parthians

In the northeast of Persia, in what is now Russian Central Asia, another people, the Parthians, were developing a quite different architecture. The Parthians pushed westward, gaining a great deal of Seleucid territory, but the two empires existed simultaneously for a long time. Combining both Greek and Persian elements, Parthian architecture made singular contributions to the development of architectural form and reaffirmed the abstract and symbolic characteristics of Persian design. The two most important Parthian contributions to architectural form were the achievement of a dome on squinches and the development of the vaulted ivan structure—both of which were to play a vital role in the subsequent development of Persian building. Unfortunately, few of these monuments remain standing and the most instructive ruins, except the Rabat-i-Safid, exist not in Persia proper but on the periphery, in Mesopotamia and in the extreme northeast, a fact which witnesses the speed with which the Parthian forces moved across the Persian plateau. Furthermore, for many years much Parthian art was confused with Sasanian, and recent scholarship is only beginning to separate these two cultures and provide identifying features for each.[56]

Although Parthian art is known to have existed from about 250 B.C., it is really with the reign of Mithridates II, of the Parthian dynasty of the Arsacids, in 123 B.C., that our knowledge of a widespread Parthian architecture begins. From the ruins of a large palace of the second century A.D. at Hatra, in what is now Iraq, it is possible to see, if not the first example of important Parthian innovations, at least enough standing structure to judge the Parthian capabilities. The main façade, built of blocks of masonry, is pierced by two large ivans (A on plan) roofed with high barrel vaults separated in the façade by two smaller rooms (B on plan) which were probably two storeys high.[57] These large ivans, parallel to each other in this instance, will later develop into the grand ivan-entrances of the Islamic epoch. Perhaps even more important is the smaller square chamber (C on plan) directly behind the southern ivan. This type of square vaulted room, here surrounded by a sort of ambulatory, will subsequently—in Sasanian

Fig. 33

47

31

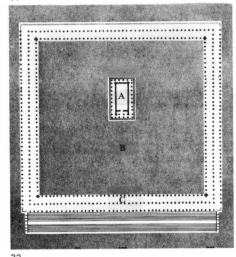

32

34a

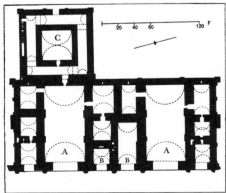

33

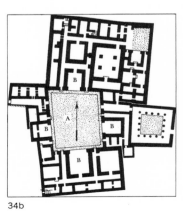

34b

times and after the Islamic conquest—become the square domed chamber so vital to Persian architecture. At Hatra, this vaulted chamber seems to have been a temple, in plan reminiscent of Achaemenid fire temples but with vaulted roofing substituted for the earlier flat covering which rested on columns.[58]

The palace at Assur, another Arsacid construction dating from the first century A.D. with additions made as late as the third century, presents an even more interesting plan—at least in terms of subsequent Persian developments. It constitutes the first known example of four ivans opening onto a central square. In plan, the cruciform is slightly irregular, with the north and west sides of the court longer than the south and east sides. With but few alterations, this is the same four-ivan plan basic to Persian mosques, madrassas, and caravanserais throughout subsequent history.

Figs. 34a, 34b

These major contributions to the development of architectural forms were indigenously Persian, but the Parthian decoration and façade treatment was closely related to Greek themes or, after the successful conquests by Trajan and other Roman emperors, to Roman forms. The façade of the palace at Assur, with its central ivan-entrance surrounded by rows of engaged columns and framed niches, is closely related to the façade of the later Sasanian palace at Ctesiphon and displays in its details derivation from Roman models. This Roman influence is felt even more strongly in the decorative use of stucco heads on the façade at Hatra. It is interesting to note that the Parthians made widespread use of stucco, both carved and painted, a technique which was to be more fully developed under the Sasanians and later in Islamic Persia.

Further, but more remote, examples of Parthian official architecture have been carefully studied, especially the treasures uncovered at Palmyra. There must certainly have been handsome palaces here, and, although no interiors have been preserved, Philostratus described "a room roofed with a sapphire vault, gleaming with heavenly light. Against the blue ground the stones . . . were like stars in the sky. Here sat the King when he meted out justice." And he tells of still another room where ". . . the moon, the sun, stars, and even a portrait of the King shone in a sky of crystal."[59]

In addition to this official and public architecture, the Parthians have also left certain religious structures of significance. The sacred shrine at Takht-i-Sulayman, later the Sasanian Takht-i-Taqdis, is surrounded by a circular wall built of enormous stones, which once enclosed the supreme fire temple of Adhura Gushnasp, from which all the other sacred fires were kindled. Today, however, with the exception of several fire altars, nothing but the ruins of this wall remain. Its masonry is of a specific and unusual character: narrow vertical slabs between large rectangular blocks. The building shown on the famous "Fortress Plate" in Leningrad rests on a masonry foundation which is identical to that of the wall of Takht-i-Sulayman.

35. Building depicted on the "Fortress Plate." (Hermitage, Leningrad)
36. Takht-i-Sulayman, Parthian. Main gate of wall.
37. Takht-i-Sulayman. Masonry wall, detail.
38. Takht-i-Sulayman. Breached wall.

Figs. 35-38   Moreover, the little concentric half circles that unite the columns on the façade of the building on the Fortress Plate are conspicuous elements over the main gate of the wall at Takht-i-Sulayman. This seems to support the recent theory that the building represented in the "Fortress Plate" was really a building at Takht-i-Sulayman.[60]

Figs. 39, 40   What is perhaps the earliest example of a domed fire temple also dates from the Parthian period. This is the badly damaged little building, a dome on four arches known as the Rabat-i-Safid. It crowns a rugged eminence about 28 miles southeast of Mashhad. In construction technique it is somewhat primitive and tentative. Instead of the harsh, but confident, squinch characteristic of Sasanian buildings, the corners here are timidly bridged with five or six partly concealed wooden beams which directly support the rudimentary masonry squinch above. The plan is irregular, with sides of unequal length supporting exceptionally thick walls, and the dome is not the true parabola of Sasanian buildings. In short, as Dr. Wilber has demonstrated,[61] this rather inept structure is really preliminary and experimental, representing an earlier stage than any known Sasanian fire temples and should, therefore, be classed as Parthian.

The Sasanians

Ardashir I, the first Sasanian ruler, built his palace at Firuzabad while, in effect, still a vassal of the Parthian Arsacids. It is, therefore, basically a Parthian structure with hints of the conscious direction eventually to be taken by the Sasanians. Called "Ardashir's Glory," its construction was a politically motivated act of rebellion and bold defiance of the last Parthian ruler, Artabanus V. The palace itself was a remarkable achievement, a king's palace, but beyond that it was also an affirmation of independence, the focus of a new epoch. Tracing his lineage back to the great Achaemenids, Ardashir wished to assert his right to their inheritance, to visibly establish a connection between himself and them. Achaemenid magnificence being impossible, the necessary regal effect was attained by sheer size; the materials and conventions of ordinary structures were utilized, but with multiplied dimensions.

Fig. 41   The façade of the palace at Firuzabad was 180 feet long. The vault of the large central ivan (A on plan) spanned 42 feet. Beyond this central ivan, which was flanked to either side by two rectangular ivans (B on plan), were three square domed chambers—the oldest known Iranian domes—supported on walls 13 feet thick (C on plan).

A smaller fortified palace, the Kala-i-Dukhtar, had been built by Ardashir, probably a few years earlier. In plan, it appears to have been a simplified version of the later Firuzabad palace: a large vaulted ivan, behind which stood a square domed chamber. In the palace at Firuzabad this plan was enlarged not only by the four lateral ivans, two to either side of the central one, and by having three domed chambers instead of one, but a two-ivan inner court (D on plan), surrounded by six small vaulted chambers, doubled the size of the complex.

35

36

37

38

39. Rabat-i-Safid, 3rd century, Parthian. Arch vault.
40. Rabat-i-Safid.

41. Palace at Firuzabad, early 3rd century.
Plan: (A) Ivan, (B) Lateral ivans, (C) Domed chambers, (D) Court.
42a. Palace at Firuzabad, detail of portal and niche. Drawing from Flandin and Coste.
42b. Persepolis, cavetto cornice. Drawing from Flandin and Coste.

Built of rough-hewn stones set in mortar, the walls of this city palace of Firuzabad were covered with plaster. Decorative architectural detail was borrowed from the Achaemenid palaces at Persepolis, doubtless with the conscious intent of creating a sense of continuity between the dynasties. Among such details appears the cavetto cornice, originally borrowed from Egypt and used with far greater aesthetic success on the flat Achaemenid doors than on this arched Parthian-Sasanian entrance or niche. Thus, the Sasanians, although continuing to develop important Parthian forms and adding valuable contributions of their own, were simultaneously affirming the validity of earlier Persian forms, particularly those linked with Achaemenid greatness.

Figs. 42a, 42b

The Sasanians, emerging in the southern province of Fars, proud of their role as successors to the Achaemenid Empire, considered it their destiny to revive former glories. Taking their religion seriously, they revitalized the principles of Zoroastrianism with its characteristic worship of natural forces. The Sun was the primal symbol, with Fire and Water as immediate objects of reverence, invocation, and cultic devotion. Fire was especially sacred as identical with the Holy Spirit and the symbol of Truth. The Sasanian period was a time of enterprise, vigor, courage and ambition; the Sasanian kings, in most generations intelligent and disciplined, achieved an empire similar in power and extent to that of Cyrus and Darius. Both art and architecture reflected their strength and character. All was in the heroic mood: large in scale, with forms energetic, inventive, affirmative, and often sumptuous in color. The interval of five and a half centuries since the destruction of Persepolis had witnessed a stylistic disruption and a lapse in the tradition of Persian design; under the Sasanians the Persian spirit was fully restored to the creative arts.

Sasanian architecture cannot be comprehensively characterized in a single formula. The monuments that have survived—too few for broad generalizations—show derivation from heterogeneous sources. Varied in style and construction, they are clearly distinguished by widely separated local habits. Moreover, there were many changes during the four centuries of Sasanian rule, especially in vault and dome constructions.[62]

Figs. 43-46

The outstanding royal Sasanian monument is the Taq-i-Kisra at Ctesiphon, in present-day Iraq. Probably built by Shapur I in the second half of the third century,[63] this noble ruin is a notable example of a Sasanian ivan. The remaining section rises above the plain like a gray cliff. Its ivan, a great open vault which spans 75 feet—wider than any vault in Europe—is 90 feet high and nearly 150 feet deep. Above this vault, the wall once continued for another 22 feet. On this façade multi-storeyed courses of shallow arcades are defined by applied colonettes, the unit varying in size with each successive course. There is no continuity of vertical axis,[64] a fact

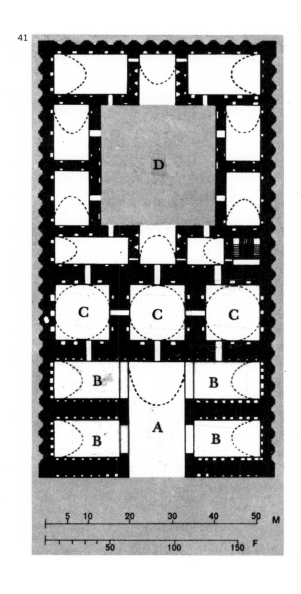

41

C C C

B B

A

B B

D

5 10 20 30 40 50 M

50 100 150 F

42a

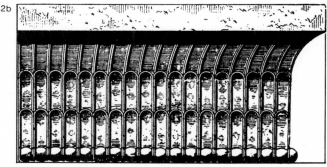

42b

which is frustrating to structural purists who feel that all weight-carrying functions should be vertically coordinated. But on this façade the colonettes are not working members, they are applied. Perhaps they stiffen the wall, which would be desirable because of its exposure to intense heat and violent temperature alterations, but they do not carry weight. Instead, their function is aesthetic and as such has several values. They emphasize the scale while they simultaneously break up the monotony and rigidity threatened by such a huge façade. Furthermore, they introduce an element of surprise, flexibility and a syncopated rhythm which is enhanced by the shifting shadows which animate the whole.

This building was not planned to demonstrate engineering but to be magnificent—to demonstrate power and wealth, to overawe envoys from other nations and to warn restless vassal states that this dynasty was too powerful to brook challenge. To evaluate this monument as façade, as its present condition now forces us to do, is somewhat irrelevant, for this ruin was but one of four sides facing in toward a vast central court; it was but one unit in an enclosed space. Nor was the ivan, as we now see it, merely an imposing gap; originally it was enclosed by a heavy gold-embroidered curtain that struck the keynote of opulence, by its great height and the richness of varied patterns.[65]

It is quite true that the façade is only a great screen, rather unrelated to the structure behind it, and that the central arch itself is not properly defined, its profile being unmarked. But the aim of this façade was to provide an impressive stage-setting for the imperial power and this is certainly accomplished. Within the huge audience hall, the Sasanian King of Kings exalted sat, arrayed in gold-embroidered blue garments. Suspended from golden chains so that it just touched his head was an immense jewelled crown weighing 600 pounds. Covering the huge expanse before him was the world's most famous carpet—Spring in Paradise, portrayed in silk, gold, and silver, encrusted with thousands of precious jewels. This was the Spring Carpet of Chosroes, later cut up by the triumphant Arabs and sold for fabulous sums. It must have represented a sizable portion of funds available to the rich Sasanian state. Judged politically, however, this carpet was probably treasure well employed, for we know how overwhelming was its effect.

Figs. 47-49 The great palace at Bishapur, also built by Shapur about the time of his victory over the Roman Emperor Valerian (260), is a more complex development of the ivan-type structure. The audience hall, a large room 72 feet square, was vaulted with a dome about 80 feet high. Each of the four sides of this room is an arrangement of triple ivans. Built of stone and brick rubble set in mortar, the extensive stucco decoration of this palace provides the best extant examples of the interior decoration of a Sasanian palace. Sixty-four elaborate niches are placed in the walls of the audience hall. Many of their decorative motifs are borrowed from Greco-Roman prototypes, doubtless a reflection of the fact that about this time Shapur took thousands of Roman prisoners. A Roman influence can also be discerned in the mosaic panels bordering the adjoining court and ivans, but, as Ghirshman points out,[66] it has here been rather happily combined with Persian taste and tradition. Close to the palace stand the remains of a contem-

56

43

44

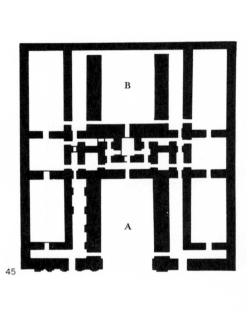

45

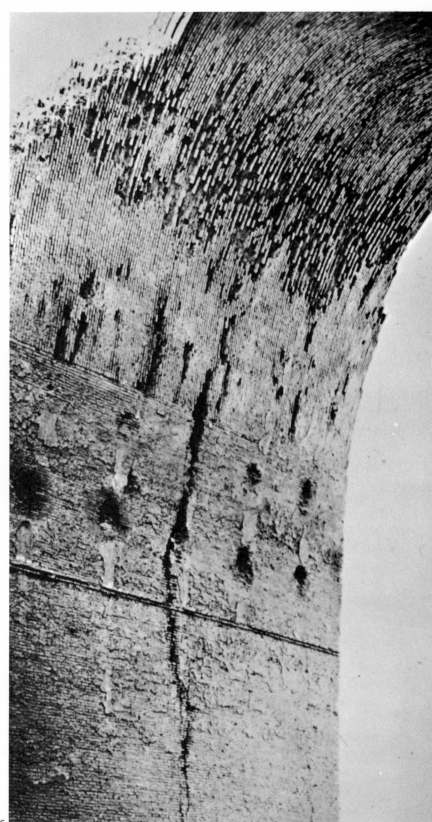

46

45. Taq-i-Kisra, Ctesiphon, 3rd century (?). Plan: (A) Ivan, (B) Former palace.
46. Taq-i-Kisra. Detail of ivan vault.

porary fire temple which, although traditionally Persian in its square plan, utilized Roman techniques of building.[67] Its decorative elements, such as addorsed bull capitals, are clearly borrowed from Susa or Persepolis.

In the fifth century palace built by Bahram V at Sarvistan a more complex development Figs. 50-54
and expanded technique is evident. The central ivan of the eastern façade, flanked on either side by a smaller ivan, provides access to the central domed chamber (B on plan). Behind this lies a square court (C on plan) whose single ivan is placed on the central axis in the blind western wall. In the northwest and southeast corners of the building are smaller domed chambers (D on plan) and the south wall of the central domed chamber gives access to a lateral exterior ivan (E on plan), smaller than the main one of the east façade. On each side of the building, but not directly opposite each other, are two narrow vaulted rooms (F on plan), each with semi-vaulted side aisles. Although reminiscent of the plan at Firuzabad, here there is more freedom and far less symmetry.

The three parallel ivans open outward, creating a feeling of accessibility, and achieve an interpenetration of outer and inner space. The rooms inside are of varying sizes and heights, and wide vaulted halls open into one another through ample arches, facilitating communication and providing ever-new interconnected vistas and flowing spaces.

Squinches were used to support the round domes, but in addition to this technique it is possible to see the use of columns as supports for the vaulting in the side rooms. As Oskar Reuther pointed out, in these narrow rooms "it was the effect of greater width that was sought —especially a relief from the sense that the walls were too restricting . . . but he [the designer] had quite a good practical knowledge of statics and understood quite well both the approximate continuation of the line of pressure of his vaults and the possibility of distributing the thrust and counter-thrust by means of a system of interior buttresses connected by arches. This is a first tentative step towards the constructional system of which Gothic architecture is the supreme realization."[68]

Unfortunately, most of the other known Sasanian buildings are even more ruined than the examples we have discussed, and although their ground plans can be redrawn from archaeological evidence, their actual appearance remains even more conjectural. The very fragmentary information we possess on palaces such as those at Kish, Damghan, Haush Quri and Qasr-i-Shirin serves mainly as evidence that our knowledge of the full range of Sasanian architecture is far too incomplete. The early sixth century palace at Damghan,[69] still only partially known, Figs. 55, 57
had a large ivan entrance behind which was the traditional domed square first seen at Firuzabad and Sarvistan. Here, however, the cupola rests on four very large and irregularly shaped pillars, thus incorporating the domed area into the larger, main room. Columns ranged along the sides of the ivan helped to support the ivan vault, thus utilizing the technique begun in the narrow side rooms at Sarvistan.

Similarly the temple and palace at Qasr-i-Shirin, probably dating from the early seventh Fig. 56
century, give evidence of much that went before. The temple, known as the Chahar Qapu, was

47. Palace at Bishapur, 3rd century.
Plan: (A) Fire temple, (B) Audience hall, (C) Court.
48. Palace at Bishapur. Reconstruction in the Louvre.
49. Palace at Bishapur. Stucco niche.

a large square room, 82 feet on each side, with arched entrances in the center of each face. Its dome, the largest known from Sasanian times, rested on four pointed squinches. Like the palace at Firuzabad some four centuries earlier, it was built of rough stones set in a bed of mortar. The nearby palace which is supposed to have been built by Chosroes II for his Christian wife,[70] is now almost totally in ruins. It was built on an artificial terrace reached by double stairways similar to those at Persepolis and in its immense scale it seems to have continued the conscious emulation of Achaemenid monuments evidenced at the very beginning of the Sasanian period. In plan, the basic elements are further developments of themes discussed above. The columned entry ivan (B on plan), which seems to have been similar to that at Damghan, leads into a square domed room (C on plan) which is once again relatively closed off but which is given extra width by lateral vaulted aisles. The remainder of the palace extends along the same axis and includes several courts and numerous rooms which were probably private apartments. The whole appears to have been set in splendid and immense landscaped gardens.

At Taq-i-Bustan, a sacred site of gushing waters near Kirmanshah, are two grottoes treated as ivans. The righthand one was carved during the fourth century and the larger one to the left dates from the fifth century, at which time it was probably proposed to carve an additional ivan to the far left, thus forming a design based on the three-ivan façade.[71] The rear wall of the large central ivan-type niche is a rock carving, representing above the investiture of a king and below the equestrian statue of a king. The king is variously identified as Peroz or Chosroes II, but is probably the latter. This niche is framed with architectural details of pilasters and cornice executed in stucco. The lateral walls contain rock carvings of royal hunts. On the face of the arch, in the spandrel, two winged figures bearing crowns flank a central royal crescent representing a diadem. The frame about this arch, instead of being firmly anchored at either end, and thus emphasizing vertical support, terminates in a fluttering ribbon,[72] indicating that it is really no more substantial than a rainbow. The flanking pilasters of the arch consist of a sumptuous cosmological tree, bursting with supernatural vitality, an impressive promise of abundance—the floral pattern appealing for fertility. Clearly, meaning and invocation by symbols rather than a display of structural forces is the purpose here. Other structures were similarly ornamented. For instance, in front of the entrance of the central ivan-niche once stood a pavilion with columns whose large cubical Byzantine-style capitals were deeply carved in rich and forceful patterns.

Despite the now ruined state of many Sasanian buildings, clues to the architectural ornamentation of the period are provided by contemporary drawings on metal vessels, as well as by the numerous remaining stucco panels that once enriched façades and interiors. These indicate that the repertoire of ornament had expanded since Achaemenid times, becoming more ornate and more lavishly disposed. There was some effort to correlate structure with ornament,[73] but most often the superb stucco panels, like other Sasanian decoration, were merely attached to the wall and were not conceived as an integrated part of the structure. The practice of designing the stucco ornamentation independently of the architecture and casting it in

Figs. 58-63

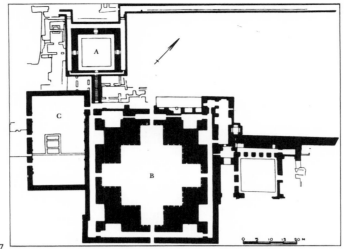

47

48

49

50. Palace at Sarvistan, 5th century. General view.
51. Palace at Sarvistan. Cross-section of the Reuther reconstruction.
52. Palace at Sarvistan. Reconstruction of facade.
53. Palace at Sarvistan. Plan: (A) Triple ivans, (B) Central domed chamber,
(C) Court, (D) Small domed chambers, (E) Side ivan, (F) Vaulted rooms.

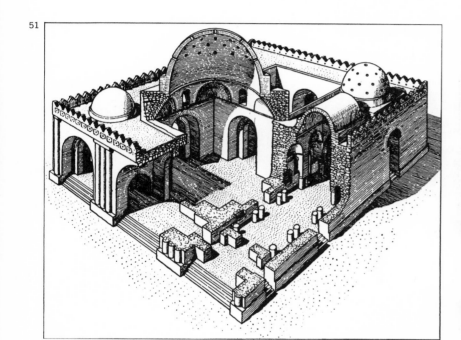

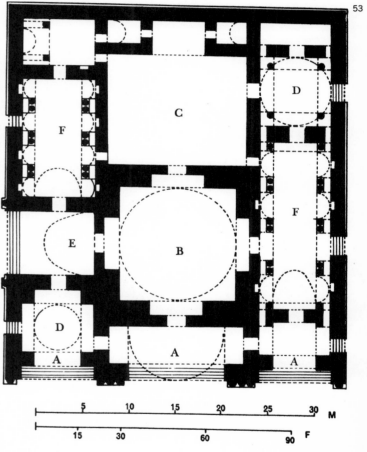

54

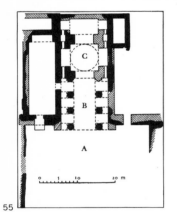

55

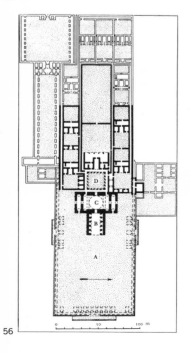

56

57

repeating molds encouraged this separation of decoration and structure. The value of a decorative design coordinated with the structure was a less urgent consideration than the force and character of the individual design itself—particularly in its symbolic affirmations. But new architectural forms, such as arches, did provide new opportunities. Thus facing the intrados of portal arches with busts in full round was for the Sasanians a new kind of royal affirmation, and at the same time offered a form of decoration later copied in European medieval architecture.

In Sasanian ornament natural forms were enlarged, embellished and schematized. The motif of the cosmological tree was greatly enriched; palmettes were given heroic scale; palm leaves assumed a great variety of forms; the pomegranate and undulating vines flourished. Fretwork and various types of imbrication enlivened many a panel, and beaded circles or carefully wrought square frames provided designs that were used not only in architectural ornament but in a rich and masculine textile art as well. By its own excellence and display of vitality, Sasanian ornament passed beyond the borders of the Sasanian empire to become a stimulating factor in Coptic Egypt, Rome, Byzantium, and medieval Europe. In addition to its westward diffusion, it exerted constructive influence eastward, across Asia, to become influential not only in India but especially in the arts of T'ang China. Figs. 64-67

Although Sasanian ornament appropriated Hellenic elements, its exuberant, self-contained vitality, whether in heraldic animals or heavy foliage, contrasts strikingly with the conventional ornament of dying Hellenism, much of which was rigid, monotonous and thin. Somewhat unusual are the stucco panels found in private houses of Ctesiphon which seem inspired by a *new* wave of Western influence, probably effected by incoming migrants from Antioch[74] during the sixth century. But the interpretation of Western forms seen in these reliefs is eager, youthful and inventive.

The colors retained in the decorations at several sites, like the late Parthian Kuh-i-Khwaja or at Bishapur, are of surprising range: red, yellow, turquoise, dull blue, light green, purple, violet, orange, fleshcolor, and white.[75] Traces of color were still visible at Taq-i-Bustan as recently as 1925. Walls and barrel vaults were covered with mural paintings—sometimes executed in true fresco technique—depicting battles, hunting scenes, excursions, and as in Parthian times these forms exhibited a variety of contributory foreign elements. Floors and walls were also treated with mosaics, large in scale, rich in color and of a realistic style mainly Greco-Roman in inspiration.

Sasanian fire temples and sanctuaries, continuing a tradition and a cult some thousands of years old, were scattered through Persia and the Sasanian empire.[76] Some, conspicuously situated, were for public participation in the ritual; others, accessible only to the priests, were for guarding the sacred fire. The forms were similar: a dome on squinches placed over a square formed by four large piers connected with arches. Sometimes a corridor protectingly surrounds the inner sanctuary. The few structures that remain, with rare exceptions, are in ruins.

58. Taq-i-Bustan, 6th century. Central ivan.
59. Taq-i-Bustan. Detail of pilaster and cornice of central ivan.
60. Taq-i-Bustan. Tree of Life relief from face of central ivan.

58

61

62

61. Taq-i-Bustan. Foliate capital.
62. Taq-i-Bustan. Lattice capital.
63. Taq-i-Bustan. Elephants, from lateral wall of ivan.

63

64

65

66

67

An important exception to the decayed state of these little Chahar Taqs is the very early   Figs. 68-70
Sasanian fire temple at Neisar, probably from the second century, which has been judiciously
restored. Its beautifully studied proportions are charming, but even more important is the
evidence of an early solution to the transition from square chamber to round dome. From the
exterior, it is composed of three distinct elements: a large square base pierced by four large and
symmetrical arched entrances, a smaller concentric square resting on the base; and a dome,
resting on the intermediate square. On the interior in each corner of the smaller square base is
a small conical vault, a squinch, connecting the round dome to the square base. In effect, these
squinches transform the interior of the smaller square into an octagon (with unequal sides, to be
sure) at its base and into a parabola at its top. The variety of stonework—from large rough
stones to quarried blocks to carefully chiseled brick-shaped stones above the arched portals—
adds to the sense of frank and simple form. Other Sasanian fire temples remain, that at Qasr-i-
Shirin from the late period and others from earlier centuries such as those at Tang-i-Chak Chak,
Kuh-i-Khwaja (Parthian), Kazarun, and Firuzabad, all testifying to the vitality and development of this form. In all these, the original ornamental stucco and moldings have largely disappeared, and the thick coat of plaster that once covered the coarse rubble walls has crumbled,
often exposing the crude underbody which, even though rather gaunt and dreary, often adds a
certain grandeur due to the simplicity and power of the form and the scale.

The plan and structure of the Sasanian fire temples were so simple and forceful that they
exerted a marked influence both East and West. In Buddhist territories, the fire temple sufficiently resembled the stupa to be acceptable. Because of its ample interior spaces it offered many
advantages and was adopted as a "hollow stupa," the interior being used for worship and filled
with images of Buddha. Westward diffusion was even more significant. Christianity had secured
a definite place in the Sasanian empire, especially under Chosroes II, and there were Christian
churches in many places (only three of which have been excavated: at Ctesiphon, Hera and
Rusafa, all in Iraq). These, and perhaps other early Christian churches on the so-called "cross
within a square" plan are, in essentials, so close to certain fire temples that one building was
occupied and used alternately by Christians and Sasanians, being compatible with the ritual requirements of each. This Christian acceptance of a Sasanian architectural type was one of the
avenues by which Persian artistic forms reached medieval Europe and exerted a marked effect
on Romanesque architecture.[77] This same Sasanian fire-temple plan was repeated in a whole
series of churches in Armenia, a type that extended up into the Balkans. Its influence in Persia
continues to the present, a virtually unbroken tradition since its inception.

68. Fire temple at Neisar, probably 2nd century. General view before restoration.
69. Fire temple at Neisar. Restored.
70a. Fire temple at Neisar, Plan.
70b. Fire temple at Neisar. Analysis of the squinch. Drawing by Godard.

68

69

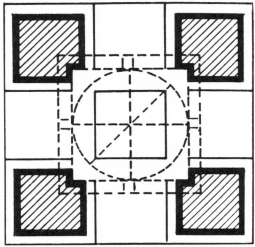

70a

70b

Architecture is more than physical structure, more even than significant aesthetic form. It is also an expression of cultural background, immediate or remote. For better or for worse, it demonstrates assumed cultural values, reveals the principle of growth, or failure thereof, in a society. Thus, an appreciation of the deeper purposes that were directing, consciously or unconsciously, the creation of a monument is essential to our comprehension and evaluation of it. No single monument can be appraised in historic isolation: for adequate appreciation, a monument must take its place in relation to others of its kind. Frequently, of course, this is scarcely possible, for time and circumstances can be strong enemies of architecture. Nevertheless, we can fill the gap a bit with evidence left by documents, traditions and sundry related artifacts.

These yield us some understanding of a remarkable Sasanian building: the Takht-i-Taqdis, built on a sacred mountaintop in northwest Persia, a point of contact between heaven and earth. Here was the reputed birthplace of Zoroaster and the most sacred shrine in the Sasanian world. The site, formerly known as Shiz or Ganzaca, is today called Takht-i-Sulayman.[78] Although the Takht-i-Taqdis was in existence only a few years (having been built by Chosroes II in 618 and destroyed by the Byzantine Emperor Heraclius in 628), it was one of the most famous buildings in history. Because of its fantastic cost, its fabulous equipment, its startling pretensions to control the skies, and as the hated temporary custodian of a section of the True Cross, the Takht-i-Taqdis aroused interest throughout the world, from Ireland to Delhi. Appearing conspicuously in popular religions of Central Europe, in literature and romance of medieval times, in countless paintings, tapestries, bronzes and models, it is at least possible that this building provided the initial concept of the Castle of the Holy Grail.[79]

The Takht-i-Taqdis is especially significant for the history of Persian architecture because it expressed so specifically the ancient Persian theory of the function of the royal throne as intermediary between heaven and earth. As at Persepolis, this function was effected here by sympathetic magic, the structure and its apparatus reproducing the firmament with an unmistakable verisimilitude that was to compel sympathetic response from the heavens.

The building, evidently a large pavilion, is described in many Arabic, Persian and Byzantine sources, including a somewhat fanciful portrait in Firdawsi's *Shah Nama*. Its splendor was incredible. Built of precious woods, cedar and teak, overlaid with much gold, its balustrades and steps were also gold-plated and only gold and silver nails were used throughout. A dome, representing the sky, was inlaid with lapis lazuli and turquoise, heavily encrusted with jewels, stars being indicated by rubies set in golden astronomical tables, and the sun and moon rendered in gold and silver. The inner sanctum was enclosed by a magnificent gold-embroidered curtain decorated with astral symbols. The nobles who attended the ceremonies in this sometimes cold spot were warmed by gold and silver braziers and in the arcades they were protected from drafts by curtains of sable and beaver. The fabulous cost of this construction, like the Taq-i-Kisra, represented a very considerable portion of the state's wealth. It was ordained by a council of (presumably all) the nobles of the empire, who apparently felt that the nation's life required it.

The whole building was set on rollers so that it could be turned in exact correspondence to the rotating sky, thus assuring the efficacy of the rituals. Even more significant was the apparatus for creating mock storms: machines for lightning, thunder and rain, all planned to induce the outer heavens to send real storms to replenish the earth and promote life. That this was a holy spot where under the King's leadership earth and sky could meet in cooperation, and that it was the spiritual center of the empire is further shown by the requirement that the day after each king was crowned at Ctesiphon, he had to begin the long hard journey to Takht-i-Sulayman—all the way on foot—in order to complete his investiture.[80]

The descriptions, some of which were based on eyewitness accounts given by men in the army of Heraclius, do not give us a specific picture of the Takht-i-Taqdis as architecture, but they do reveal the motives that inspired its creation. Again we are confronted with the Persian royal confidence in a magical and beneficent function far beyond any thought of practical shelter or convenience. Thus, the Takht-i-Taqdis continued the invocational character of the program set forth centuries earlier at Persepolis.

Similarly, the Chahar Taq, or fire temple, of Nawbahar was another in a long chain of efforts to bring the world of man into accord with the cosmos. Around its wooden dome, reputed to have been 150 feet high and 150 feet in circumference, were 360 adjoining rooms, corresponding to the days of the year. Like the Taq-i-Kisra, it was sumptuously decorated with patterned silk wall-hangings or walls inlaid with jewels (probably outlining constellations). It was built by the Barmakids (ancestors of the ministers and confidants of Harun ar-Rashid) and, like Persepolis, its purpose was to celebrate the spring festival. The very name Nawbahar means the new or earliest spring.[81] The structure must have been very solid as well as high for Abu ibn Kays attempted its demolition but finally was balked by the massive structure and had to give up this plan.[82]

One of the reasons that so little remains of so many imposing buildings is the fact that after the third century only comparatively inferior materials were used. Sasanian builders, if they preferred cut stone, were hampered by a break in the tradition of stone construction and design, but at the same time they also lacked a mature masonry technique. The characteristic buildings were generally built of coarse broken fieldstone or roughly shaped blocks of stone set in thick, fast-setting mortar beds. There was also available, especially in Mesopotamia, excellent brick, both fired and sun-dried, which was faced with stucco, a brittle and perishable material. Frequently wooden beams were added for greater flexibility. Only occasionally was cut-stone masonry used and then for foundation or detail, or for facing a rubble core.

With limited architectural resources, Sasanian builders suddenly had to meet urgent demands from the new dynasty, which felt that it must proclaim itself as promptly as possible with impressive monuments. Despite these handicaps, some handsome and imposing buildings were achieved, and some splendid ruins exist today. The most important and influential Sasanian contributions to architecture were in the development of the dome and its setting on squinches and in the achievement of huge vaults built without centering. The tentative division of massive weights into structural functions, the concentration of loads on separate fixed points (as at Sarvistan), and the suggestive use of transverse vaults also provided important groundwork for further development. All of these were significant for Western developments and were fully deployed in subsequent Islamic architecture.[83]

Yet, despite some undoubtedly imposing and expressive monuments with lavish and vigorous ornamentation, Sasanian architecture, on the whole, was not a fully realized art. It was to be the destiny of subsequent periods to refine what was ambiguous or clumsy in Sasanian hands, to clarify Sasanian structural forms, bringing their great potential to full maturity.

III. Early Islam: New Purposes

With the speed and violence of a desert whirlwind, the Arabs burst out of their ancestral homes, shattered Persian military power at Nihavand in 637 and, within a few years, sent the surviving Sasanian rulers fleeing toward China—a shocking disaster to a proud people. Surprisingly, the continuity of Persian life was not really severed; daily life, local government, and even some of the arts for a long time proceeded about as usual, and essential elements of Sasanian culture continued to operate within the new framework. The conquering forces of Islam imposed no architecture because they had none to impose. However, Sasanian architecture—inventive, audacious, impressive as it was—because of its somewhat elemental structural forms had relied too heavily upon inert masses for stability. It was the achievement of Islamic Persia to refine these powerful forms and to develop their potentials into an architecture of exceeding beauty. The result was to be lighter, more sensitive, more varied and more expressive than its antecedents.

The organization of the Islamic Empire, dominating a culturally diverse area, opened new avenues of communication, augmenting commerce, and creating an expanding economy which in time supplied the wealth needed for a new and urgent era of building—both secular and religious. Mosques, colleges, tombs, bridges, forts, hospitals, caravanserais and libraries were needed everywhere.

Older Persian religions, particularly Zoroastrianism, were gradually displaced by the new faith. The Moslem religion, more humane and democratic, created new loyalties; its simplified duties replaced the complicated priestly hierarchy which, with its exacting ritualism, had stood between man and God. Islam proclaimed both the brotherhood of all and the fatherhood of God, giving a new dignity and value to the common man. In Persia, conversion to Islam was not so much by the sword as by persuasion:[84] the demonstration of economic and political advantages involved an attractive new status for the individual. Almost immediately, Islam became the central and conspicuous fact in the Persian mind, competing in authority with political sovereignty. Replacing the grandiose palaces that had so ostentatiously proclaimed the pride and power of kings, the mosque, with its more communal and democratic character, became as immediate and important as the cathedral in medieval Europe. The humility and dedication of genuine piety gave to these new cultural foci a certain simplicity and dignity.

From the mosque five times a day came the call to communal prayer, and on Friday the call for attendance. But one need not await the call or the sacred day, for the mosque is open to all people at any time. It belongs to all Moslems on an equal basis, and the homeless wanderer has the same claim on its spiritual and physical hospitality as the proudest resident prince. Even today, incoming caravans repair immediately to the mosque where access is never questioned and any vagabond sleep. Moreover, the mosque became the basic educational institution, from elementary grades through sophisticated theology, including grammar (a subject more significant than in our Western schooling), philosophy, and popular lectures. A college, *madrassa*, was often attached, and each mosque had its own library.

The mosque was also a political institution of central influence and varied functions. Here are still posted royal decrees, notices of war and mobilization, tax assessments and exemptions. Here monarchs proclaimed their authority and, in the name of Islam, cursed their enemies. To be mentioned in the Friday prayers was an essential confirmation of sovereignty. The mosque was often a court of justice; there contracts were frequently drawn and signed, business transactions completed, gossip and news exchanged. Scribes did a flourishing business there, and parts of the mosque complex were even used as prisons or morgues. As the mosque is, and has been from the beginning, spiritually coextensive with the whole life of the people, it often becomes physically integrated with the city—indeed can become its very focus. With its various appendages it was a veritable *civitas Dei* set in the midst of the *civitas mundi*. In cases where this integration of the two worlds was complete, the mosque merged with surrounding buildings. Hence it had neither external walls nor façade, save for the portal, and its area was frequently difficult to define.

Architecturally the mosque may be wholly an interior court design, conceived to exclude the outer world and emphasize its inner concentration. These courts are always characterized by repetitive elements—arcades or columns—that give it coherence and at the same time define

71. Tarik-Khana, Damghan, 8th century. Columns, looking toward quibla wall.
72. Tarik-Khana. Plan: (A) Court, (B) Mihrab aisle, (C) Mihrab.
73. Tarik-Khana. Columns and vaults.

its purpose: fulfillment of the deepest kind of unity. In the mosque is focused the life and meaning of the community.

For the most part, the first mosques were extremely simple ("mosque" means merely "a place of prostration"), often not unlike the layout of a camp.[85] But, in addition to the armies of Islam, the rapidly increasing number of converts soon required something more adequate and practical, not merely for protection in the cold regions of upland Persia but also for reasons of dignity and prestige. Compared with lavish Sasanian structures, the hastily built Moslem places of worship (with only a few notable exceptions) must have seemed shabby and unimportant. Use of the same building by more than one religion—a practice which continued for more than a century—could be only temporary, ill-suited as these structures were to the requirements of Islam. Ritual requirements at first were satisfied merely by defining an open space, outlined by a ditch or reed paling.[86]

Almost immediately after the advent of Islam in Iran, there was a great surge of building. New religious and secular buildings were continuously required, and they had to be created out of local materials, techniques and styles. To be sure, no Persian building from the first two Islamic centuries has survived, but contemporary descriptions tell us much.[87] Thus, we know that these earliest mosques, often ambitious undertakings involving great expense, continued the ancient Persian architectural tradition of sumptuous ornament.

There were three basic mosque types: the pavilion—a dome over a square chamber (the Sasanian fire temple adapted to Islamic ritual); the open ivan—a simple barrel vault in the tradition of the Taq-i-Kisra; and the open court (the so-called Arab plan)[88] surrounded by arcades. Eventually, all three types were merged. Within three centuries, many important mosques, to say nothing of caravanserais, bazaars, and other types of structures, were built. Little survives, but contemporary accounts speak of these mosques with enthusiasm for their beauty, lavish decoration and impressive size. For such a building program Persia was able to supply competent, experienced architects who, under the Sasanians, had been grounded in the already long traditions of Persian architecture. For about two centuries, Sasanian materials and building methods continued in use, and even as late as the fourteenth century Sasanian structures were still conspicuous throughout the land, providing ideas and serving as models for new structures. The vast arch of Ctesiphon repeatedly stirred rulers to emulation, challenging the capacities of architects for more than a thousand years; and the solid, solemn fire temples were readily adapted to serve as tombs; Imamzadas, of the venerated saints.

Figs. 71-73

Except for a few crumbling walls and archaeologically revealed groundplans, the oldest existing Islamic structure in Persia is the little Tarik-Khana in Damghan, built toward the end of the eighth century. The original building, although partly rebuilt and naturally decayed by some 900 years, is sufficiently intact to convey its quality. The layout is the typical inner-court plan: a large almost square court surrounded by arcades of tunnel vaults set on huge round piers $11\frac{1}{2}$ feet high and almost 6 feet in diameter. The whole design is simple,

71

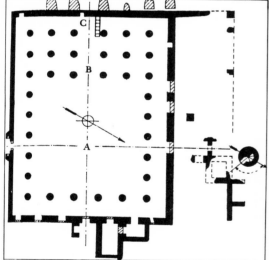

72

73

indeed rather obvious, yet most competent judges have found it curiously imposing: it gives an "impression of grandeur and sovereign beauty; one of the most magnificent buildings in Islam."[89] It certainly expresses dignity and confidence, but also humility. In materials, structure, and technique, it is a purely Sasanian building. The only innovation lies in the slightly pointed arches which are the first recorded in Persia. Even the radial lay and the dimensions of the burnt bricks and the columns themselves are identical to the same features in the nearby Sasanian palace.

But how can a purely Sasanian building speak with the authentic voice of Islam? Despite its strongly Sasanian character, the Tarik-Khana is not Sasanian, for its personality is definitely changed by the contribution of Islam.[90] This is of crucial importance, for it implies that form rather than material or technique is the primary source of its strong emotional effect. This form is at least in part a result of ritual requirements which demanded no complicated offices or services and were therefore completely compatible with utmost simplicity. The plan calls for a wide, unencumbered space with a single focus, the *quibla* wall, behind which lies the *mihrab,* an arched panel marking the direction of Mecca toward which the faithful must direct their prayers. A mosque must be horizontally extended to accommodate many worshippers on the same level, thus creating physical breadth and an aura of serenity. The huge piers of the Tarik-Khana, strong beyond the requirements of structure, provide calm assurance. The unhurried rhythm of the arches, the powerful vaults designed with frankness and economy, the low roof which deepens shadow, all unite in an ensemble of harmonious proportions and solemn effect. Thus, a form governed by new purposes and attitudes, emotionally supplemented, in the Tarik-Khana was deployed to a new effect.

Many other important buildings were built in the subsequent century but of them only verbal notices survive: the two great mosques at Bokhara and several at Rayy, the citadel of Semnan, a caravanserai built by Harun ar-Rashid on the road to Tus, the mosque of Sari and the mosque at Qazvin finished in 868.[91] Similarly, the Dar al Imara built by Abu Muslim at Merv *circa* 747 is today only a memory,[92] but it was especially significant because of its traditional symbolic intent. Essentially the plan was that of the Sasanian fire temple: a large domed building open on all four sides, with four tunnel-vaulted ivans, each giving onto the square central court. It was also an obvious representation of the "Four Quarters of the World" and, like the Persepolis portal, an affirmation of world sovereignty. Abu Muslim used to sit in the very center of this building, perhaps as a ritual act, seeking support for his audacious scheme to overthrow the Umayyad dynasty and to place a Persian in the seat of Islamic power.[93]

In their present state of somber simplicity, the earliest Islamic monuments would probably have seemed to their builders impoverished and monotonous, for the architecture of the period was already committed to rich decorative effects, exuberant but sophisticated. These consisted largely of superlatively designed and executed polychromed stucco. The earliest remaining fragments—examples from Nishapur, probably of the late eighth century; from the Masjid-i-

Figs. 74-76

Jami in Shiraz, of the late ninth century; and from the Masjid-i-Jami in Nayin of the mid-tenth century—are of great beauty and elegance. The mosque at Nishapur had marble columns, gold tiles, walls with polychrome carved stucco and profusely ornamented roofs. It is reported that at Damghan "magnificent ornaments with precious marble" were used.[94] Both the Dome of the Rock in Jerusalem and the Mosque of al-Walid in Damascus had set commanding examples of ornate decorative effects, but it is interesting that contemporary accounts repeatedly give the Persian mosques at least equal rank in splendor. Fragments of clear fresh color testify to the sophisticated and clearly developed level of ornamentation which must have been reached at this time.

From Parthian times on, carved and polychromed stucco had been a major factor in architectural embellishment. The variety of Persian invention, style and mood seems to have been quite inexhaustible, ranging from the unadorned to the brightly colored, from huge symbolic floral patterns covering whole walls to small and delicate insets carved with a jeweller's finesse, from static patterns of staccato punctures to designs of long and sinuous melodic lines. With the acceptance of Islam, panels of stately inscriptions began to appear, marching in slow rhythms across swiftly scrolling spirals. Sometimes, as in a fragment from the Masjid-i-Jami of Shiraz, these stuccos are essentially two-dimensional, lucid and graceful; at other times they are massive, multi-leveled and of almost bewildering opulence.[95]

The Samanids

The final acceptance of Islam brought a much needed peace and was accompanied by a prosperity that furnished the economic basis for creative energies. By the second half of the ninth century, a genuine Persian renaissance was developing in Khurasan (which then included Transoxiana and Afghanistan). There, under the brilliant Samanid dynasty which ruled the Turan region from Bokhara and Samarkand throughout the tenth century, a new yet characteristically Persian culture emerged. The tenth century was one of the most exceptional and creative in Persian history.[96] Persian literature flourished; all the arts and sciences were pursued with a seriousness and enthusiasm that is reflected in contemporary pottery, which for sobriety and force ranks with the world's greatest.

Only one monument survives from the period, but that is one of the finest in Persia: the Figs. 77-79 mausoleum of Ismail Samanid. Built in Bokhara sometime prior to Ismail's death in 907, this is an edifice of imposing force and originality. Both in structural development and in its brilliant decorative deployment of material it exerted a strong influence on subsequent Islamic architecture.[97] It is almost cubical, roughly 31 feet on each side, with a low hemispherical dome and, at the corners, four small ovoid domes of Sasanian derivation. An open-arcade gallery, just below the cornice, surrounds the building. The walls, which slope inward slightly, are fortified at the four corners by huge, three-quarter inset columns, made more emphatic by dark shadows. In form and emphasis the building has a time-defying solidity, appropriate for a memorial. Its

74. Nishapur, 8th century. Stucco ornament.
(New York, Metropolitan Museum of Art, Rogers Fund)
75. Masjid-i-Jami, Shiraz, 9th century. Stucco ornament.
76. Masjid-i-Jami, Nayin, 10th century. Stucco ornament.
77. Tomb of Ismail Samanid, Bokhara, 907.

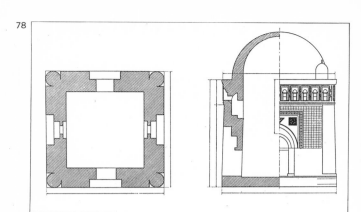

78

79

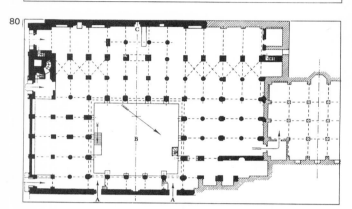

80

81

simplicity and impressive scale (although it is actually a small building), its harmonious and thoroughly studied proportions, its vigorous and inventive ornamentation, combine to rank it among the masterpieces of Persian architecture.

Judging by the number of buildings reported to have collapsed during the first centuries of Islam, the techniques necessary for stability of domed buildings had not been fully developed prior to Ismail's tomb, the only building of the period to have survived in this region. The problem of setting a dome over a square chamber is here carried beyond the simple solution of Parthian and Sasanian times. Consisting of three supporting arches which curve down from the crown of the arch to the walls, the squinch carries the thrust of the dome downward —somewhat in the fashion of a Gothic flying buttress. This ingenious and constructively sound solution is but one example of the way in which the simple mass of earlier buildings was analyzed and developed in a functional manner. Similar examples, such as the four double-arched portals with their framing panels, the massive corner columns that seem to support the gallery, and the interior colonettes, are likewise all individually defined features which are organically related to the whole.

Quite as commanding as the powerful form and robust construction is the decorative energy of the surfaces. Here brick was used with a vivacity and intensity that had no precedent, prophesying the superiority of Persian brick masons who, especially in the subsequent three centuries, were to create masterpieces of vaulting. The deeply shadowed texture of the walls, recalling wicker-work,[98] veils the harsh reflected glare of sunlight. Much of the ornament seems to be derived from techniques evidenced in carved wood—a confirmation of various statements by Istakhri that a good deal of wood was used to build the early mosques of this region.

In the region of Turan, this impressive monument was followed by a whole series in a somewhat similar style, and early Mongol architecture continues many of the same features. In Central Asia proper, the tomb of Jalal ad-din al-Husayni, at Karakanid, Usgen (built in 1152, some 250 years after the tomb of Ismail), has the same imposing cubic form, heavy ornament and a similar—if more refined—portal arch, which, however, bears the notable addition of carved terra-cotta, delicate and intense.[99] Subsequent mausolea became increasingly concerned with decoration and although architecturally clumsy and inept, devoid of monumental character, they nevertheless had carved stucco of extraordinary finesse and imagination.

In the tenth century mosque of Nayin, on the north edge of the Central Desert, the horizontality that had dominated the Tarik-Khana or the solidity of Ismail's tomb gave way to the old Persian urge for verticality, seen in the lofty columns of Persepolis, the elongated Seleucid columns at Khurra, and the high vaulted ivans of Sasanian times. This urge reappeared at Nayin in sharply pointed tunnel vaults, which are nearly three times as high as they are wide.[100] Excessively slender columns flank the mihrab (the outer columns are 16 diameters high, the

Figs. 80, 81

inner 13) and convey a spirit of excitement through attenuation which is quite unlike the spirit of the earlier Islamic monuments. The exuberance of ornament at Nayin is also Persian in character. The piers, soffits of the quibla arches and the mihrab itself are covered with superb stucco patterns, deeply carved and formerly polychromed. In subject, too, these patterns recall ancient Iranian traditions, celebrating the theme of fertility—most welcome to a community on the very edge of a great desert.[101] Of course, such highly developed ornament had its antecedents, the most notable of which is Amr Laith's Masjid-i-Jami in Shiraz, built about 894. The scrolling acanthus pattern seen in a fragment of stucco which ornamented one of the mihrab arches at Shiraz has more elegance, freedom and liveliness of movement than the Nayin stucco, although it is also closer to Hellenic designs.

Probably there were so many monuments as fine or finer than Nayin that the geographers, who are so constant in their praise of notable examples but never mention Nayin, regarded it as architecturally inferior.[102] Its court façade lacks unity and focus and, compared with the massive concentration of Ismail's tomb or the quiet assurance of the Tarik-Khana, it seems fragile and insecure. The trend toward attenuation had perhaps developed too rapidly.

Fig. 82   Under the shadow of the eastern Elburz mountains, facing the vastness of the Asian steppes, there stands in stark majesty a supreme architectural masterpiece: the Gunbad-i-Qabus, the tomb tower of Qabus-ibn Washmgir. From its spreading plinth to the tip of the conical roof, it rises a full 167 feet, with another 35 feet or so underground. It is built of time-defying hard-fired brick, now bronze and golden tan in color. The interior dome, now turned greenish-blue, is covered with tightly fitted bricks, some molded in varying sizes in order to fit exactly the inward sloping areas of the walls. On the exterior, ten powerful right-angled flanges project from the circular body, vertically uniting base and roof. Kufic inscription panels between each flange (both at the top and near the bottom of the tower) tell us that it was built by Qabus in 1006–7. Except for these inscription panels and the flanges, the monument is totally bare of ornament.[103]

Qabus was an extraordinary man, ruling Gurgan intermittently from 976 to about 1012. A scholar and patron of scholars, a poet and patron of poets, a calligrapher, astrologer, linguist, chess player and doughty warrior, he was also unreasonably suspicious and, in the end, was assassinated by his exasperated nobles. His life was such as to engender a longing for security and repose, as well as a defiance of fate—all qualities eloquently expressed in the design of this monument. It owes its power to great height and bleak singularity, to the sheer concentration on simple mass and powerful form which allows no argument or distraction. The structure is stripped clean, a warrior in mortal combat with Fate, as it were, a monarch-poet wrestling with eternity. Solemn, formidable, it makes an affirmation of death and death defied. Is there any funerary monument so expressive, so commanding?

The Gunbad-i-Qabus is the earliest and most expressive of a series of some fifty monumental towers still standing. These towers, which cover a period of seven hundred years, vary

86

83

84

83. Pir-i-Alamder, Damghan, 1021.
84. Chihil Duktaran, Damghan, 1058.
85. Sei Gunbad, Rezeieh, 1277.
86. Tomb of Ala ad-din, Varamin, 1287.

85

86

87

88

87. Tomb Tower, Shrine of Bayazid at Bistam, 1313.
88. Gunbad Abdullah, Damavand, 12th century.
89. Tower of Toghrul, Rayy, 1139.

90

91

93

94

95

96

enormously in size, form and ornamentation. They have been found in nearly every part of Persia. The great majority are round, beginning with the tomb tower of Pir-i-Alamder (1021) Figs. 83-85 at Damghan and at Lajim, Mazanderan (1022), and continuing through the fifteenth century. Towers with prismatic flanges like the Gunbad-i-Qabus continue into the fourteenth century Figs. 86-90 with the tomb tower at Bistam (1313). There is an important group in which the body of the tower is composed of an engaged cluster of almost round shafts, as at Jar Kugan, at Radkan East Fig. 91 (1280–1300), and at Kishmar (fourteenth century) where the circular shafts alternate with prismatic flanges and both are elaborately ornamented. Another type, with coupled columns which begins with the Rabat-i-Malek, or the tower at Jar Kugan, reappears in the Kutb Minar of Delhi. A few of these towers are octagonal, beginning with the Gunbad-i-Ali at Abarquh Figs. 93-95 (1036) and continuing through the fourteenth century in tombs at Qumm and the Imamzada Jafar at Isfahan (1341) and even later. Some are square, such as the Gunbad-i-Surkh at Maragha of the eleventh century or the tomb of Shahzada Muhammed at Sari in Mazandaran of the Fig. 100 fifteenth century. In addition to the variety of plan, these towers differ also in base and terminus: some have no bases, others a low socle—square, round or hexagonal. They may be crowned with ovoid domes, as in the large but comparatively low towers, or they may have stalactite cornices leading to tent or polyhedral domes. Some towers are not over 30 feet high while others, like the graceful Monar Sarban at Isfahan of the eleventh or twelfth century, reach nearly 150 feet. Clearly, the formal inventions were myriad and even more variety was made possible by combining more than one form, as in the minaret and tomb of Arslan Jadhib (997– Fig. 104 1028 at Sangbast.

These towers faithfully reflect period, local styles and the genius of individual architects. The rugged Gunbad-i-Ali (1056) at Abarquh, crowning an abrupt little eminence, is built of heavy rubble and its walls show a decided entasis. Most towers are of plain brick but, beginning in the early eleventh century, decorative facings were devised of cut and raised brick laid in an infinite variety of patterns, rhythmically arranged in contrasting zones separated by collars or narrow bands of emphatic design. Rich shadows not only subdue painfully bright reflections but they also provide a scale whereby the height of the tower can be immediately gauged and appreciated. In twelfth century towers (for example, the Mu'minin Khatun at Nachshirvan, Armenia) deeply recessed panels and a network of raised brick in patterns of colored enamel give a rich and quiet surface that does not detract from the tower's monumentality. Blue enamel brick insets, frequently outlining huge rectangular Kufic inscriptions, were common, and by the fourteenth century mosaic faience was used for cornice and friezes.

The earlier towers of Maragha (a special study in themselves)[104] are masterpieces of brick construction and compact energetic form—particularly the square Gunbad-i-Surkh (1147) Fig. 92 which, with its ingeniously designed brick patterns and its ponderous corner column, recalls the tomb of Ismail Samanid. Its secondary ornamentation consists of inset carved terra-cotta panels placed above the arched panels. Later examples are more lavishly decorated, for instance the Gunbad-i-Kabud (1196) which has sunken pointed arched panels on each face, the whole overlaid by a geometrical framework in blue faience and enriched by a dense stalactite cornice and a blue on white inscription band. This sumptuous combination is saved from weakness by the massive form and stout engaged columns framing the panels. In other Maragha towers, the insets of blue and white faience make a particularly lovely contrast to the soft red tone of the brick.

Figs. 97-99

Another remarkable minaret built *circa* 1149 by the Ghorid Sultan Ala ad-Din at Jam in Afghanistan, rises spectacularly out of the heart of a deep rocky gorge.[105] It is two hundred feet high, in three stages of studied proportions and of firm stance, densely covered with deeply cut stucco. This stucco consists of an especially rich counterpoint of floral and geometric ornament wrapped around interweaving bands of Kufic. This handsome inscription contains a whole chapter of the Koran, the *Maryam sutra*—973 words! The minaret is in perfect condition, save for two flaring platforms that have broken away. It is a work of mind and spirit, an exultation and commemoration of military and political triumph, confronting and dominating the bleak mass of unfeeling rock which surrounds it. This is a work of psychic intensity.

Figs. 96, 100-102

Scattered all through the province of Mazandaran and up into the Elburz Mountains are some striking and often handsome tomb towers, frequently combined with mosques. Of rustic local style they are often quite touching in their simplicity. The best of them, however, are from the fifteenth century and most are distinguished as a simple mass with a top frieze of slightly corbeled blind arcades. They sometimes have an astonishing similarity to eleventh century Romanesque towers. Most of them are in native red brick, although some are brown or tawny

Fig. 103

or even plastered. They are all dignified, generally unpretentious, and occasionally powerful in form. Throughout Persia, but mostly in the southern regions, is a very striking tower form resembling a sugar loaf. These consist of some ten or fifteen receding courses of plain convex panels stacked one on top of another in diminishing sizes, rising to quite a sharp point—an architectural fantasy that has a good deal of charm. Very similar to each other, their history is still to be written; their dates are uncertain but are probably nineteenth or possibly eighteenth century, although reputed to be earlier.

Perhaps the antecedents of all these towers were the cairns and poles erected by earlier Central Asian tribes to commemorate their victories. Their ultimate source, however, is in the more potent tradition of the "high place"—a tradition thousands of years old in the ancient East and of ageless concern in Persia. Affirmations of nonmaterial value, the focus of reassuring spiritual power, are evoked by these stately memorials. The inscription on the tomb tower of Mu'minin Khatun at Nachshirvan emphasizes the time-defying intent of these structures: "Everything passes; may this remain."

99

100

101

99. Tomb of Ala ad-Din, Jam, *circa* 1149.
100. Tomb of Shahzada Muhammed, Sari, 15th century (?).
101. Imamzada Sultan Muhammed Tahir, near Babul, 1470.

The Ghaznavids

The renaissance of Persian culture initiated under the Samanids was transmitted to their successors, the warlike Ghaznavids, in the form of architectural ambitions and traditions, sophisticated taste, and enthusiasm for literature, science and art. Mahmud of Ghazna (997–1030), an eccentric and ferocious conqueror who amassed enormous wealth in his conquests, was a passionate devotee of architecture, on which he lavished immense sums and great energy, utilizing workmen from all quarters of his realm. Of his sumptuous architecture there remain only two victory towers and the impressive ruins of Lashkari Bazar.

The tower of Mahmud and the similar one built by Masud II nearly a century later were originally topped by cylindrical shafts. The body of each tower, externally shaped in a series of convex panels framed by emphatic flanges, was enriched with geometric interlaces, bold Kufic inscriptions and intricate leaf designs of carved terra-cotta. The great palace complex of Lashkari Bazar,[106] in Afghanistan, is a walled-in area of 7 x 2 kilometers. A monumental ensemble, it included a grand esplanade, a huge royal palace (538 feet on one side and 260 feet across the façade), a large central court and several subsidiary courts, a reception hall reminiscent of Persepolis and Firuzabad, a mosque, bazaar, various private structures, and extensive gardens with pavilions, canals and fountains. The whole was planned as a unit along a common axis. Of its many significant features one of the most important is the repeated court plan which has four portals, one in the middle of each side: the typical four-ivan mosque plan.

Ornamentation was varied, including not only carved stucco but also, in the great reception hall, large mural paintings of people in handsome costumes. (Today these are badly damaged, but originally they were rich in color.) The buildings themselves recall the ninth century Abasid palaces at Samarra and Ukhaydir but repeat some features of Firuzabad and Persepolis.[107] The material is brick, fired and crude, with timber inserts as binders. The forms of construction include large ivan vaults, domes, and pointed arches.

Mahmud inspired similar ambition among "his nobles, who built magnificent palaces, mosques, pavilions, gardens, reservoirs, and aqueducts in the provincial capitals."[108] His son, Masud I, continued this passion for building. Not satisfied with the inheritance of a series of gardens and palaces, he created his own and, accordingly, constructed a royal city, Gawhar Shah-i-Masudi. This city had a symmetrically arranged pair of palaces, one for summer and one for winter (domed), a large audience hall and, apparently, an ivan—all the costly work of some twenty years. But the poet, Nizamir-Aruzi, tells us a lot in three lines:

> How many a palace did great Mahmud raise
> At whose tall towers the Moon did stand agaze
> Whereof one brick remaineth not in place.[109]

The mausoleum of Arslan Jadhib at Sangbast from the early eleventh century with its single minaret (possibly there were once two), in its massiveness and use of four portals continues a style

99

102. Imamzada Ibrahim, Amul, 1519.
103. Tomb near Burujird, late 18th century (?).
104. Tomb and minaret of Arslan Jadhib, Sangbast, 997–1028.

inherited from Sasanian times. These four portals especially, so inappropriate for a tomb, witness the continued dominance of Sasanian tradition. The severity of the immediately preceding structures such as Ismail's tomb or the Gunbad-i-Qabus seems definitely ameliorated by the rounded corners and deep chambers, which might once have been externally concealed by a gallery, as well as by the squinch arch that is much higher and more graceful than the too compressed round-backed squinch of earlier times.

Central Persia—The Buvayhids

If Khurasan under the Samanids and Ghaznavids took the lead in the renaissance of Persian culture and the initiation of a new era in architecture, Central Persia under the regime of the Buvayhids was simultaneously developing a somewhat different cultural pattern. Apparently animated by the finest Iranian traditions, the energetic rulers Fakhr ad-dawla and Adud ad-dawla undertook extensive building, of which almost nothing remains. Their vizier, Sahib ibn Abbad, himself famous as scholar, poet and administrator, was also a discriminating patron of all the arts, combining a genuine enthusiasm with fastidious taste. A new architectural style was forming in Shiraz and Isfahan, where the sahib built a mosque, that according to reports was very beautiful but too fragile to endure. Adud ad-dawla's palace and library in Shiraz was a vaulted two-story building containing 360 rooms, each of different shape, each decorated in different style and color. According to Ibn al-Balkhi, Firuzabad too had a worthy hospital and a fine library.

Aside from sections of the Masjid-i-Jami in Isfahan, the oldest standing monument representing this new dispensation is the Shrine of the Duvazdah Imam in Yazd, dated 1036. Here, the ancient problem of setting the dome on a square is all but perfectly solved (the dome is a little too low). In earlier solutions, the zone of transition was narrow and compressed, obviously only a mechanical adjunct without beauty or character in its own right. But in the Duvazdah Imam this zone is fully developed; it becomes a partner in the whole, equal in height and in aesthetic function to the dome above and the chamber below. Visually, it is actually the dominant member of the ensemble.

How high should the squinch be? And how should the space within its arch be filled in to display, not too rudely, the crucial function it performs? The tripod squinch of the mausoleum of Ismail Samanid, though harsh, is obviously quite strong; that at Sangbast is high enough, yet the back appears shallow and weak. At the Duvazdah Imam, however, a highly ingenious solution is provided to these questions. The interior of the squinch is composed of three arched panels, consisting of a deep half-dome flanked and supported by two lower and shallow quarter-dome panels, all merging upward and outward to reach and carry the ring of the dome. It is bold, simple and powerful, effectively suggesting the structural energies at work. This form was destined to be carried to perfection in Seljuk architecture, developed so brilliantly in Isfahan.

Fig. 374

102

104

103

IV. The Seljuks: Structure as Beauty

Seljuk architecture, noble and powerful, structurally sophisticated, was neither sudden nor accidental. Rather it was the culminating expression of a Persian renaissance that had begun in the early tenth century with the Samanids. This renaissance reached its apex under the Seljuks, for although artistic production of a high order continued beyond the twelfth century, a perceptible decline in creative energy became evident. This is often true when the momentum of a great epoch has passed its maximum and there is a tendency for the monumental and heroic to ease off into the romantic and reminiscent.

Cultural Background

In addition to her own constant resources, Persia had assimilated much from the economic and intellectual wealth of the Persian-dominated Abbasid Caliphate established in Baghdad about the middle of the eighth century. The productive stimulation of different, and often competing, societies was steadily enlarging and energizing Islamic cultural life and thought, supplying richer content and new models, both aesthetic and intellectual. Most significant was the appropriation and preservation of classical Greek culture. Through well-organized translations financed by Caliph Mamun (813–833), Greek philosophy and science became known in Persia, where its influence was crucial as indeed it was to be in development of the European Renaissance. Galen, Plato and Aristotle were assiduously studied by all leaders of Persian thought. Moreover, the Abbasid Caliphate bequeathed an intense appreciation of learning in its most serious forms. "Seek ye knowledge even unto China," commanded the Prophet Muhammed and, next to prayer, learning was regarded as most sacred, preferable even to unreasoned piety. Mansur (754–75) contributed much to the esteem of learning and his patronage of poets and scholars made serious discussion groups fashionable. Such associations were enthusiastically adopted, providing an effective way to distribute and stabilize the new culture. Throughout this early Islamic period, although Persian genius was essential for the administration of the great Islamic Empire, Persia's own national personality was frustrated and depressed.

During the tenth century, however, Persia produced a constellation of poets, philosophers, mathematicians, astronomers, physical scientists, historians, geographers and lexicographers— most of them brilliant, many of unequaled eminence, all with a high degree of originality, boldness and cultural breadth. Despite turmoil and wasteful conflicts, the Samanid reign in Persia was a literate and civilized era. In comparison, the same years in Europe were dark indeed.

By far the most important element in the initiation of the native Persian revival was Firdawsi's poem the *Shah Nama*, completed in 1010. One of the world's greatest epics, it entered immediately and permanently into the heart of the nation. From the coming of Islam, which Persia enthusiastically welcomed and profited by, no independent artistic creation can be cited before Firdawsi. Although Arabic had displaced Farsi, the Persian language (which was steadily being weakened and corrupted by imported words and idioms), Firdawsi wrote his poem in Persian words, cleansing the language of foreign intrusions and giving it a fresh and vigorous personality. In all of his fifty thousand lines he used no more than nine hundred and eighty-four Arabic expressions; the rest were purely Persian.[110] Not only did he restore to the Persians the use of a renovated and magnificent language, but his work also created new confidence and patriotism. The *Shah Nama* demonstrated the glory of Persia's past, revived her traditions, renewed popular festivals, promoted national enthusiasm and was at the same time the prophecy of her future. At this critical moment in Persian history the nation's ethos received a powerful impetus.

Through his accomplishment, Firdawsi mobilized the resources of Persia. If Firdawsi stands out as the greatest poet, he was not alone to contribute to his nation's cultural enrichment, for Persians increasingly indulged their natural aptitude for mathematics and the dawning physical sciences. The spirit of intellectual independence and creativity was stirring through all Persia, and the accomplishments of this era would help to guide it through catastrophes to come.

The rulers, a number of them true scholars and even poets, rivaled each other in patronizing poets, artists and scholars. The honor of being a patron was regarded as an obligation of royalty and a valid claim to status and public esteem. The libraries of the time tell the story of a widely shared culture, in which learning was revered. Sahib ibn Abbad, vizier of the Buvayhids and successful ruler of most of Persia before his death in 996, had a vast library of certainly more than two hundred thousand volumes.[111] Each mosque had a collection of books, and magistrates were encouraged to collect and preserve them. The Gadi of Nishapur designated a house with a library especially for the use of visiting scholars, and even supplied them with living expenses. One of the most famous libraries was compiled by Adud ad-dawla and installed in a special building in Shiraz. A long vaulted hall opened onto numerous rooms where books were housed in specially made cases and a systematic catalogue provided.

Of course, Persia's passion for learning was shared with the rest of Islam; Ibn Nadim of Baghdad, for example, published (*circa* 988?) an immense catalogue of all the known books of the period, both Moslem and non-Moslem. These libraries were put to wise and generous use, many of them open to all applicants, and stipends—including allowances for paper and pens —were generally provided.[112]

From this background there emerged a series of scholars, scientists, designers and artists, who effected impressive achievements in many of the arts. Both the Buvayhid and Seljuk periods produced some of the most remarkable textiles ever achieved: designs of solemn power, marked originality, elegance and imagination as well as unsurpassed weaving technique. There are specialists who regard the pottery of the period, mostly from Nishapur and Samarkand, as the finest ever made.[113]

The second half of the ninth century saw the appearance of a number of encyclopaedias and general histories. Lexicographers and grammarians, working effectively for the development of language as an instrument of precision and communication, added to the new era of dawning knowledge. Each of the learned professions produced a number of great thinkers, many of whom were competent in several areas. Al Razi (*circa* 850–923), the famous physician, was more than the greatest clinician in Islam; he was also a chemist and a physicist whose influence spread through the Moslem world to make itself felt in Renaissance Europe. His ablest colleagues were mostly Persian. One, al Dinawari, was simultaneously lexicographer, historian, botanist and astronomer. In the tenth century, al Tabari (838–923), author of a ten-volume history of music which contained much valuable historical and even archaeological material, also created a systematic star catalogue, astronomical tables and ingenious astronomical instruments. There were numerous lesser philosophers and historians whose work was on a very high level indeed. Mathematics and astronomy were vigorously pursued and were well summarized in a Persian encyclopaedia of 976 entitled *The Keys of the Sciences,* and a small society of scholars of varied subjects, the "Brethren of Sincerity," published valuable joint commentaries.

Intellectual activity reached its climax during the first half of the eleventh century.[114] Among a flourishing group of scholars were two of the world's greatest, two who gave the period universal distinction: Ibn Sina (Avicenna, 980–1037) and Alburini (died 1048). Possibly the greater of the two was Ibn Sina—prolific, versatile, brilliant, comprehensive, a great organizer and insatiable worker. He was a born mathematician, poet and astronomer who made important contributions to physics and was one of the world's first great figures in medicine and the related field of pharmacology. As a medical authority, he was greatly honored throughout Europe and his medical treatises were basic texts at Oxford and Montpellier as late as the seventeenth century.

In the second half of the eleventh century, Omar Khayyam, the well-loved poet, was also an original philosopher and a great mathematician. He recognized thirteen different forms of cubic equations (with suggested solutions) and, in 1074, he formulated a new calendar of "remarkable accuracy, probably better than our own."[115] He is still widely regarded as a brilliant algebraist. Another quite different spirit who influenced the same age was al Ghazali (1038–1111), a man of intellectual power, deep feeling and utter dedication. He was outstanding as poet, philosopher and theologian but, in the spirit of the times, he also had working knowledge of a number of the sciences and wrote original astrological treatises and a general summary of astronomy.

Into this highly developed civilization came the conquering Seljuks, an Irano-Turkish stock, their leaders already familiar with the Persian culture established in Central Asia under the Samanids and Ghaznavids. They must have been impressed by the Ghaznavid magnificence, but their austere way of life and the tempering effect of their native plains of Central Asia inclined them to a more vigorous and less opulent style.

The Seljuks, led by Toghrul Beq (1031–63), conquered Persia in various campaigns from 1037–51, expelled the remnants of the Buvayhid regime and established a dynasty of great rulers rarely matched in history: Alp Arslan (1063–72), Malik Shah (1072–92), and Sultan Sanjar (1117–57)—all sincere and serious men, born to rule nobly. Humbled by their recent conversion to Islam, they had a notable sense of ethical responsibility.[116] Alp Arslan and Malik Shah were supported by the famous vizier Nizam al-mulk (1020–92), one of Asia's greatest statesmen who was also an ardent Sunni. His deep interest in theological questions, coupled with the general intellectual pursuits of the time, resulted in a flowering of madrassas which, although born in Persia, became prominent throughout Islam.[117]

Seljuk Architecture

The power and nobility of Seljuk architecture is doubtless best exemplified by the Masjid-i-Jami of Isfahan, one of the greatest mosques in the world. From earliest times Isfahan, by virtue of its central location and natural beauties, had been destined for greatness; it was inevitable that its Friday mosque should be outstanding. As a magnificent structure in a city chosen to be Persia's capital during widely separated epochs and under a variety of rulers, the Isfahan Jami is not purely Seljuk, but those portions which date from Seljuk times are, even today, its chief glories.

More than 800 years of Persian architecture are revealed in this great mosque's twenty distinct structures, varying in date from the eleventh to eighteenth centuries. During its long history it has been much fought over, repeatedly damaged, reconstructed, and all but ruined. Nevertheless, it endured all and in its thirty or so historical inscriptions—still not perfectly interpreted—it adds documentation to our appreciation of its majestic forms.

A four-ivan court (196 x 230 feet) is enclosed by arcades and two-storey open galleries faced with mosaic faience on buff brick. A deep ivan, embellished with especially strong faience revetments opens into a spacious domed sanctuary built, as the inscription states, by order of Nizam al-mulk at the beginning of Malik Shah's reign (1072, almost certainly before 1075). Some of the earlier buildings are still visible, however, and it is possible that the lower section of this sanctuary itself may date from the late tenth century. This chamber—spacious and noble, of compelling grandeur—supports a huge dome, 50 feet in diameter, which rests on deep trilobed squinches (their form developed from the Buvayhid Duvazdah Imam of Yazd). The squinches, in turn, are supported by huge cylindrical piers that are crowned by Abbasid-looking stucco scrolls, certainly of earlier date than the dome.[118] The sanctuary is surrounded by arcades and corridors covered by an amazing variety of domical brick vaults, some with stout ribs and an independent supporting framework in the Gothic manner (thus indicating the possibility of a contributive relation).[119] Frequently these vaults rest on columns that vary in date from pre-Seljuk to the Safavid period.

All of the ivans were rebuilt or redecorated on a Seljuk base, showing that the basic plan of the Jami existed during the Seljuk period. The half-domed northwest ivan, externally a ribbed structure, is on the interior filled with huge stalactites (probably eighteenth century, for the reornamentation is dated 1744). Other worthy components of the Jami complex include a vaulted winter prayer hall (*circa* 160 x 83 feet) built in 1447 and largely undecorated; a chamber with the superb early fourteenth century Oljeitu mihrab; and a madrassa built in 1366 with an interesting transverse vault and entrance ivan. However, these are just parts of a large and intricate structure that defies brief description.

Figs. 105-108, 110

Figs. 114, 116

Figs. 115, 117-131

Figs. 111-113

Aesthetically, the most important unit in the Jami is the small but superlative north dome Figs. 109, 132 known as the Gunbad-i-Kharka, dated 1088, and located at the opposite end of the central axis from the sanctuary. This is perhaps the most perfect dome known. Its solemn, memory-gripping power is not a matter of dimensions (65 feet high and 35 feet in diameter), but of design. Every feature has been meticulously studied and, with the perfection of a sonnet, fused into a completely unified whole. Mechanically it matches the mathematical requirements of the ideal dome, achieving an accuracy at critical points that approaches exact duplication.[120] In each corner, four narrow arched recesses framed by slender angle colonettes, form the downward extension of the squinch. From floor level, these colonettes lead the eye swiftly up to the typical tri-lobed squinch. The squinch itself is enclosed by a larger arch that, together with identical arches along the side walls, supports an octagonal ring of sixteen shallow panels merged with the base of the dome.

All arch forms, including the dome, are of the same contour and constitute the key ele- Figs. 133-135 ment or motif that, beginning in the corners, with successive comprehensiveness enclose one element within the other until their multiplicity is resolved and merged in the dome—the inevitable conclusion of the complex upward movement. The dome is thus the culminating point in a vertically rising stream of force. Such natural and logical succession of identical forms, so precisely defined, endows this space with a compactness and perfect unity that makes it as moving as anything in Persian architecture. The subdued bronze color of the brick, relieved only by inconspicuous dark gray and white carved terra-cotta insets, adds to the solemn impression. The sense of utter finality however comes from the perfection of form itself. This single-shell dome, having survived without a crack for almost 900 years in a country of earthquakes, testifies to the "subtle mathematics and impeccable mechanics" of its Seljuk architect. Like the Gunbad-i-Qabus, it was "built for eternity."[121]

Other important Seljuk mosques were built in the style of the Isfahan Jami and, fortunately, several survive in relatively good condition. The Friday mosques at Ardistan (*circa* Figs. 136-139 1180), Zaware (1153) and Gulpayagan (1120–35) are all in approximately the same style but, giving up the uninterrupted verticality seen in Isfahan's north dome chamber, they show a strongly marked horizontality in the zone of transition. Rather somber in tone, their decora- Color Plate II tion—as at Ardistan—is in simulated brick bonding and applied stucco or terra-cotta insets, giving a discreet but quietly intense quality to the buildings. Structural functions are emphatically revealed and each mosque has an air of dignity and independent authority.

105. Masjid-i-Jami, Isfahan, 11th–18th century.
Plan: (A) Court, (B) Domed sanctuary chamber, (C) North dome chamber (Gunbad-i-Kharka),
(D) Sanctuary ivan, (E) Northwest ivan, (F) Northeast ivan, (G) Southeast ivan.
106. Masjid-i-Jami, Isfahan. Northwest ivan, 1150,
with stalactite decoration, probably of the 18th century.
107. Masjid-i-Jami, Isfahan. Sanctuary ivan (before recent restoration),
with 15th century mosaic decoration probably on a Seljuk base.
108. Masjid-i-Jami, Isfahan. Southeast ivan, 12th century with later repairs.

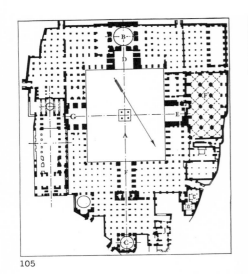

105

106

107

108

109. Masjid-i-Jami, Isfahan. North dome (Gunbad-i-Kharka), 1088.
110. Masjid-i-Jami, Isfahan. Sanctuary dome and 15th century minaret.
111. Masjid-i-Jami, Isfahan. Rear of half-dome of northwest ivan.
112. Masjid-i-Jami, Isfahan. Rear of sanctuary ivan and dome, *circa* 1072.

110

111

112

114

115

116

117

118. Masjid-i-Jami, Isfahan. Vaults, south corner.
119. Masjid-i-Jami, Isfahan. Vaults with intersecting arches, south corner.
120. Masjid-i-Jami, Isfahan. Columns and vaults, northeast side.
121. Masjid-i-Jami, Isfahan. Detail of vaults, west corridor, *circa* 1075.

121

122

123

122. Masjid-i-Jami, Isfahan. Vaults and piers, northwest side, 14th century.
123. Masjid-i-Jami, Isfahan. Northeast ivan.
124. Masjid-i-Jami, Isfahan. Columns and vaults, northeast side.
125. Masjid-i-Jami, Isfahan. View into northeast ivan.

124

125

126. Masjid-i-Jami, Isfahan. Star vault.
127. Masjid-i-Jami, Isfahan. Star vault.
128. Masjid-i-Jami, Isfahan. Star vault.

127

128

129. Masjid-i-Jami, Isfahan. Vault (Herzfeld no. 60).
130. Masjid-i-Jami, Isfahan. Vault (Herzfeld no. 61).
131. Masjid-i-Jami, Isfahan. Domical vaults.
132. Masjid-i-Jami, Isfahan. North dome chamber
(Gunbad-i-Kharka), 1088. Cross-section.
133. Masjid-i-Jami, Isfahan. North dome chamber.
West corner of interior.

129

130

131

132

133

134. Masjid-i-Jami, Isfahan. North dome chamber (Gunbad-i-Kharka), 1088. Dome and squinch.
135. Masjid-i-Jami, Isfahan. North dome chamber. East corner of interior.
136. Masjid-i-Jami, Ardistan, *circa* 1180. Plan: (A) Court, (B) Ivans, (C) Domed sanctuary chamber.
137. Masjid-i-Jami, Ardistan. Detail of entrance ivan.
138. Masjid-i-Jami, Ardistan.

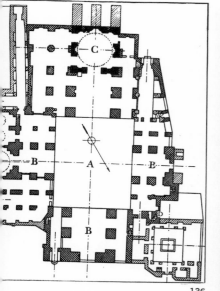

136

137

138

139. Masjid-i-Jami, Ardistan, *circa* 1180. Soffit of arch, looking toward dome.
140. Masjid-i-Jami, Qazvin, 1113–1115. Detail of upper wall.
141. Haydariya, Qazvin, early 12th century. Corner detail.
142. Haydariya, Qazvin. Upper wall.

139

140

141

142

143

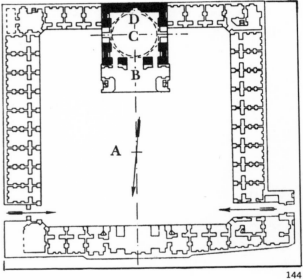

144

143. Haydariya, Qazvin, early 12th century. Detail of squinch.
144. Haydariya, Qazvin. Plan: (A) Court, (B) Ivan, (C) Domed sanctuary, (D) Mihrab.
145. Haydariya, Qazvin. Lower wall.

146

147

148

146. Alaviyan, Hamadan, late 12th century. South corner detail.
147. Alaviyan, Hamadan.
148. Rabat-i-Malik, wall, before 1078.

The large Masjid-i-Jami at Qazvin (1113–15) is impressive by virtue of its serene sanctuary space, capped by a large dome (52 feet in diameter). The groined squinch is almost primitive in its emptiness, quite without the mediation of subordinate forms to fill it in, which for centuries had been a major concern of architects. The high plain dado emphasizes its utter simplicity. But this was no weakness or blunder of the designer's, for originally almost the whole quibla wall was occupied by the largest mihrab in Islam. We can only guess how beautiful it must have been from the exciting contemporary mihrabs of the nearby Haydariya and the tomb at Alaviyan.[122] However, we are certain that its quality was superb because of other details   Fig. 140 which remain, paramount among which is the double inscription frieze that circles the entire chamber. The upper is a splendid Kufic and the lower a fine Nashki, both in white against a blue ground of vines and tendrils—for sheer loveliness perhaps not equaled in Islam. The wall is rescued from inertia by lively bonding and great ornamental loops of outset brick that describe sweeping curves. With a gigantic and intricate mihrab set in this strong architectural framework, the total effect must have been majestic, and the very simplicity of major forms would have contributed substantially to the impression.

A beautiful little madrassa, the Haydariya (early twelfth century) is also in Qazvin, today   Figs. 141-145 incorporated into a larger nineteenth century mosque.[123] Perhaps the finest Kufic in all Persia is seen in its stucco frieze while its carved stucco mihrab is also splendid. Its deep corner squinches, formed by high pointed arches, are echoed in the decorative arched panels surrounding the upper wall. Intricate brick lays, simulated brick bonding and subtle stucco ornamentation provide constant, but unaggressive, detail. In a tomb at Hamadan, the Alaviyan, dating from   Figs. 146, 147 the second half of the twelfth century, the interior is completely covered with deeply carved stucco of extraordinary richness. Somewhat in the style of the Hardariya, this is a *tour de force* of opulent imagination. To explore its recondite harmonies and decorative meaning is an endless pleasure.

These great Seljuk monuments of Central Persia were rivaled by several structures built to the northeast, in Khurasan and the region of the Oxus.[124] Of these, the Rabat-i-Malek is one of   Fig. 148 the most imposing ruins of the Islamic period. Only part of one wall of this caravanserai remains. This fragment alone suffices to show that here (possibly as early as the first half of the eleventh century) was built a massive and forbidding structure of plain brick, simple as becomes a frontier fortress. A row of almost cylindrical piers (five diameters high) are connected at the top by arches whose form is clearly derived from a squinch, thus relieving the blank walls. A narrow, ornamental frieze marks the plain cornices. This building, which must have been impressive in medieval Islam, hints at a source of the Seljuk builders' preference for forthright and powerful forms.

In an utterly desert region, on the road that runs from Nishapur to Merv, Sultan Sanjar finished in 1155 a combined caravanserai and palace, the Rabat-i-Sharaf.[125] From the exterior it is a formidable fort of high blank walls and strong bastions. A handsome portal is formed by an arch within an arch, the outer powerfully framed in raised brick, the inner framed with a Kufic inscription in stucco. Within, two large four-ivan courtyards were both equipped as mosques and each had a fine stucco mihrab. The interior is ornamented with bold and ingenious patterns of raised and cut brick, such as had distinguished earlier towers like the Pir-i-Alamdar of Damghan and the minaret of Sava.

Sultan Sanjar was buried at Merv in a mausoleum worthy of a noble and tragic figure. Constructed after his death in 1157 by a devoted follower, this tomb is a ponderous and solemn cubical chamber, about 90 feet square and was surmounted by a blue-tiled dome (now partly collapsed), also about 90 feet high. The interlocking framework of the ribs seen on the interior seems to carry the weight of the dome but, in reality, it is probably more decorative than structural.[126] The crucial transition from sanctuary block to dome above was beautifully achieved by means of corner galleries which concealed the squinch, so awkwardly exposed on the exterior of earlier Seljuk domes. The circular drum of the dome, often previously just a bare octagon, is similarly arcaded and the galleries, decorated with pierced brick in ornamental lays, mitigate the severity of mass without compromising the simplicity of the structure as a whole. The main entrance is on the east, facing the rising sun; a comparable opening on the west was closed by a grill. The other two sides are blank, thus providing a plan more suitable for a tomb than the four-opening fire-temple scheme used in some earlier mausolea. Brick latticework at the corners admitted light to the corridor around the base of the dome, a further development of the tomb of Ismail Samanid and one that anticipates the mausoleum of Oljeitu at Sultaniya. The plain walls are enriched with a typically Seljuk plaster coating marked out in simulated brick bonding with decorative insets of terra-cotta. This mausoleum is the last, and one of the finest, examples of Seljuk architecture.

Fig. 149

V. The Meaning and Function of Persian Decoration

It is through design in its deepest sense that the Iranian genius for visual beauty has found its most adequate and characteristic expression. To the twentieth century Western mind, words like "ornamental" and "decorative" too often suggest something of secondary importance. In architecture, simple and massive forms certainly have independent value of their own but they also provide the substructure for ornamentation. Ornament can both embellish architectural form and exist as an aesthetic achievement in its own pure design. The inherently symbolic character of Persian design, coupled with the iconoclastic ban against figural and other naturalistic representations, endowed Persian ornament with a seriousness and intensity unfamiliar in Western culture. Because so much aesthetic talent has been so seriously concentrated on ornament, a more sympathetic and detailed study of it is required. In no other architecture has ornament played such a vital and creative role as in Persia.

A genius for lucid and vigorous decoration was already a striking feature of the prehistoric pottery of this region, and sumptuous embellishment, mentioned in the earliest descriptions of buildings, has been archaeologically confirmed. In fact, important structures of all periods in Persia have been aglow with color, often resplendent with gilding and mural painting or enriched by carved stucco or ingenious patterns in brick or tiles.

With the Islamic period there began a new chapter in the history of architectural ornament and the relation of structure to decoration. Within the slowly maturing tradition of color and pattern as an essential of the building art old themes re-emerged, slowly infiltrated from earlier contacts with India, China and the Hellenic west. The discovery and control of new materials and techniques was nowhere else exploited with such zest and knowledge.

132

IX

X

XII

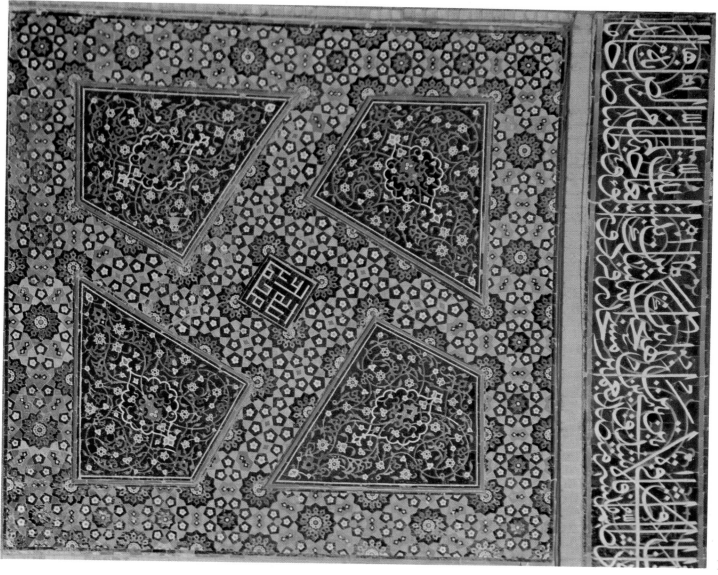

XIII

XIV

XV

XVI

XVII

XVIII

XIX

XXI

XXII

XXII

The theological prohibition against the representation of living forms, although not formulated by Muhammed himself, expressed a real dread of possibly contaminating the new religion with idolatry. Muhammed was aware of the Near Eastern disposition to see magical symbolic powers in natural objects and phenomena, and he was anxious to keep religion pure from such distractions.[127] Hence, within the mosques and in the decoration for mosques or tombs, we find few representations of actual living forms.[128] However, even the orthodox caliphs of Baghdad, proud and luxury-loving, curious and open-minded, did not hesitate to adorn their great palaces with human figures (largely of Hellenic inspiration); in privacy, confident of their power, they thought to escape theological censure. Similarly, in the palaces of Persia itself figural representation was common. From ancient and especially Sasanian times, there was abundant precedent for animal forms, and familiarity, sympathy and talent all made animal representations vivid. For the representations of human beings, there was less precedent, so that although human figures were represented both in pottery and in stucco panels during the Islamic period, they were for the most part closely related to architectonic form.[129] Even though figural compositions of the enthroned king surrounded by his courtiers are often graceful and highly decorative (and one or two individual figures are not without merit), all these figural types must be observed with tolerance and judged for their decorative significance. They were probably all richly polychromed and, when viewed together with patterns of geometric designs, dados, tiles, and occasionally mural paintings placed above them, the effect must have been quite beautiful.

All the arts of Persia are closely interrelated and all express a common cultural inspiration. The great Islamic art of calligraphy, with its standards of rhythm, precision and expressive form instructs and disciplines other arts. Poetry, universal and indispensable in Persian life, together with philosophy, overt and implicit, nourish all cultural expressions. Analogies between Persian poetry and visual design are numerous: rhythm and rhyme, stress and resolution, surprise and fulfillment merely head a long list of characteristics that have their counterparts in each.[130] Both are distinguished by a lively appreciation of sensuous delight as well as the abstract. The talent for rational abstraction enabled major aesthetic creations to escape a particularity, turning them toward generalized expressions of timeless significance. A decisive element in the development of abstract motifs was the Persian predeliction for mathematics and philosophy. Faith in the controlling power of significant forms shows itself early in Persian art and is a central feature of its finer poetry.

Not only are the motives of poetry and visual ornament deeply akin, but at times they also share the same faults. In both, the urge for ingenious elaboration (a *horror vacui* is a temptation which betrays many poets) can crowd the theme and extinguish mood. Designers were more restrained by the limitations of visual perception but, even more, by the accepted canons of lucidity and order which their mathematical aptitude and training favored.

Through many centuries, with but few exceptions, Persian patterns continued to be lucid and rational, thoughtfully as well as imaginatively planned. The most intricate compositions of the Islamic period were built upon familiar, traditional themes: the sacred tree, the lotus in myriad forms, the undulating vine that turns back on itself, leaf and flower motifs of infinite variety and subtle geometric interlaces built up from six or eighty stars. The primary themes are three: symbolic plant and natural forms (from prehistoric time expressing fertility and abundance); geometric schemes (especially since Parthian times, due partly to Greco-Roman and Chinese contributions) affirming control of interlocking forms, and calligraphic compositions (from the Islamic period).

That which to a hurried Western viewer may seem a surfeit of opulence is to the Persian, who values contemplation, an invitation to leisurely exploration, a promise of endless delight. Familiar with the decorative language, he can read the ornamentation as if it were a poem, or he can lose himself in following, unraveling its subtly planned intricacies. Inventiveness in ornamental patterns is as infinite as the potential combination of notes in Western music—always some genius comes to open up fresh variations and new vistas. To the Persians, the conventions, traditions and formulae of decoration were not impediments or restrictions but were to be used as guides, as supports, for new inventiveness and variety.

The sources of Persian architectural ornament are as wide as their contacts; they acquired from all: from Western Asia, Mesopotamia, Assyria and Egypt as well as from the East. From Darius' inscription at Susa and Achaemenid carvings we know many themes common to all, the sun rosette and the Ahura Mazda symbol of the winged disk, originally Egyptian, to mention but two. From Sasanian times, Persians imported textile patterns from the east and from India, perhaps, the pointed arch and vaulting schemes as well as handsome stone carving. From China, in medieval and later times, came figures like the Dragon and Phoenix, and the Chinese cloud band, common in faience as well as carpets and manuscripts. Rome contributed to sculptural ideas and techniques, and Hellenistic characteristics spread through the country in the centuries following Alexander's conquest, but neither of these Western influences deeply affected the habits of a people for whom the abstract and symbolic had a prior and permanent attraction. The appropriation of these various themes and styles was complicated and often obscure, but whatever their origins they eventually became absorbed into the repertoire of Persian art and became Persian in character and use.

134

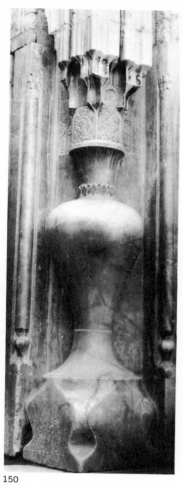

150

151

152

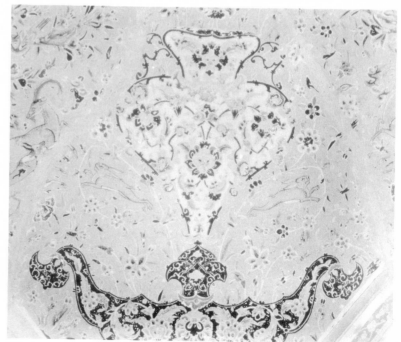

153

The abstract decorative patterns that embellish Persian monuments—especially the great mosques—are far more than prettification. What appears to Western eyes as merely decorative is indeed decorative but it is also affirmation through traditional and pictorial symbols. One particularly universal symbol, the cosmological tree of many seeds issuing from the vase of the waters of life, was used on Sumerian seals, Achaemenid columns, and in Sasanian carvings. During the Islamic period it reappeared as angle columns on the dado courses of the courts or portals of most mosques. These consist of the vase, the shaft decorated with foliage and a stalactite capital representing floriation. Their life-affirming function is clearly demonstrated in the cemetery of the fifteenth century Shrine at Gazur Gah, where a beautifully carved marble tree form is attached to the gravestone, an assurance of life denying the victory of the grave. The portal of the Masjid-i-Shah (and many other mosques) is defined by a twisted triple cable molding which represents the living vine, rendered in bright turquoise faience and issuing from a large vase, which is frequently of golden-toned marble. The vase is an almost indispensable element in all floral ornament, especially from the fifteenth to nineteenth centuries, but it has prototypes in prehistoric times.

Figs. 150-153

In addition to traditional visual symbols, inscriptions play a major decorative role. Much as the Gothic architects presented in vivid pictorial realism the story of the Christian religion, so the Persian designers, addressing a more literary audience, presented Islam in the actual word of the Koran. Each imbued his revelations with high aesthetic principles that transcended both kinds of literalism; each was able to emerge into the realm of pure spirit.

Calligraphy in Persia, as in the Far East, is ranked as a major—indeed elemental—art. The Arabic alphabet, the most decorative of all scripts, was cultivated with passion and was developed by the Persians into an amazing variety of beautiful forms which ingenious architects incorporated into every part of the mosques so that the building virtually *became* the word of God. These inscriptions may range from gigantic Kufic letters high enough to cover whole walls to tiny fluid Naskhi inscriptions hidden in a stalactite panel. As frieze or cornice, they may encircle an entire building and frame all arches. Combined with other designs, they may be buried in geometric ornament or become monograms in decorative medallions. They range from powerful affirmations to barely whispered suggestions. In reading one kind of script, other quite different types are excluded from attention, but to the unhurried worshipper, they will gradually reveal themselves until by echo and refrain the whole building seems to be breathing the divine message of its inscriptions.

In addition to verbal communication, the work of a master calligrapher also communicates a specific emotional quality, and an abstract form of its own. Thus, the austere and noble Kufic proclaims authority and power while the infinitely graceful Thulth—as firmly composed as a fugue—is often of an intensely emotional beauty.[131]

Both structural and decorative forms have cosmic reference. The dome, although it provides the ample unencumbered interior space needed for ritual as well as practical purposes also,

154

and quite consciously, represents the vault of heaven. Floral and geometric patterns were both treated as segments of an infinitely extensible whole that in imagination was coextensive with limitless space.[132]

Despite dazzling achievements in polychrome ornament, Persian designers also knew the value of pure white.[133] In many places, unadorned white was used with impressive effect, enhanced by proximity to areas of intense blue. Often the white stalactite half-domes, especially in portals, pile up like sunlit summer clouds. Such contrasting effects are characteristic in Persia: the dark green oasis contrasts with the bright glare of the desert wilderness; in towns the monumental buildings, rich and intense in color, provide a startling relief to the drabness of streets and the blank whiteness of houses.

The relation of Persian ornament to structure has often been misunderstood and is frequently cited as a seductive misalliance, as if this decoration were just gorgeous fabric applied to the surface. In good examples, ornament is visually organic with the structure, often appearing as if inherent in the material, like the graining of wood or veining of marble. It identifies, defines and emphasizes the component elements and their functions by means of patterns appropriate in scale and character, as in a superb fifteenth century niche of the Masjid-i-Jami in Isfahan. A tiny colonette, a huge dome, wall panels, arches and dados will each have clearly separate decorative treatment and the implied movement of the pattern will accord with stresses and directions in the structure itself as well as adding new qualities of richness and vitality.

Thus, in the façade of the Masjid-i-Ali (1522) at Isfahan, the wall is carefully distinguished from the vertical, presumably weight-bearing members by the surface design. The patterns on the curtain wall are static and directionless while those on the pilasters are powerfully and unmistakably driving upward. The compulsion of the design intensifies, even exaggerates, the mechanical operation of each section. Of course, such a balance between the values of revealed construction and embellishment is not always maintained. It is in itself an imperfectly defined ideal, varying with available materials, technical competence and changes in taste. The result is ornament which can range from bleak mechanics to an almost suffocating luxury.

In the architecture of any period, the coordination of structure and ornament is often imperfect, with structural values concealed, frustrated or over-emphasized. It is more usual, however, to see ornament used to enhance, to give added life to the mechanical forms. The huge arabesques wheeling over a dome increase our sense of its rotundity; the tight band of a dense inscription just below the swelling of a dome sharpens our sense of expanding inner pressures above it; and stout verticals of retangular Kufic give an unmistakable feeling of reinforced support.

The many forms of Persian ornamentation are rendered in different materials: brick in countless forms; stucco; to a lesser degree, wood (in exquisite patterns for railings and ceilings); metals, for window gratings and ceremonial doorways (generally repoussé over wood); and polychrome faience, in mosaic fragments or solid tiles.

Fig. 217

Fig. 154

Brick

Brick was an accepted building material throughout the whole ancient Near East, for the hand-molded plano-convex brick had been invented in Persia by the third millennium B.C. Major Achaemenid buildings, composed largely of stone, as well as Sasanian buildings, occasionally of cut stone but more generally of filled stone rubble, are related in their masonry technique to brick construction. There were good reasons for the Persian preference for brick (other than the scarcity of timber): it is more durable than stone, far less expensive, permits of rapid construction and, because of its superior elasticity, demonstrates quickly the physical forces at work in the structure. These are qualities that encouraged instructive experiment and final achievement. For the creation of mass, for ingenious solution of structural problems, or for inherent decorative possibilities, brick offered many advantages which the Persian explored to the utmost, always with sympathetic regard for the nature of the material. Nonetheless, though brick was in general use, its decorative possibilities were not exploited until well into the Islamic period; stucco had been more or less supreme as a surface ornament during most of the long preceding period. The potential beauties of brick, such as various types of bonding, ornamental end-plugs, contrasting textures, pattern inlays and overlays, began to be thoughtfully realized only in the tenth century.

The use of brick endows the general appearance of any building with specific qualities; it does not permit of sharp corners and moldings, cannot create the feeling of weight, permanence, and hardness that result in formidable stone construction. Instead, it makes for softer contours and quiet mass, even while it allows equal possibilities for monumentality, which is primarily a question of form and scale. At Qala-i-Bist, in the tenth century Ghaznavid arch, we Fig. 155 see a variety of flush bondings. The geometric patterns formed here compensate for the monotony of uniform brick lays, thus creating a lively and interesting plane.

With the Seljuks, brickwork was carried to a perfection, both aesthetic and constructional, that has perhaps never been equaled since. The dome of the Masjid-i-Jami in Isfahan is of an unsurpassed majesty, and the time-defying, stark strength of the Gunbad-i-Qabus is unique. These bricks were not the ordinary building bricks of modern times, but were huge, slightly irregular, square blocks, heavy, and hard. Frequently they measured seven by nine inches and weighed five or six pounds. The best of the fired bricks ring like metal. According to the space they were to fill, they varied in shape and size—cut, molded, flat or curved, especially for the colonettes and angle columns much favored in Seljuk building. Small brick ends (bats), especially when slightly off color, produced a tapestry-like effect. When the contrast was more marked, these inset squares outlined large patterns; the first simple geometric schemes were later developed into huge rectangular Kufic letters. This brickwork brought the wall quietly to life, giving the building an expressive vitality. In Azerbaijan and Mazandaran, in the later twelfth century, these insets were enameled in bright turquoise. Contrasting with the soft red brick of the region, especially when mingled with pure white, the effect is still very beautiful.

139

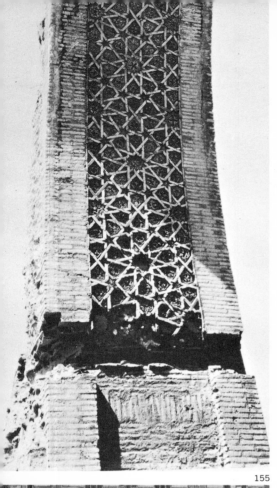

155

156

157

158   159

160

161

155. Qala-i-Bist. Detail of soffit of 10th century arch.
156. Gunbad-i-Surkh, Maragha, 1146. Detail of brick column.
157. Turbat-i-Shaykh Jam, early 15th century. Enamelled brick panel.
158. Tomb of Zayn ad-Din, Tayabad. Enamelled brick panel.
159. Tomb of Zayn ad-Din. Enamelled brick panel of Kufic; inner medallion and upper frieze are Thulth.
160. Do-Dar minaret, Isfahan. Detail.
161. Masjid-i-Jami, Isfahan.
Brick patterns, interior of the north dome chamber.
162. Tomb of Chujuk-Bika, Samarkand.
Brick patterns with stucco embellishments.

162

163   164   165

166   167   168

Early in the eleventh century, in addition to the varieties of flush bonding, various sizes of brick and new bondings and joints were devised. The joints were treated in several ways: a deep, raked line between the ends created a dark vertical shadow which was in sharp contrast to a thin, light horizontal mark between the outer edges of the brick. This combination of vertical and horizontal lines made possible a great variety of patterns, as in the late tenth century tomb at Sangbast. Other schemes were developed and the surface was further enriched by bricks, both sunk and set forward, whole courses being built out by projecting, overlapping units which
formed richly shadowed zones, as at the Damghan minaret or the Pir-i-Alamdar, one of the first structures to employ heavy outset patterns. The end gaps were filled with plugs of molded plaster or finely carved terra-cotta or with handsome little medallions.

The elemental repertoire included squares, triangles, disks, dentals, crosses, swastikas, chevrons, diapers, fretwork and grilles, accented by diagonals—a veritable mosaic of brick-work. Of the various kinds of strapwork, some were precast and applied. Bold Kufic inscriptions entirely composed of outset bricks added force and interest to the handsome abstract forms. The various shadows thus produced were worked into elaborate patterns spiraling or merely en-circling, which added animation and beauty to the exceedingly simple forms of the early memo-rial towers. The brickwork of the Chihil Duktaran of Isfahan (1107),[134] is simple, but elaborate patterns were again utilized in towers such as the handsome cylinder of the minaret at Sava (1110), which is more ingenious than ever in its design.

How competent these brick builders were is demonstrated by the impressive number of
surviving monuments. Besides the single-shell domes of the Masjid-i-Jami of Isfahan, still in-tact after nearly 900 years, there are almost a dozen slender, delicately tapered minarets (over a hundred feet high!) still standing in the Isfahan area alone[135]—and this in an earthquake coun-try. They can only be the products of first-class brick, first-class mortar, first-class craftsmen, and superior designers. Furthermore, a number were made of sun-dried brick and even these lasted for at least a few centuries, a tribute to all concerned.

The variation in the size, shape and color of the bricks and in their decorative lays made surface texture so attractive that the very sober and unostentatious Seljuk builders sometimes gave up applied plaster ornament altogether, as in the north dome of the Isfahan Jami. This de-nial could only have been temporary, however, for patches of large scrolling arabesques still adhere to the roughly contemporary sanctuary dome and also decorated the impost blocks of the piers. The ivan vault of the Ardistan Jami is thickly covered with a network of interlacing arabesques.

It is in the north, in Azerbaijan, that brickwork reached its ultimate beauty. In the
Fig. 156 Gunbad-i-Surkh, as Godard, Schroeder and others agree, we have perhaps the most beautiful example of brickwork known. The angle columns are composed of ten shapes of cut brick, in-volving at least eight molds perfectly adapted to the curving profile of the colonette. Here also

ingenious and sometimes deceptively simple patterns are worked into the panels, but the undecorated brick itself is of such fine quality that it seems to meet all decorative requirements.[136]

More important than its function as decorations was the use of brick to indicate the direction of pressures, as in the older vaults of the Isfahan Masjid-i-Jami. Here the constructional use of brick was truly remarkable. These line directions vary in sensitive response to changing pressures, pressures that they designate and emphasize, clearly intensifying the sense of powerful but securely composed forces. The commanding energy of these Seljuk vaults comes as much from the brick patterns which emphasize the structural forces as from the basic structural shapes themselves. Fig. 372

Sir Edward Lutyens said, "Do not speak of Persian brickwork but rather of Persian brick magic."[137] The wide variety of arches and intersecting vaults and all their curious shapes proclaim an unrivaled virtuosity in brick construction. One element that remained in use for centuries is a little triangular concave panel, evidently based on the form of a squinch, which with its pointed apex bending outward seems almost to lean on space. These cell-like elements assembled in groups constituted the first stalactites, beginning in the portal of the Gunbad-i-Qabus and eventually coming to fill squinches and hollows in many parts of a structure. They appear as supports for the platforms of large minarets and, like little squinches, mark the transition from the corners of a square base into the circle of a dome. The static properties of such panels are somewhat dubious, and within a short time after their appearance plaster and applied materials rather than brick were widely used for their construction. It may be that the tenacious mortar used in the early brick versions accounts for some of their surprising forms and functions, but they are all energetically beautiful, imparting a vivacity and sense of useful work successfully accomplished. Figs. 169, 170

Despite its great beauty, however, exposed brick was thought to be a bit harsh. Thus, imitation brick bonding was created in order to enhance true brick, even while retaining its genuinely decorative quality. This was accomplished by covering a raw brick surface with smooth hard plaster, which was then marked out in interesting brick patterns. Brick end-plugs of great beauty and variety were then inserted. The bricks could be tinted in any way that gave coloristic charm and unexpected variety. This use of simulated brick began toward the end of the Seljuk period, as at Ardistan, and reached its most sumptuous expression in the vaults of the mausoleum of Oljeitu at Sultaniya. At Varamin, the rhythm and delicacy of the brick end patterns, almost colorless, created a tranquil charm well suited to worship and devotion. Figs. 171-173

Brick also produced a most suitable substructure for more elaborate plaster finishes or decorative encrustation. Its concession to the plaster coating encouraged the development of stucco ornament of the richest kind, and the end of the twelfth century saw the fulfillment of these possibilities in great stucco mihrabs. Color Plates IV, V

169 170 171

173

172

169. Gunbad-i-Qabus, 1006–1007. Stalactites.
170. Masjid-i-Jami, Varamin. Stalactites of sanctuary portal.
171. Tomb of Oljeitu, Sultaniya, 1305–1313. Simulated brick gallery vaults.
172. Tomb of Oljeitu, Sultaniya. Detail of simulated brick, end plugs and stucco.
173. Tomb tower of Imad ad-din, 1390, Qumm. Niche of stucco, brick and other materials.

Stucco

From earliest times, stucco—carved, molded, painted—was one of the major elements in Persian architectural ornament, extensively used and highly developed. For nearly 2,000 years the Persians have devised, experimented with and perfected types of stucco treatment, producing a series of masterpieces in a succession of styles that are unequaled anywhere. Too frequently, stucco is disparaged, for it is felt that this medium does not sufficiently resist the designer, that it enables him to create light fantasies without a sense of responsibility or thoughtful planning.[138] The actual execution of stucco patterns, requiring a carver's skill, is not extremely difficult, but design is. The merit of Persian stucco lies primarily in its design—really great design is always a disciplined and imaginative work of genius. It is significant that stucco patterns as well as designs for luster faience, mosaic faience and painted ornament were frequently made by the same artist.

Even the carving itself is not always so easy. First the wet plaster is applied to the wall in a large mass to form the foundation of the design which is blocked out in its major forms; then, as it stiffens to the consistency of cheese, the essential motifs and figures are carved and small sections of new plaster are added as necessary. Finally, after the plaster has dried almost stone-hard, it is cut and polished until it gains clear and lively contours—all rather more difficult than it sounds and far more resistant than brush or pencil. The final process is a plaster coating, thinner than cream, that can yield a surface almost like polished marble, but it is more suitable for a mat surface and subtle polychromy. Furthermore, the stucco carver does not have the stone-cutter's advantage of working in a homogeneous, stable material; because his plaster is always in process of hardening, he must completely finish one section at a time. Some stucco patterns are quite deep, practically three-dimensional, and have to be built up in layers—as many as three to six, possibly even more[139]—each worked separately.

The patterns are often quite complex, five or six components interwoven and moving in various and contrary directions. The carver must foresee how the final forms will develop out of the starting points in the first (deepest) layer, at which point there can only be hints of what they are going to look like when brought to the surface and integrated with other elements. Memory, imagination and precision are all required if the result is to be rational and consistent, rather than confused, for confusion is indeed a danger if improvisation tends to overcome discipline and thorough planning.

Just where this art began and became a serious architectural feature is not clear, but we have examples from the first century A.D. that imply a considerable prior development.[140] Hellenistic motifs from the early Parthian period, rich in color and of complicated patterns, forecast the elaborate polychrome incrustation of later Persian structures. In the enormous ornamental repertoire of Sasanian stucco appear many characteristics which seem not to have been used in Parthian times.[141] We know that the walls of the Sasanian buildings, some of brick but mostly of crude rubble, were thickly plastered and that their ornament was characterized

147

by large and bold motifs,[142] which went beyond the floral designs to include animals and human figures. A significant feature of stucco ornament of Sasanian times is the use of the *double entendre*, patterns that can be interpreted in sharply different ways. This double meaning becomes very important in later Persian ornament. In textiles it developed into the use of the void pattern so that, in addition to the dominant figure of any design, the empty spaces themselves outline significant motifs, thus giving what the Persians delighted in: concealed and recondite meaning that rewarded search beyond the obvious.[143] This interest is related to the theory of double truth, indeed to the whole tendency toward allegorical interpretations that became a source of bitter strife between the orthodox Shi'ites and the Sufis.

Fig. 176   In the early Islamic period, stucco was often of great beauty. For instance, the lively scrolling vine of the ninth century found at Shiraz is a charming and vital design reminiscent of Hellenistic forms from Firuzabad, some 500 years earlier. At Nayin, less than a century later, the ornamentation was not merely sumptuous and firm but subtle and original as well. It was distinguished by exceptionally beautiful Kufic calligraphy and by some new forms that must have been somewhat experimental as they were not repeated in later stucco. The encasement of a solid column with entwining vines, although objectionable to functional purists, was pictorially significant, the primary delight of the Persians being not in architectonics but in the expression of the primal hope for fertility and abundance. Abstract formal perfection, which the Greeks carried to such a high level, was of less interest to the Persians than symbolic meaning: spiritual encouragement (by prophetic representations) and consolation in the painful struggle to achieve a more fertile earth.

Fig. 177   Painted wall panels continued from earliest times and only in the Islamic period were they gradually rivaled by carved stucco. Interesting painted panels were disclosed by the 1937 Metropolitan Museum expedition to Nishapur. Although perfectly flat in movement and scale, these panels have relation to the development of carved stucco. Some of these tenth century panels discovered at Sabz, near Nishapur, are suave and subtle, especially a group of little triangular squinch panels such as mark the transition from square room to the ring of a dome. On them in clear fresh colors were framing bands of red and dividing lines of yellow, striped in red and black, all framed in black. The patterns—palmettes, undulating vines, vases, rosettes—were in white enlivened by red against a ground of bright blue. One of the panels, composed of large intertwined leaf forms, terminates alternately in hands and eyes; it is difficult to interpret but possibly symbolic of life.[144] The designs exhibit a strong self-contained movement, but are much less varied or developed than the stucco carving at Nayin.

Figs. 178-185, 191   During the early Islamic period probably all stucco was colored and, frequently, lavishly gilded but, from the middle of the eleventh century, stucco decoration seemed to give way temporarily to the magnificent development of brickwork. The change was neither immediate nor complete (nor permanent) for, despite the austere beauty of the brickwork of the Isfahan north dome, stucco lost none of its authority. Thus, in an almost contemporary madrassa, the

174

175

176

177

182

183

184

185

186

187

186. Alaviyan, Hamadan. Stucco mihrab, 12th century.
187. Pir Hamza Push, Varamin. Stucco mihrab, 1180.
188. Mashid-i-Jami, Rezeieh. Detail of the stucco mihrab, 1277.
189. Masjid-i-Jami, Isfahan. Mihrab of Oljeitu, stucco, 1310.

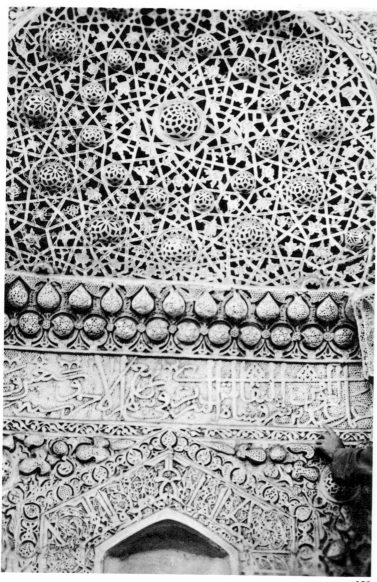

188

189

191

192

190

193

Haydariya of Qazvin, stucco was used for the superlative inscription frieze, for the facing of the arches and for the complex mihrab of originality and power. This fine stucco was even surpassed in the late twelfth century Alaviyan of Hamadan where the interior was completely covered with carved stucco, a work of maximum intensity which focused on an elaborate mihrab.

In the Alaviyan, carved stucco is of remarkable character, opulent in its inventiveness, consistent in design, unified in effect and of impeccable workmanship. Architectural form here is fundamentally clear and forceful, somewhat resembling the Isfahan north dome. Deeply sunk, high arched wall panels in pairs reach up into the squinch, marking the four corners, each framed by a cluster of four nearly round colonettes. The dado, friezes and squinches are likewise all structurally emphatic and provide a dominant rhythm that controls the multiplicity of forms and surfaces. The ornamentation is not merely added prettiness, it is a powerful component in its own right. The massive, sweeping curves of arabesques in the arched panels are three-dimensional, protruding thickly from the background with great force, enriched by complicated starlike punctures. Colonettes and moldings are treated in similar fashion, thus supplying a repetitive surface that gives consistency and uniformity to the whole interior. The climax is, as it should be, in the central panel of the mihrab: the focus of worship. Of this whole *tour de force* Herzfeld, moved by its eloquence despite misgivings concerning the artistic worth of stucco in general, wrote: "Here ornamentation, through the fusion of all factors, is brought to a most intense fortissimo. Words cannot describe it, it must be seen."[145] Herzfeld is right about the insufficiency of words to describe this astonishing creation, but exclamations are not enough. The intent of this great design is the old invocation for abundance and affirmation of fertility. It is expressed here in an overflowing wealth of floral forms: huge leaves, fantastic blossoms, tiny flowerettes, interweaving vines and tendrils—not realistic, but imagined, special and magical, representing an exuberant ideal for an uncertain world.

The patterns, closely interwoven, are really conceived as distinct units, each with a character that must be maintained and kept self-consistent no matter how closely allied to other members. The relative importance of each factor follows a definite scheme of subordination and coordination with varying functions, somewhat like the voices of a fugue or like the complex and separate ornamental systems of sixteenth century carpet design. However rational and systematic the relations are between components, their unified purpose must not be too evident; it must, and does, present a real problem of comprehension, sufficiently baffling to require effort and concentration. Such complexities tend to detach the serious worshipper from his human world, to entice him into an exercise of contemplation, thus making more vivid and convincing the spiritual world from which he derives life and strength. As a device for temporary frustration, a delayed and hence more gratifying resolution, the elaborations are different for each form. Even identical forms are given different values by the patterns of the surface punctures, various kinds of honeycombs or little circular star forms, always concealing their likeness with

Fig. 186

155

ingenious differences. The same variations are to be found in other major forms in the interior of the Alaviyan: colonettes, moldings, panels, are all subtly differentiated, and the rich inscription friezes, continuously modified, add further elements of movement and vitality.

All this at Hamadan was controlled by a master designer who never permitted confusion but managed to maintain throughout a rational and well coordinated composition. Somewhat by contrast, later mihrabs, such as the ambitious fifteenth century one of the Masjid-i-Jami at Varamin, did not wholly avoid weakness and confusion. Others were more directly emotional, like the mihrab panel at Pir-i-Bakran, whose muscular sweep instantly imparts a feeling of power. To contrast with this, a light open framework was superimposed, smaller in scale, elegant and rapid rather than momentous. Almost all of this framework has broken away, however, and its effect can only be imagined from the remaining upper fragments which show an ingenious knotting, an indication of the allegro movements which once played against the ponderous force of the main panel.

It must be remembered that carved stucco was widely and expertly developed throughout the whole Islamic world. There are early and splendid examples in Cairo, Baghdad and Jerusalem as well as many other places.[146] But these inventive and often very handsome stuccos are mostly geometric pattern. Floral magnificence and exploitation of its fluid possibilities was capable of stimulating more symbolic and emotional responses. The full development of this lyrical type of carved stucco was chiefly due to Persian inspiration and workmanship.

Figs. 186-188

The Persian mihrabs were largely the works of individual designers. In fact these works fall into several well-defined groups, each exhibiting a similar style and feeling, but the differences between these groups are not due to temporal sequence. Instead, they are evidence of artistic independence and vitality. The exuberant, complicated three-dimensional type continued for over three hundred years.[147] The precise elegant mihrab of the Pir Hamza Push at Varamin, dated 1180—almost contemporary with the Alaviyan—is as far apart from it in feeling as Holbein from El Greco; and the lacelike character of the stucco mihrab at Rezeieh (1277) is of still another conception.

Figs. 189, 190

The beginning of the fourteenth century (and the astonishing recovery of Persia following the Mongol invasions) was marked by a rapid succession of superb buildings, all of which featured fine quality stucco decoration. The new mihrabs in general were less emphatic, flatter and in more carefully studied proportion. The most famous of these is the mihrab of Oljeitu (1310) in the Isfahan Jami, more architectonic than some of the more demonstrative examples from the Seljuk period. Its components are more rationally composed, clearly differentiated and carefully proportioned. The framing inscription, calligraphically superb, is carved against exquisitely designed blossoms, leaves and threadlike tendrils. The central panel includes two different types of calligraphy against scrolling foliage (some with unusual asymmetries), while across the top is a rich but regular panel of double-row lotus, a favorite fourteenth century motif. Across the lower panel is an abstract pattern of interwoven Kufic. Many other stucco mihrabs

194

195

196

197

198

199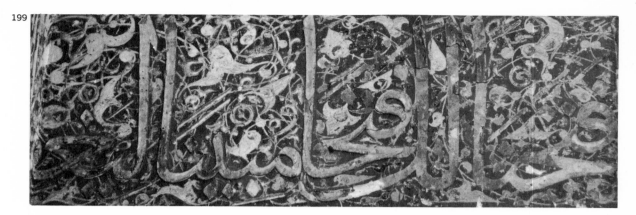

200

201

202

203

deserve a more detailed study than is possible here. Some, like that of the Shrine of Bayazid at Bistam, are masterpieces where new and fascinating lacelike patterns of stars are enclosed in intersecting geometrical framework.

Stucco was effectively employed in a variety of subsidiary ways. In the fifteenth century madrassa of Khargird, the ring of the dome in one of the side oratories is supported by a ring of stalactites, plaster coated and embellished with brick. The monotony of side walls was relieved by myriad little arched panels in low relief stucco, varying in width and with all verticals staggered. All are delicately and precisely executed, giving the whole wall a rich texture and subtle mobility. Figs. 192, 193

In Central Asia, carved stucco and terra-cotta were developed with bewildering variety and perfection of finish. The elegantly varied panels in the soffit arches of the mausoleum of Sanjar at Merv (1157) alleviated the severity of the ponderous cube, but in many monuments, especially smaller tombs in Samarkand, the virtuosity of the terra-cotta ornamentation is overwhelming. Sometimes the building is hardly more than a framework supporting panels, friezes and moldings, all carved with quite astonishing richness. The inscriptions are superb and their spiral floral ground are often of great beauty and fine technique,[148] but as architecture most of these buildings are inferior and their structural weakness is not redeemed even by the breathtaking ornament which distinguishes them.

Such intensive elaboration requires a basic structure of simple mass that clearly dominates ornamentation. This is found in the major buildings of Persia proper, as well as in the great creations of the fourteenth and fifteenth centuries of Central Asia. From the early fourteenth through the fifteenth century, terra-cotta patterns were effectively used interspersed with geometrical strip-work of enamel tile or, similarly, in a subordinate capacity to fill in spaces left between the framework of tiles. The result was a sharp contrast of surfaces, both in texture and design. Beautiful examples are found at Yazd and, especially, in the façade of the Khanequah at Natanz. Fig. 211

In the fourteenth century especially, the stucco workers in conjunction with the calligraphers executed magnificent inscription friezes in which the rhythm and movement of the Kufic and Naskhi letters were intricately intertwined with elaborate floral groundwork. Often two inscriptions of contrasting sizes were used in the same frieze, the smaller usually above; each was distinct but mutually enhancing. More often than not they consisted simply of white lettering on a gray or sometimes blue ground.

These inscriptions, which create great excitement among sophisticates of calligraphy, must really be studied *in situ*. As pure design they are most rewarding but they have also been regarded by Muslims as having magical properties. This reverential concentration on calligraphy, beginning at least as early as the ninth century, the honors accorded the great practitioners of this art and the large number of calligraphers of first-rate competence to be found Figs. 194-208

204

205

206

207

208

204. Shrine of Shams ad-din, Yazd. Stucco inscription, 15th century.
205. Pir-i-Alamdar, Damghan. Painted stucco inscription, 1021.
206. Sharistan, Isfahan. Painted inscription, 12th century.
207. Masjid-i-Jami, Yazd. Painted inscription frieze.
208. Isfahan. Tile inscription fragment, 16th century.
209. Ardabil. Inscription medallion, 1310.
210. Masjid-i-Jami, Isfahan. Braided Kufic inscription, northeast ivan, *circa* 1310.

209

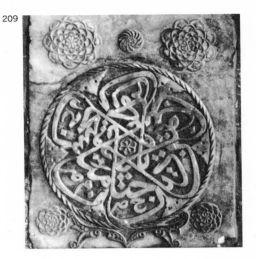

210

211. Masjid-i-Jami, Yazd. Panel of mosaic faience and carved terra-cotta.
212. Shrine of Imam Reza, Mashhad, chamber of Allahvardi Khan, 1612.
Mosaic faience panels of wall and vaults.
213. Isfahan. *Haft-rangi* tile panel, late 17th century.
(New York, Metropolitan Museum of Art)

Figs. 209, 210   among all classes gave rise to one of the greatest of decorative styles. There was an immense concentration of effort to develop the ornamental potentials of Arabic into scores of alphabets, each with its own strictly controlled character and rules. Into this effort went severe training, discipline, artistic passion and—especially in Persia—inventiveness. As side friezes, inscriptions encircled entire buildings, supplemented by panels, moldings, medallions and monograms. They ranged from a minuscule inscription in some unexpected spot to gigantic Kufic covering whole walls or domes with letters ten to sixteen feet high.

Figs. 212, 213   Although few examples still exist, we know that at least some realistic stucco panels also were executed, mostly for private palaces. Figurative designs from the other arts of the period (murals, miniatures, pottery and arts of the book) warrant an expectation that figural stucco was also highly successful. Other types of stucco treatment developed slowly, and by the sixteenth and particularly the seventeenth centuries we have a combination of almost three-dimensional relief richly polychromed. Some of this work was done with the elegance of fine engraving, apparently an effort to give greater substantiality to the work of the painter and to realize an insistence on the aesthetic values of texture. For example, the ceiling of the Chihil Sutan has all of its patterns slightly raised and delicately carved; enriched by gold leaf and shown against the ground of vivid blue, pale green and maroon, it must have made a sumptuous combination. Similarly, in the palace of Ali Qapu at Isfahan there are handsome panels that copied quite closely some of the great woven textile panels of the day.[149]

In Persian stucco work a high degree of inventiveness was maintained over long periods and the variety of components used in stucco decoration is quite astonishing,[150] even greater than in the stucco of Western Islam, ancient though it is. Some of these elements changed and developed very rapidly, but others (like the guard stripes, which were very ingenious but simple) were often repeated with only slight modification over a period of centuries. Even today there are very skillful stucco workers in Persia creating handsome things, sometimes very well designed. In too many cases, however, they have become victims of the nineteenth century Western preference for pictorial realism, and naturalistic rosebuds have less to recommend them than the magnificent imaginary blooms of earlier stucco. The power of design, which requires effort, talent and discipline, easily degenerates as exacting standards give way before such superficial demands. But, in the hands of the greatest Persian designers, stucco was always especially adapted for the expression of floral abundance and surging vitality. In the great mihrabs, it was capable of sustaining attention, a confusing (but not confused) complex of multiple strands, emerging suddenly by deep inner compulsion, creating new forms and magical blooms. When beautifully designed and executed, stucco was the acme of opulence; patterns were lively and intricate in their movement, free but rhythmic, providing the worshipper with an opportunity for intoxicating self-obliteration and for an intensely felt awareness of an ultimate reality.

211

212

213

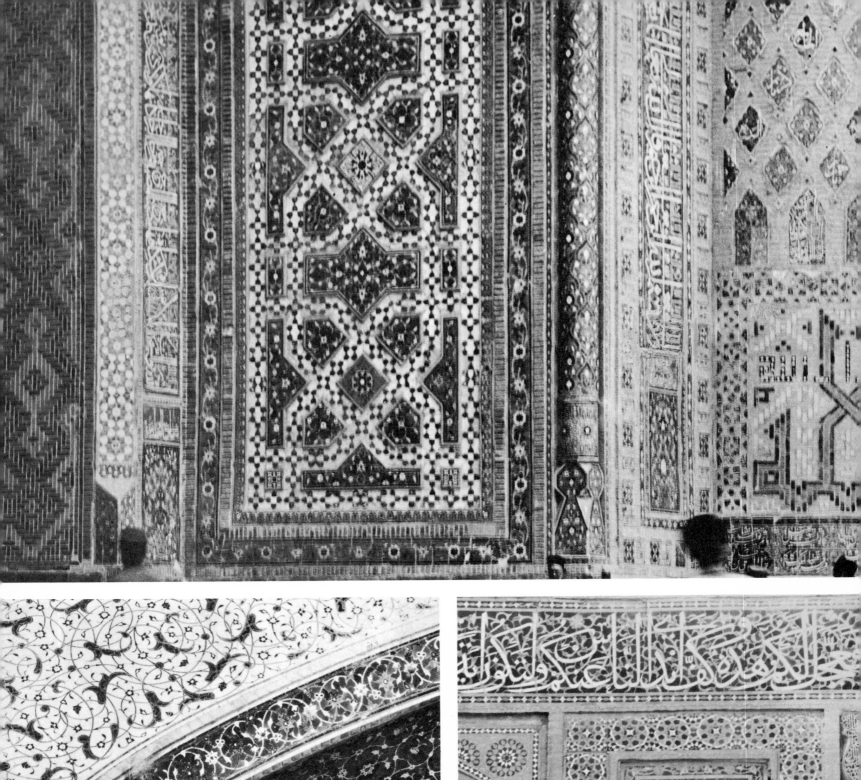

214. Mosque of Gawhar Shad, Mashhad. Detail of mosaic faience decoration of sanctuary portal.
215. Harun-i-Vilaya, Isfahan. Detail of mosaic faience decoration of portal spandrel, 1513.
216. Masjid-i-Jami, Yazd. Mosaic faience panel and inscription frieze.

Tile and Mosaic Faience

Rivaling stucco but never completely displacing it was the impressive development of enameled tile, considered Persia's greatest contribution to ornament. The luster faience mihrabs which Color Plate XV appeared at the end of the thirteenth century were exquisite, even startling in their beauty.

The demand for complicated floral ornament, both abstract and roughly pictorial, had been well established in the ornamentation of the tenth and eleventh century Korans. The use of tiny fragments of cut tile appeared first in Maragha in the beginning of the twelfth century and suggested the possibilities of combining finely divided units of such tiles instead of the earlier single, solid colored tiles. This technique of faience mosaic was continuously developed and improved until, by the fifteenth century, it reached a degree of luxuriance—a purity and intensity of harmonious colors—hardly ever equaled in architectural ornament. It quite literally has to be seen to be appreciated, for so much of its appeal lies in fluctuating tones, changing light and reflections; even then, however, it seems impossible.[151]

Whole buildings are invested with these brilliant colors and fluid designs that look as if they were no more difficult to create than painted patterns. In the Persian climate painted designs could not last in good condition for more than a few generations, whereas mosaic faience retains its color indefinitely and is as fresh six hundred years later without loss of luster.

The process of making mosaic faience is actually fairly simple, although it does require a specialized skill. The great advantage of the luster faience over *haft-rangi* or multi-colored tiles, is that various colors attain their maximum brilliance at different temperatures, ranging from 800° centigrade for lead glazes up to double that number for tin and cobalt. The average temperature for the *haft-rangi* is about 1050° centigrade, but individual colors have varying temperatures for their maximum brilliance. The red glazes, for instance, give an excellent tone at around 850°. Thus, by using separately fired faience elements, each color can be employed at its maximum intensity.

The design pattern is drawn to exact scale on heavy paper or on a smooth plaster of paris bed, and the designer indicates the different colors needed for each element. A collection of all the tile colors, each at its most perfect tone, is then cut by chisel, rasped and fitted into small units that are placed color downward on the pattern, cut so that there are interstices beween the units. The whole can then be covered with stiff plaster. Sections can be removed as needed and are thus quite manageable. Using such a process, the elements of faience mosaic do not constitute an absolutely mechanically even surface. The slightest divergence in the bed or the setting

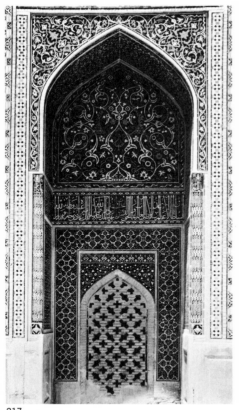

217

218

219

220

217. Masjid-i-Jami, Isfahan. 15th century niche, with mosaic faience decoration.
218. Masjid-i-Jami, Isfahan. Detail of sanctuary ivan, with mosaic faience panels.
219. Masjid-i-Shah, Isfahan. Window grill, north ivan.
220. Shrine of Imam Reza, Mashhad. Mosaic faience panel, late 15th century.

(and these divergences always occur) changes the planes of each piece so that all reflect at almost microscopically different angles, giving the whole a lively play of reflections. This is always true of mosaic faience unless a craftsman's mistaken ambition for expensive mechanical accuracy eliminates the distinct advantage of such variations.

At first colored faience, generally blue, was set into a contrasting buff brick ground to form large patterns. Within a short time, the use of colored faience was expanded to form solidly colored areas, especially effective for domes. By the fourteenth century, the faience mosaic technique, various colored shapes assembled like jig-saw puzzles, was worked into complex patterns, sometimes covering many hundreds of square feet of surface. Perhaps the most perfect examples are from the fifteenth century: the mosque of Gawhar Shad in Mashhad and the Blue Mosque in Tabriz. The most perfect example of early Safavid mosaic faience is perhaps found in the Harun-i-Vilaya of Isfahan (1513), signed as the "work of the poor mason, Kusayn." The court façade and portal, all that remain of the original building, are distinguished by superlative color, particularly the intense turquoise ground, and by the drawing of arabesques, spiral tendrils and blossoms of a grace and precision worthy of any manuscript. Nowhere is the dominant turquoise so pure and brilliant, even in the gem itself. The portal of the Masjid-i-Ali, just opposite the Harun-i-Vilaya, is of similar superior color and quality.[152]

Figs. 214, 215

Color Plates XVII, XVIII

Color Plates X, XIV

By the time of Shah Abbas I, in the late sixteenth and early seventeenth centuries, mosaic faience covered entire buildings. In doing so, the quality of many individual panels doubtless deteriorated, especially because of the introduction of enamel *haft-rangi* tile as a replacement for mosaic faience throughout many interiors. Obviously, this change was necessitated by the great number of larger surfaces to be covered, for the setting of square tiles was much faster, and creation of the patterns by painting rather than laboriously cutting each fragment by hand was both faster and easier.[153] In total effect, however, these great colored areas—still composed of relatively small component panels—are really quite splendid. In ornamentation as well as structure, the Safavid period represents the culmination of Persian traditions. At this time all of the different decorative techniques were combined: from the delicately painted plaster of the Sava mihrab through faience mosaic to painted enamel tiles and including even the oldest technique of enameled brickwork. This fostering of varied techniques must also have been greatly aided by the mobility of the craftsmen, for from inscriptions we know that the Safavid work at Sava was accomplished by a mason from Yazd, that the Masjid-i-Ali portal at Isfahan was made by a craftsman from Tabriz, and that parts of the Shrine at Mashhad were done by artists from Isfahan and Shiraz.

Figs. 216-224

167

221. Shrine of Imam Reza, Mashhad. Portal vault with mosaic faience stalactite.
222. Shrine of Imam Reza, Mashhad. Tile panels.
223. Tomb of Khwaja Rabi, Mashhad. Mosaic faience panel, 1622.
224. Musalla, Mashhad. Mosaic faience panels, late 17th century.

222

223

224

VI. The Mongols: Destruction and Grandeur

The Mongol invasions, begun by the ferocious Genghis Khan in 1218, formed one of the most hideous episodes in history. Whole provinces were depopulated by savage massacre, cities obliterated, and precious libraries consumed in the campfires of the barbaric invaders. With blind destructiveness, the Mongols ruined the lands they conquered, striking a near-fatal blow from which Persia never fully recovered. For several generations the country, devastated and demoralized, had neither mood nor capacity for building, but by the end of the century the Mongol conquerors—tamed and instructed by Persian culture, by Islam and even Buddhism—started rebuilding. Fortunately these invaders were more than butchers and devastators, for their victories were due less to sheer numbers than to superior military skill, effective intelligence services, fantastic physical endurance and the personal ambition, even audacity, of their leaders. The sum of these qualities, when combined with Persian rationality and aesthetic tradition, ultimately resulted in fourteenth century architecture of powerful scale and sumptuous ornament.[154] Their near-total devastation gradually played itself out and Hulagu Khan (1217–65), grandson of Genghis and chief of all the western forces, began to think of building projects. Although this is partly attributed to a somewhat belated desire to create as well as destroy, it must also have been the result of necessity and the convenience of having a developed architecture.

Under Hulagu, building and reconstruction commenced all over Persia. Basic plans and structural types remained traditional and, specifically, Seljuk, but the proud and ambitious Mongol princes were determined to surpass everything that had preceded them. They had con-

170

quered the world, destroying much of it, and would now try to parallel that achievement by expressing their mastery in visible and permanent form. An increased scale became apparent: domes were of immense size and towers very high. Façades were energized by groups of tall, narrow pointed arched panels, a revival of parallel salients and recesses that alleviated the mass of the early ziggurats and temples, now artfully composed in groups of three. There was also a marked intensification of the old Persian verticality and exceedingly tall and narrow portals were much favored.

Hulagu ordered the reconstruction of some ruined cities, such as Kuchan, built himself a fine palace, a Buddhist temple at Khoy and about 1260 established at huge cost the famous observatory at Maragha, employing an architect named al Urdi. His successors built many palaces and gardens, and under Arghun Khan (1281–92) architecture began to revive on a substantial scale. These rulers were by turns Buddhists, Christians, Sunnis and Shi'ites, shifts which were reflected in the erection of a number of Christian churches and monasteries as well as in the reconstruction of the lofty ivan at Takht-i-Sulayman under Abaqa Khan in about 1275. Many fine buildings appear to have been built in Shiraz in the late thirteenth century but none of them survive.[155]

This building activity was greatly augmented under Ghazan Khan (1295–1304), a fervent convert to Islam. Refined under Persian tutelage and disciplined by Islam, he ranks as one of Persia's greatest rulers and innovators, initiator of a new and important period in Persian architecture. As he himself said, "I inherited a ruined country," but once his regime was consolidated and the country's economy re-established, he and his associates planned with such limitless enthusiasm and built with such furious energy, irrespective of cost, that within a decade they had created a series of superb monuments.

Typical of Ghazan's reconstruction effort was his order that a mosque and bath should be built in each town, the profits from the bath to support the mosque. His greatest achievement was the suburb of Sham, two miles south of Tabriz—in variety, organization and magnitude hardly rivaled by anything since Persepolis. Ghazan apparently drew plans himself and personally directed the workmen. The mausoleum, today marked only by rubble, was once a complex of some twelve buildings—monasteries, madrassas, a hospital, library, philosophical academy, administrative palace, observatory and palatial summer residences, as well as arcades and gardens of exceptional charm. All were dominated by the mausoleum itself, once an imposing twelve-sided, towerlike structure, 50 feet in diameter, surmounted by a dome about 250 feet high, with a deep stalactite cornice, a richly gilded inscription frieze and surfaces liberally faced with faience tiles of lapis, turquoise, and black arranged in various geometric designs.

171

225. Tomb of Oljeitu, Sultaniya, 1305–1313.
226. Tomb of Oljeitu. Niches, 15th century restoration.
227. Tomb of Oljeitu. Stucco vaults of the gallery.

Fourteen thousand workmen worked four years to complete the structure, which was still standing, only slightly damaged, four hundred years later despite severe and frequent earthquakes.[156] Perhaps inspired by his sovereign, Rashid ad-din, Ghazan's vizier, created a university city in Tabriz that surpassed even the ancient complexes. It included twenty-four caravanserais, fifteen hundred shops, thirty thousand houses, special quarters for scholars who assembled there from all countries, hospitals, dispensaries and gardens—"for solidity and strength" surpassing all comparable structures.[157]

By the command of Oljeitu, Ghazan's younger brother and successor (1304–16), there arose on the beautiful open meadows of Sultaniya a wonder city planned to be the imperial capital. Begun in 1305 and dedicated in 1313, it was built magnificently as well as rapidly. The result was a complex almost the size of Tabriz, dominated by Oljeitu's mausoleum, one of Persia's supreme architectural achievements. The building was the climax of a congeries of subordinate buildings no longer extant. At one time it was planned to receive the bodies of Ali and Hussein, early saints revered by Persian Shi'ites, but this was rendered impossible, partly because of Oljeitu's conversion to the Sunni branch of Islam.

The mausoleum is octagonal in form, rising to a beautifully poised, high profile dome, 177 feet high and 80 feet in diameter, solidly covered with light blue faience tile. It rests on a wide and rich stalactite cornice and a gleaming blue-patterned minaret rises from each of the eight angles, framing the dome like a diadem. The second-storey galleries open outward, anticipating the Khwaja Rabi, Gadam Gah, and the Taj Mahal. Its imposing scale provides for an interior of great power. Here space is ample and majestic—not mere emptiness but space more intensely realized than an open landscape. The walls, though 25 feet thick, are made less conspicuous by the stately rhythm of eight huge and soaring arches. Mediated by shallow stalactites, the angles between these arches seem to melt quietly into the circular base of the enormous dome. All components are fused into a unity of serene grandeur. The tribunes let in an abundance of well diffused light and their railings ingeniously provide the horizontality necessary to measure and enhance the strong verticality of the other forms. Despite its size, the dome is as buoyant, as light and secure as the vault of heaven which it brings to mind. There are no wide, empty walls to dilute or retard the harmonious upward flow, no thin multiple verticals to aggressively speed the effortless movement; there are only powerful scale and studied proportions.

The walls were originally faced with light golden-toned brick, punctuated with small, dark blue faience tiles strung out to form large inscriptions of rectangular Kufic, but in 1313 the interior was redecorated with plaster. Evidently the best designers of the time created these fine ornaments, which were often worked in low relief. Designs were varied, consisting of huge lacy medallions or painted mosaic and floral patterns in garnet, soft rust, dark blue and gold on a light ground. Everywhere sacred inscriptions proclaimed the divine message, framing all arches, crowning the dado, encircling the base of the dome; their undulating scripts kept alive a gentle flowing movement. The vaults of the outer twenty-four galleries (three on a side) were decorated with painted panels of intricate geometric ornament, exceedingly lovely in

Fig. 225
Color Plate III

Figs. 226, 228, 229

Color Plates IV, V
Figs. 227, 230

228. Tomb of Oljeitu, Sultaniya, 1305–1313. Interior, transition from octagon to circle of the dome.
229. Tomb of Oljeitu. Wooden balcony grill, possibly Safavid.
230a and 230b. Tomb of Oljeitu. Gallery vaults, plaster-faced brick.

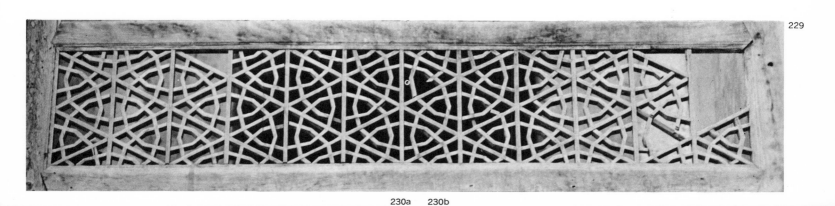

229

230a

230b

231

232

233

design and color. These were set in simulated brick bonding with handsome end ornaments.[158] The intrados of the window arches were quietly enlivened by carved stucco, sinuous, subtle and suave.

Throughout, structure and ornament were united: majestic scale, harmonious proportions, rich and glowing colors all combined in a quiet equilibrium, endowing the building with a unique presence. Structurally the building is a masterpiece. "Loads and thrusts are properly concentrated on a relatively small number of points," and the huge dome is the work of a consummate technician having been "built without buttresses, pinnacles or shoulders of any kind." The thickness of the dome shell diminishes from base toward apex, a necessity in terms of both lightness and stability. This diminution in thickness was obtained by a series of steps which would naturally give a rough and irregular profile to the dome. The architect overcame this, however, by providing a smooth auxiliary outer shell which could carry the glazed tile on a smooth and even contour. The result is, in fact, a double dome which, although unusual was by no means a new idea, for there already existed famous wooden double domes in Baghdad and Damascus.[159]

At Sultaniya, the dome stands "simply by virtue of a perfectly conceived and constructed profile."[160] Here grandeur and tranquility both dwarf and magnify; here man is both diminished and ennobled. There are larger enclosed spaces—the Gol Gunbad in Bishapur, the Pantheon in Rome—but perhaps none that combines in such transparent unity, power, repose and sovereign beauty. It is the visible realization of the poet's dream: "a palace as massive as the mountain, resplendent as the stars, wide as the land, lifting itself into the sky."

Almost concurrently, Ali Shah, a wealthy and ambitious patron of architecture who is said to have been the architect of Sham and the mausoleum of Oljeitu,[161] began work on the Masjid-i-Jami in Tabriz (begun 1312 and finished by 1322). In this mosque we again find the colossal scale initiated by Ghazan Khan, for it is probably the most massive brick structure still partially standing. The sanctuary ivan was a vault 100 feet wide and 158 feet deep; the distance between portal and mihrab was over 215 feet. The springing of the vault, which must have been over 150 feet high, began about 80 feet from the ground, and it seems probable that a pair of minarets, whose bases rested at the same level, once rose some 116 feet higher to a height more than 200 feet above the ground. The ivan portal faced a marble-paved court (937 x 750 feet), which was surrounded by a stone-vaulted arcade supported on coupled octagonal alabaster columns, richly decorated with gold. The largest doors (about 9 feet square) were closed by single slabs of polished alabaster which must have been visible from far away; others were of gilded bronze plates over wood. Arcades and ivans were faced with faience tile or mosaic faience and a huge inscription in gold and white against a floral ground wound around the entire building. The interior was equally sumptuous: a mihrab of gold luster faience, bronze columns with silver and gold inlay, window grilles with bronze balls inlaid at the crossings, and masses of silver and enameled glass lamps to light the sanctuary. All combined to create an ensemble of

Fig. 231

177

234

235

utmost splendor, sustained by the mass of the structure. The immense vault collapsed within a few years, although the building continued in use for several centuries.

As these structures were finished, thousands of craftsmen were scattered throughout the country, carrying architectural and artistic skill into several provinces. The revered shrine of Bayazid at Bistam (an almost incoherent assemblage of structures ranging in date from the tenth century and including a minaret dated 1120 and an austere tomb tower of about 1300, similar in style to the Gunbad-i-Qabus but less austere), was further elaborated by Ghazan Khan and the young Oljeitu in the early fourteenth century. An outstanding stucco mihrab of 1267 and fine stucco panels testify to their activities there.

A similar but more homogeneous complex of considerable beauty was built at Natanz, one of the loveliest mountain towns in Persia. Abrupt hills, ample trees, rushing streams and the remains of former palaces made it an ideal retreat for people from Kashan and Yazd, both fiercely hot cities. Abundant game also attracted a good many visitors from Isfahan. What nature created man successfully adorned with an uncommonly beautiful ensemble of religious structures which form a group of compact and unified buildings. Although the walls of each unit are contiguous to those of another, the component buildings are all distinct, highly individual and, for the most part, in good condition.

The four-ivan type Masjid-i-Jami fortunately is dated 1304–1309, and there is evidence that it occupies an older site. Rather small, crowded, a little ungraceful in proportions—perhaps evidence of insufficient funds when built—it nevertheless is characteristic of the period except for the parsimony of its ornamentation. The spiritual focus of the ensemble at Natanz is the tomb Fig. 232
tower of Abu Samad, built in 1307. Though small (only 19 feet square), this tower is of great aesthetic and emotional power. It is crowned by an octagonal tent dome which in its original state—faced with bright blue tiles—must have appeared in rich contrast to the golden buff of the 123-foot high minaret which was added in 1324. The interior walls of the tower are pure white except for a gray inscription band of deeply carved stucco that encircles the top and the slender angle colonettes, also of gray carved stucco. Broken by shallow bays on each side, the walls thus contain twelve vertical elements all of which lead swiftly upward toward an exciting climax of adroitly composed stalactites that fill the peak of the dome like a sunlit summer cloud.

Light, pouring in through eight windows, is softened by handsome double grilles, shed downwards in a magical but serene glow. No direct outside light reaches the worshipper below, only a buoyant radiance. The lower part of the chamber was formerly faced with very fine golden luster tiles focussing on a splendid mihrab (now in the Victoria and Albert Museum in London). The adjoining Kanequah (1316), a monastery or pilgrim's refuge, is completely in ruins except for one of the most beautiful façades in Persia. Much of its exceptional quality is probably due to workmen who were released from the tremendous constructions Figs. 233, 234
at Tabriz and Sultaniya. This might well explain the contrast in degree of sophistication and refinement of ornamentation between the Kanequah and the Masjid-i-Jami which had been built while all the best workmen were concentrated in the North.

236

237

238

236. Masjid-i-Jami, Varamin, 1322. Sanctuary portal.
237. Masjid-i-Jami, Varamin. Outer portal.
238. Masjid-i-Jami, Varamin. Oratory vault.
239. Masjid-i-Jami, Varamin. Sanctuary corridor.
240. Masjid-i-Jami, Varamin. Detail of portal.

239

240

Because of the vigor and variety of its decorative patterns, as well as the intensity and clarity of the turquoise blue facing tiles, the Kanequah is a fine and instructive example of the period. The portal arch is high and graceful, its spandrels enriched by large disks. Recalling the tomb of Ismail in Bokhara, the main mass of the façade is a basket-weave pattern instead of the usual floral patterns and arabesques. Additional embellishments consist of a surface design in patterns of outset enameled brick, interlocking circles and other geometric figures, supplemented with dense friezes and panels of rectangular Kufic or framing bands of stately Naskhi. The squinches, recesses and subordinate panels are also sumptuously decorated but the total impression is one of harmony.

In the early fourteenth century, the city of Varamin—like Natanz—became a center of building, having gained in importance with the decline of Rayy, so thoroughly devastated by earlier Mongols. The tomb tower of Ala ad-din (1287) followed the typical northern scheme, Fig. 86 with thirty-two right-angled flanges and a conical blue tiled roof, ornamented with an inscription frieze and a strapwork cornice band of the characteristic blue faience and terra-cotta. The now ruined Masjid-as-Sharif (1307) leaves few traces of its former magnificence but the Masjid-i- Figs. 235-237, 240 Jami is still one of the most attractive mosques in the country. According to its inscriptions, this Jami was begun in 1322 and finished in 1326 under the aegis of Abu Said, the last of the Il Khanid Mongols. It was planned and constructed with great care, its studied proportions resulting in unusual grace. Although unostentatious, it discloses a richly varied scheme of ornamentation, consisting of intricate patterns of blue faience strips relieved by buff terra-cotta. Delicate diapers of shadow lines in the raised or cut-out brick trace out religious messages in huge rectangular Kufic, confirmed by deeply carved Naskhi inscription friezes. The piers are faced with painted plaster, narrow bands in carved stucco simulating decorative bonding, all meticulously executed.

The sanctuary interior reverts to the typically Seljuk scheme of three distinct horizontal Figs. 238, 239, 241 sections (square chamber, zone of transition, and dome), a practice which in contemporary buildings was being displaced by vertical panels and arches which carried the dome weight straight to the ground. The chief distinction of the building lies in its perfection of the four-ivan plan, harmoniously incorporated into the total structure. Natural and easy transitions lead one from the outer portal to the climax of the sanctuary mihrab and the dome which dominates the rest of the building with dignity and grace. An inscription indicates that the architect of this impressive building was Ali Qazvini.

Among the many other fine monuments of the period,[162] the mausoleum at Pir-i-Bakran Figs. 242, 243 near Isfahan (dated 1303 but rebuilt in 1312) is an impressive example of the single-ivan structure, still reminiscent of the Taq-i-Kisra. Its elaborate decoration, including fine faience and rich stucco, is marred by occasional incoherence, for within the same recess it is possible to observe marked differences of design and conception—a lack of detailed consideration that results in a loss of unity.

183

242

243

242. Tomb at Pir-i-Bakran, near Isfahan, 1303, rebuilt 1312. Stucco panel of interior recess.
243. Tomb at Pir-i-Bakran, near Isfahan.

In Yazd, the Masjid-i-Jami,[163] like so many important mosques, was the focus of a complex of buildings of various periods and styles in various states of conservation. The site of a Sasanian fire temple, it also saw a period of great wealth and power under the Saffarids. Its major features, however, were begun in 1324 and continuously developed for forty years, even after the dissolution of Il Khanid power. Architecturally it is of high quality. A portal ivan opens into a court at right angles to the main axis. A high ivan vault, leading into the domed sanctuary, focussed on one of the finest mosaic faience mihrabs (1365). On either side were oratories, both distinguished by transverse vaults at right angles to the longitudinal axis—a brilliant innovation of Sasanian times that covers with adequate strength a wide span. The high walls being thus relieved of structural function, it was possible (as in the south oratory) to cut windows into either end of the vault. The ivan and sanctuary are especially marked by the urge to verticality and the portal minarets are the highest in Iran. The ivan tunnel vault is exceptionally high for its width and the upward movement everywhere is emphasized by slender angle colonettes, some of which have a height of 100 diameters. The Masjid-i-Jami of Kirman (dated 1349, rebuilt in 1559) also is a large four-ivan structure whose tall portal arch is rather similar to that at Yazd. Its richly colored mosaic faience is of outstanding quality.

Color Plates VI, VII

Figs. 244-248

Fig. 249

The most notable contemporary structure to the east, in Khurasan, is the noble mausoleum at Tus.[164] Imposing by virtue of its size, isolation and compact mass, it is reminiscent of Sultan Sanjar's mausoleum at Merv, especially since in both an external second-storey gallery masks the zone of transition. Further comparison with the thirteenth century Jabal-i-Sang at Kirman, more clearly Sasanian in character than the later tombs, sets the development at Tus into perspective.[165] Although much smaller, the structure at Tus also has affinities in its stately proportions with the mausoleum of Oljeitu. Deep vertical channels which impart an appearance of great energy to the façade have their prototypes at Sultaniya, and some stucco panels recall those of the shrine of Bayazid at Bistam—considerations that warrant a date early in the fourteenth century. There are no polychrome revetments, only the plain white plaster coating. Beautiful proportions, the careful arrangement of all elements in multiples of three, the wide reveals and broad framing of the four great arches that are carried down to the ground and the concealment of the squinch mechanism are all factors which work together to create a sense of stability and repose.

Figs. 250, 251

Fig. 252

Following the death in 1335 of Abu Said, the last Il Khanid sovereign, political disorders, dynastic quarrels, and conflicting ambitions of local principalities prevailed. Nevertheless, real economic prosperity was sustained by the continuance of policies laid down by Ghazan Khan and considerable architectural activity continued throughout the country. The most important post-Khanid monuments occur in Central Persia. In the environs of the sacred city of Qumm are still standing some fifteen tomb towers, all of the fourteenth century. Mostly octagonal, with inward-sloping walls, conical or polyhedral domes and rich interiors, they are decorated with vigorous polychrome and carved ornament. The tomb tower of Imad ad-din (1390) is a late but fine example of this type. Some stucco ornaments at Qumm closely recall those at Sultaniya,

Figs. 253-255

185

244

245

246

247

244. Masjid-i-Jami, Yazd, 1324–1364. Portal showing buttresses.
245. Masjid-i-Jami, Yazd. South corner of interior.
246. Masjid-i-Jami, Yazd. Mihrab, 1375.
247. Masjid-i-Jami, Yazd. Mosaic faience and carved terra-cotta panels.
248. Masjid-i-Jami, Yazd. South oratory, 13th century.
249. Masjid-i-Jami, Kirman, dated 1349, rebuilt 1559. Portal dome.

248

249

250. Tomb at Tus, early 14th century (?).
251. Tomb at Tus. Interior, detail of the squinch.
252. Jabal-i-Sang, Kirman, 13th century.

especially in color scheme. The pyramidal shape of most of these tombs may indicate that the ideal of the sacred mountain was still effective. Since the Il Khanid state had disintegrated so rapidly after the death of Abu Said, there was no royal patronage for these structures. Thus, they expressed the standards and tastes of the community in general which, judging by other buildings throughout the country, was very high indeed.

The architecture of the Il Khanid Mongols is closely dependent on its antecedents, being in fact a coherent development from previous Seljuk styles and techniques. The relationship between the two styles is so close that in some instances, like the Alaviyan of Hamadan, opinions differ as to whether a building is Seljuk or Mongol. But in general, Mongol architecture had a distinct character of its own, and in many features contrasted with Seljuk practice. Although a more colossal scale was introduced in Mongol buildings, they were also much lighter, with structural elements such as corner piers broken up into sharply marked bays and re-entrant angles. Structural components were multiplied and their functions differentiated. In general, solids were diminished, voids increased, while illumination was more ample and better planned. Buildings were more complex and better integrated, details more refined, and there were more effective deferred climaxes. Furthermore, domes, which usually accounted for the upper two-thirds of a structure, were more gracefully united with the buildings they crowned, the rugged forthright energy of the Seljuk squinch was skillfully ameliorated, and there was increased sensitivity of feeling for harmony, proportion and elegance in the building as a whole.

Structural problems, more severe than those of Seljuk times, were successfully and ingeniously solved; transverse vaults were perfected (at Yazd and Isfahan) and building with brick was carried to its ultimate triumph (tomb of Oljeitu, Sultaniya). There was greater emphasis on attenuation and verticality: higher ivans, closely coupled portal minarets, slender colonettes, higher arches, elongated panels. Courts tended to become narrower and the four-ivan plan was perfected.

Finally, all the techniques of ornamentation were still further and quite enthusiastically developed. In the Turan, where the tomb of Ismail Samanid continued to exert strong influence, ornamentation became the primary concern, sometimes replacing a sense for structural forms.[166] Decoration became overwhelming, concealing or even misrepresenting structure, but this ornament was of fascinating beauty, a repository of the whole grammar of decoration. Such buildings, virtual jewel boxes, provided Timur with examples of concentrated magnificence, examples which he continued to elaborate within nobler architectural forms.

Compared to the finest monuments of the fourteenth century, even the greatest of the earlier buildings (e.g. the Tarik-Khana, Gunbad-i-Qabus, the north dome chamber of the Isfahan Jami) were, despite their exceptionally moving powers, somewhat abstract and limited. Splendor and magnificence, legitimate and important in architecture, came in chiefly with the Mongols and their successors, whose buildings generally were saved from mere ostentation by grandeur of scale, harmonious composition and ornamentation that was brilliantly designed and perfectly executed.

253. Tomb tower of Imad ad-din, Qumm, 1390. Interior.
254. Tomb tower of Imad ad-din. Exterior.
255. Tomb tower of Imad ad-din. Interior of dome.

254

255

VII. The Timurids: Refinement and Opulence

Because of political chaos, Persia toward the end of the fourteenth century was an easy victim for the furious ambitions of Timur, or Tamerlane, as he is frequently called. By 1394, that ferocious warrior was in the heart of Persia. Again whole cities were leveled, entire populations massacred, and the fourteenth century, which began with the rapid creation of beautiful monuments, ended in disaster, heightened by the destruction of many of its finest buildings. Timur had much of the same ruthlessness as his Mongol predecessors, but his ravages were less random than those of Genghis. He spared many cities and sacred monuments. He admired outstanding buildings and systematically collected all kinds of artisans whom he carried off to Samarkand. His conquest of the greater part of Asia provided him with limitless wealth, workmen and special materials, but Persian refinement and architectural skill dominated. Assembling all these resources at Samarkand, he rapidly built a series of imposing structures, and the Registan, the central plaza of Samarkand, became one of the most imposing civic centers the world has ever seen.

Persian architecture of the fourteenth century was based on Seljuk forms and construction, but took on new scale and magnificence thanks to the domination of Mongol personalities. Similarly its architecture of the fifteenth century continued the principal forms of the Mongols, but with greater refinement and consistent skill. This was accomplished under the direction of the Central Asian conqueror, Timur. His successors, Shah Rukh, Ulugh Beg, Baysunghur, Abu Said, were all enthusiastic exponents of Persian culture and presided over a veritable Golden Age which saw all of the arts —including the arts of living—carried to new heights of perfection.

192

Under Timur's imperious driving force, Samarkand, already architecturally rich, once more became "the focus of splendor." He assembled skilled engineers and competent architects from all his far-reaching domains: Fars, Iraq, Azerbaijan, Damascus, and Baghdad, in addition to hundreds of stone-cutters from India. "I was determined to build a Masjid-i-Jami in Samarkand which should be without a rival in any country," Timur announced. But, although it had a minaret at each corner, a dome covered with finely polished marble, and a roof carried on 460 columns, the building was not as imposing as he had expected, so he put the architect to death—a warning to timid designers.

Even more ambitious was the conqueror's own palace at Kesh (1345–46), his birthplace. Intended to overawe all who saw it, it was twenty years in building, and not quite finished when Clavigo saw it in 1405.[167] In plan, the building was somewhat novel for the period with a triple-ivan façade reminiscent of Firuzabad. Reception chambers led out at right angles to the central ivan-entrance. The portal arch itself was 165 feet high,[168] flanked by a pair of round towers, like minarets, rising out of a twelve-sided base. The center ivan opened into a huge marble-paved court (300 paces wide) at right angles to the entrance. On the opposite side, another great ivan led into a large reception hall tiled with blue and gold, with a ceiling of gold, enameled tile and rich mosaic faience, occasionally relieved with deep-cut stucco. The building beyond contained galleries and numerous chambers to the height of six stories. All was encrusted with enamel tiles.

The huge rear wall of the reception hall was covered with the finest mosaic faience in quietly fluctuating tones of turquoise, lapis, milk-white, mirror-black, green and aubergine embellished with gold.[169] Such an expanse completely covered with many strong and varied patterns could have been intolerable, but the opulence was organized and controlled by a firmly designed geometrical framework of harmonious proportions. Rectangular panels of mosaic faience, varied in size and design emphasis, with low relief framing floral bands or calligraphy are symmetrically organized. The contribution of each panel is carefully appraised and apportioned with sensitive regard for the total effect. Intense major patterns are concentrated in limited areas while symmetrical repetitions and framing borders provide relief. A wide cornice of a deeply cut Kufic inscription gives weight and authority to the whole. The entire ensemble was surrounded by extensive lawns and orchards.

No monarch in Asia could boast of anything comparable. It was a perfect expression of Timur's imperial power and pride, fortunately formulated and controlled by Persian aesthetic genius and experience. Its gigantic ruins, still glowing with color, confirm Clavigo's account.

256. Gur-i-Mir, Tomb of Timur, Samarkand, 1404.
257. One of the minarets at Herat, *circa* 1417–1437.
258a,b,c. Minaret at Herat. Three details.

256

257

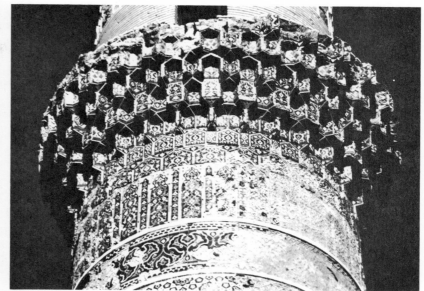

258a

258b

258c

259. Madrassa at Khargird, finished 1444–1445. Façade.
260. Madrassa at Khargird. Detail of façade.
261. Shrine of Shams ad-din, Yazd. Portal with painted stucco, 15th century.

Among Timur's other very numerous structures, the Mosque of Bibi Khanum in Samarkand, begun in 1398 and finished in 1404, was almost as impressive as the palace at Kesh. An entrance portal, 130 feet high and 56 feet wide, led into a large court (300 x 200 feet). The whole building, including its eight minarets and three domes, was covered with enameled tile. Clavigo thought it the noblest building in Samarkand and today it is certainly a majestic ruin.[170]

One of Timur's most famous buildings, the Gur-i-Mir (1404), his own tomb, is still a monumental and dramatic structure. Externally it is divided into three equal parts. A bulbous dome, 112 feet high, is enriched with 64 almost round flutes and flanked by minarets 83 feet high. It is set on a high but narrower cylindrical drum which causes a sharp constriction at the base of the dome. This drum, in turn, rises out of a chamber which, on the exterior, is octagonal. Portals pierce each of the major four sides, again reminiscent of ancient Sasanian practice. The dome is covered with bright blue tiles and the high drum, ornamented with a huge inscription of rectangular Kufic, is of golden-buff bricks—a beautiful contrast characteristic of the fourteenth century. The interior is also impressive, with an alabaster dado, gray-green jasper cornice, black limestone niches and a marble balustrade. (In 1454 Ulugh Beg added a new portal of superb mosaic faience, designed by Muhammad ibn Mahmud of Isfahan.)

Timur, who "built more extensively than any other Asian monarch,"[171] was responsible for a number of buildings—mosques, palaces, madrassas, tombs—in other cities of the Oxus region as well as in Samarkand. In order to get a full picture of the magnificence of his architecture, we must again supplement the meager appearance of what remains with written accounts. These speak of mural painting, of the marble and porcelain imported from China, of fantastic carvings from India, screens of silver and gold, lavish silk hangings and probably ought to have included other embellishments like carpets, which are not specifically mentioned but which we know of from contemporary miniatures. The will, the organization, colossal costs and much personal supervision were supplied by Timur; but the buildings, although probably overly gorgeous at times because of Timur's personal predilections, were Persian in conception, structure and proportions.

Shah Rukh, Timur's son and successor, was responsible for the ambitious musalla and madrassa at Herat, begun in 1417 and almost finished in 1437. In contrast to his violent father, Shah Rukh was a peace-loving and constructive monarch, who promoted all forms of art and beauty. His great madrassa at Herat was comparable in scale and magnificence with Timur's finest in Samarkand. The court was 357 by 195 feet, surrounded by eight minarets lavishly decorated with mosaic faience and several domes. Of all this there remain only six minarets, each crowned with stalactites and set on a base of carved marble, and the mausoleum of Shah Rukh's wife and queen, Gawhar Shad. Architectural evidence indicates that Qavam ad-din of Shiraz was the architect.

The madrassa at Khargird (completed in 1444–45) is an individual and thoroughly unified building, also designed by Qavam but finished by Ghiyath ad-din, another Shirazi. It is a carefully proportioned, four-ivan madrassa. The court is square, with ivans of equal height and the portal pavilion of three domed chambers is decorated with painted ornament, delicate carved

Fig. 256

Figs. 257, 258

Figs. 259, 260
Color Plate VIII

197

262. Shrine of Abd Allah Ansari, Gazur Gah, rebuilt 1428. Oratory.
263. Turbat-i-Shaykh Jam, early 15th century.
Portal with mosaic faience decoration and small dome with *haft-rangi* tiles.
264. Turbat-i-Shaykh Jam. Interior of sanctuary dome.

stucco and intricate stalactites. The tile and mosaic faience of the court are exceptionally force-ful in pattern and rich in color. The admirably organized façade, low and wide, centers on a deep portal of modest height; the symmetrical walls to either side of the portal are enriched with pointed arches, inset with rectangular panels and terminate in low corner towers. The whole façade emphasized horizontality and repose—a new note in Timurid architecture. In the shrine of Shams ad-din at Yazd the painted stucco decoration emphasizes the structural function of various architectural elements. Contemporary, and also unusual, are the shrine complex of Abd Allah Ansari at Gazur Gah (rebuilt by Shah Rukh in 1428), and the Masjid-i-Kali at Turbat-i-Shaykh Jam, a low dome behind a very high ivan portal.

Figs. 262-264

Figs. 265, 266

The first, and the greatest surviving, Persian monument of the fifteenth century is the beautiful mosque of Gawhar Shad (1418) now abutting the shrine of the Imam Reza in Mash-had. Its portal continues the Samarkand style of arch within arch, enriched by a succession of bevels and reveals that give it depth and power. The thick, tower-like minarets, merging with the outer corners of the portal screen, extend to the ground and, together with the high founda-tion revetment of marble, give the ensemble the impression of solidity necessary to support its exuberant color. The entire court façade is faced with enamel brick and mosaic faience of the finest quality. The full scale of colors includes a dominant cobalt blue and turquoise, white, a transparent green, yellow, saffron, aubergine and mirror-black—all tones fluctuating through several shades. The patterns, lucid and vigorous, are artfully adapted to their decorative role, whether for eye-level panels, or dome ornament meant to be effective at a thousand feet. Mo-notony, difficult to avoid in such a large area, and a distracting intricacy that might compete with the essential architectural forms are both forestalled. This is accomplished by the energy of the faience floral patterns and brick geometrical schemes; by the emphatic rhythm of the arcades, open galleries and deep recesses; and especially by the striking contrast of the ivans.

Figs. 267-269

The sanctuary ivan is in pure white, while in the other three ivans the ground color of the vault is pale red, carrying large white-outlined Kufic inscriptions of light turquoise that appear green against the reddish ground. The whole decor is interlaced with an unusual amount of white, which adds clarity and excitement to the total effect. "It needs no acquaintance with other styles to acclaim this court, among the buildings now existing, as the most beautiful ex-ample of color in architecture ever devised."[172]

The architect was Qavan ad-din of Shiraz, who is responsible for so many of Shah Rukh's great buildings. Although most of the great Timurid monuments were built in the north of the empire, the architectural and decorative genius came from Shiraz and Isfahan. If western Persia had been impoverished by the recruitment of its best designers and craftsmen to work in the north, by the middle of the century the west had resumed its supremacy. The reign of Jahanshah, ruler of the Qara-Qoyunlu, a Turkoman tribe which was taking western territory from the Timurids, saw in Isfahan examples of the art of mosaic faience carried to new perfec-tion. A recess in the court of the Masjid-i-Jami in Isfahan, dated 1447 and designed by Sayid

265

266

265. Mosque of Gawhar Shad, Mashhad, 1418. Sanctuary portal.
266. Mosque of Gawhar Shad. Detail of minaret.
267. Mosque of Gawhar Shad. Detail of ivan.
268. Mosque of Gawhar Shad. Detail of northeast ivan.

267

268

269

270

271

Mahmud, is equal in design (though not in color) to Khurasan work; while the portal of the Darb-i-Imam, also in Isfahan, a memorial to two Imams built in 1453, is one of the finest examples of decorated architecture in Persia.[173]

There are other fifteenth century monuments in Mashhad, of which the most distinguished is the ruined Sunni Masjid-i-Shah, built about 1350. Its dome form is perfect—striking and pure—infinitely better than the neighboring dome on the mosque of Gawhar Shad. On its interior, a bold frieze, green on bright orange and white, crowns the dado, creating an effect of intense excitement.

Figs. 270, 271

Further north, Saliha Khanun, the daughter of Jahanshah, was patron of the Blue Mosque of Tabriz (1465). This is one of the few completely roofed mosques of Persia, a necessity in the severe climate of Tabriz. That the dome and minarets have collapsed in this region of severe earthquakes is no reflection on the structural design of the building, which was boldly planned and carefully built. With its new kinds of polychrome ornament, of fresh and beautiful use of color and exquisite workmanship, this building must have been a formidable rival to the mosque of Gawhar Shad. The architect, according to the portal inscription, was Nimat Allah ibn Muhammad Bawvab.[174] The Timurid influence shows in the long (170 feet) façade, terminating in round corner towers that originally carried very high minarets. The richly decorated half-dome portal leads into an octagonal domed sanctuary (52 feet in diameter) which was carried on eight arches. Across the front of the sanctuary is a domed corridor and similar corridors run along each side of the sanctuary, resulting in an enlargement which allows the accommodation of more worshippers than would have been possible in the sanctuary itself. In the rear is another sanctuary which may have been meant for a tomb chamber. In all, there were nine domes.

Figs. 272-276
Color Plate XVII

The ornamentation throughout is bold and dramatically varied. As in many mosques, a stout cable molding of intense turquoise frames the portal arch. Inscriptions in gleaming white stand out against the dense fabric of foliation, all rendered in mosaic faience of unparalleled richness and intricacy. Some patterns in the portal are worked in relief, punctuated by square medallions of Kufic, while still others recede into the deep maze of foliation. On piers and arches, large-scale, well-spaced escutcheons in intense cobalt and turquoise are embedded in plain golden-buff bricks. The sanctuary dado uses emphatic, continuous geometric patterns in white on an almost black ground.

The inner sanctuary is faced with huge slabs of Maragha marble bordered with a carved Naskhi inscription. Above this facing are closely fitted hexagonal tiles of deepest lapis lazuli ornamented with gold. Clusters of white stalactites relieve the intense ornamentation and are placed at the apex of the pier angles leading to the dome. The exterior of the main dome was covered with white arabesques in relief on a turquoise ground; the smaller dome with white stars, also in relief against a black ground. Throughout, a wealth of pure and intense color, dominantly a beautiful tone of light blue, has been combined with powerful and original pattern, harmoniously distributed with imagination and perfect judgement.[175]

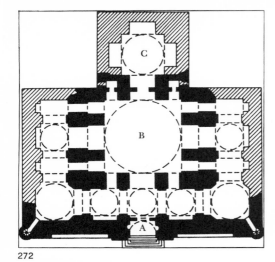

272

273

274

275

272. Blue Mosque, Tabriz, 1465. Plan: (A) Entrance, (B) Domed sanctuary, (C) Second domed sanctuary.
273. Blue Mosque. Detail of mosaic faience.
274. Blue Mosque. Portal.
275. Blue Mosque. Portal recess.
276. Blue Mosque. Pier and arch, detail of mosaic faience.

276

VIII. The Safavid Culmination

The Safavid regime was initiated by the dashing Shah Ismail I (1499–1524) who launched his dynasty with a burst of energy. The greatest artists of the day thronged his court, producing many buildings, most of which have been destroyed. Some modest but structurally unimportant monuments from his reign such as the Masjid-i-Ali and the Harun-i-Vilaya of Isfahan are still standing and their decoration fulfills the most exacting ideals.[176] That so few monuments still exist is due at least in part to the devastation of the Turks who, in the first half of the sixteenth century, repeatedly invaded and occupied Azerbaijan, the heart of Shah Ismail's territory.

Ismail's successor, Shah Tahmasp I, enjoyed a long and eventful reign (1524–76). His contribution is seen above all in exquisite masterpieces of the decorative arts rather than through great architectural monuments. His large palace at Qazvin, with its mosaic faience revetments—doubtless of high quality—must have been handsome, but unfortunately it was totally ruined in an earthquake. Much of the early Safavid architecture was constructed of unfired brick, a rather fragile material. No great building exists today which can definitely be assigned to Shah Tahmasp, and even in contemporary documents the only construction specifically described was the Masjid-i-Shah in Qazvin (begun by Shah Ismail). That building was said to be the largest and fairest mosque in Persia, but it would not withstand the earthquakes that did not even crack the Seljuk dome of the nearby Masjid-i-Jami. This fact is a revealing comment on the building methods and materials of Tahmasp's time.

Under Tahmasp, a reconstruction of the Shrine of Ardabil was successfully begun, and many palaces, mosques and some particularly lavish pavilions dazzled European visitors. Various reparations and additions were undertaken, such as the subsequently rebuilt golden minaret and small portico at Mashhad and the revetments of the southwest ivan of the Masjid-i-Jami at Isfahan. Some important city walls (Teheran) were also built. The history of Persian architecture could almost skip his reign, but one curious piece of provincial architecture dating from Tahmasp's era is worth particular note: the Palace of the Khan in Baku provides us with an example of the use of traditional Persian forms in conjunction with independent local stone building techniques. In this building, the most striking feature is the material, large stone blocks, which almost overwhelm the small portions of rather delicately carved stone. Figs. 277, 278

While the advent of the Safavid dynasty engendered enthusiastic national pride, it was at the outset entangled in wars which frustrated any capacity for architecture on a grand scale. Moreover, the brilliant development of other arts—miniature painting, carpets and textiles— was then at an apogee. These arts were more in keeping with the somewhat effeminate character of Shah Tahmasp, whose particular tastes diverted interest from architecture itself.

With Shah Abbas I (1589–1627) the great period of Safavid architecture opened. By virtue of his resolute ambition, exceptional capacity and artistic sense, and aided by the wealth that his able government had fostered, he initiated a new period in Persian architecture in which the rich, sensationally colored and imaginative details developed by his predecessors became unified into serene and meaningful ensembles of immense scale and grandeur. Although marked by no great structural innovations, and although certainly not Persia's most supreme period, this architecture represents the culmination and final expression of Persian Islamic architecture. During the reign of Shah Abbas I, planning and overall design continued to be important, absorbing components so that ornament receded into structure, diverse elements became subordinate to a splendid entity, whether in a single niche, building, complex shrine, or a great city such as Isfahan. In effect, an architecture which was distinguished by skillful planning, refinement of proportions, and the combination of elegance with strength of design attained some new and important qualities of beauty. Isfahan, designated the capital by Shah Abbas I, was reconstituted with so many new mosques, palaces, bridges, avenues and parks that European travellers referred to it as "half the world" and wrote rapturously of its beauty. Chardin, a dependable observer, reports that in 1666 Isfahan had 162 mosques, 48 madrassas, 182 caravanserais and 273 baths.[177]

The great central maydan at Isfahan, scene of maneuvers, processions and games, especially polo, is surrounded by two-storeyed arcades which focus on the recessed portal of the

277

277. Palace of the Khan, Baku, mid-16th century.
278. Palace of the Khan. Detail of portal
with carved stone spandrels and stalactites.
279. Masjid-i-Shah, Isfahan, 1612–1638.
Plan: (A) Maydan, (B) Entrance, (C) Vestibule, (D) North ivan,
(E) Court, (F) Sanctuary ivan, (G) Domed sanctuary.
280. Masjid-i-Shah. View across the maydan.
281. Masjid-i-Shah. Sanctuary portal.
282. Masjid-i-Shah. Corridor near sanctuary.

278

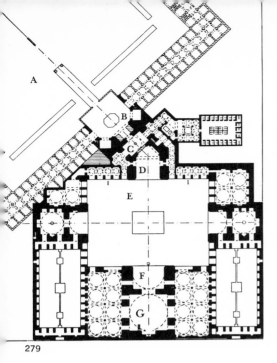

279

281

282

Masjid-i-Shah. Opposite, at the north end of the maydan, is the royal caravanserai and bazaar, at the middle of the west side is the palace of the Ali Qapu—the seat of government—and facing it, across the maydan, is the private oratory of Shah Abbas, the mosque of Shaykh Lutf Allah.

The Masjid-i-Shah was begun in 1612, but despite Shah Abbas' impatience it was inevitably slow in building, not receiving the final marble revetments until 1638.[178] This monument represents the culmination of a thousand years of mosque building in Persia. The formative traditions, the religious ideals, usage and meanings, the plan which had slowly matured from a combining of earlier and simpler types, major structural elements, and ornamentation are all fulfilled and unified in the Masjid-i-Shah, with a majesty and splendor that places it among the world's greatest buildings.

Figs. 279, 280, 283

The whole mosque is of majestic proportions, built up on a wide base. The half-domed arch of the outer portal on the maydan is 90 feet high, and the flanking minarets are 110 feet high. The minarets flanking the sanctuary are higher still, while the sanctuary dome soars above all. The recessed outer portal, almost a building in itself, forms a welcoming embrace, inviting and guiding the throngs outside into the refuge, security and renewal the mosque provides. The outer façade is enriched by galleries, recesses, masses of gleaming stalactites and long bands of brilliant white inscriptions. It is completely faced with polychrome faience mosaic in dominant tones of blue above a lower course in golden-toned marble revetments. The two panels which flank the actual entrance within the recess carry the design of a prayer rug, a reminder of the mosque's essential purpose. At a distance, the imposing mass of this façade, sometimes almost etherealized by its glowing misty blue, quite dominates the maydan and, by contrast with the modest royal palace, proclaims the overwhelming priority of religion over secular power and the central place of religion in the life of the city.

This outer portal faces north, as required by the placement of the maydan, but since the axis of the mosque itself must be in the direction of Mecca (hence northeast to southeast), a difficult adjustment was necessary to avoid a sense of dislocation. This problem was solved triumphantly. Through the outer portal one enters a noble vestibule (C on plan), a feature of Persian monumental buildings from much earlier times. This vestibule is circular and thus has no particular direction; it can therefore serve as a pivot on which the axis of the building is turned. It opens into the high vault of the north ivan, and from its shaded depths one suddenly faces the sun-bright court. Across this court rises the vast sanctuary portal, the gateway to another world of splendor and concentrated power.

Figs. 281-289

The mass of the sanctuary building is simple, its components and their relations clearly defined. The dome, the portal frame and the minarets make a harmonious and invigorating composition of their contrasting forms: the rectangle of the portal intersects the hemisphere of

210

the dome; both are cut vertically by the tall minarets; and the curve of the portal arch repeats the curve of the dome. As one moves, even slightly, about the court, these elements quietly stir, alternating in dominance. The dome sinks or looms high with sovereign authority, while the portal frame and minarets assume new relations.

Color Plates XXIV-XXV

If the glory of the color and the grandeur of the portal screen and dome are almost overwhelming, comprehension is steadied by the rhythmical repetition of the structural elements, symmetrical arcades, balanced ivans, the calm of the wide ablution pool, and the unifying effect of an evenly distributed enveloping color. Over the dome wheel festoons of intricate arabesques in dark blue and golden yellow. The dome, elegant and sensitive in contour, slightly bulbous, set on a high drum, is simple, of remarkably clean and expressive outline, and is uncluttered by buttresses, supports, or supplementary constructions of any kind.

Both the ground plan and the structure of the building reflect the doctrinal simplicity of Islam, proclaiming and demonstrating an essential precept: the equality and the unity of the faithful, who are all assured of unmediated and clear access to the Divine Mercy. Circulation and communication are everywhere facilitated, nowhere impeded. The common floor level is at no place broken by steps, railings, or screens. There are no closed doors, no tunnel-like corridors, no choir, ambulatory, sacristy, no separate structures such as altars, no restricted areas, no privileged positions, just as there are no exclusive ceremonies, no sacred ritual objects, no hierarchy. The very walls merge into their gardenlike floriation or open onto real and natural gardens. Because of the concentration of the bearing load on octagonal stone columns, wide vistas open up and voids are at a maximum. The high and ample vaults and the imperative rhythmical intersection of their sweeping curves define areas that flow freely into one another in successive waves toward the mihrab. Worshippers are visible to one another as they follow in unison the prayer ritual or individually share in the meditative atmosphere created. Mutual awareness and shared worship are at the heart of Islam and here structure has become the handmaiden of faith.

The ornamentation is wholly traditional, repeating the ancient Iranian motif of symbolic appeal for fertility and abundance. Almost the entire surface of the building is covered with enamel tile, depicting a vast display of floral wealth that is abstract and imaginative. From the great golden sun in the apex of the dome, distributing its vitality through an infinite mass of quivering foliage, to the high vaults and panels gleaming with myriad starlike blossoms or opulent palmettes, to the flowing tendrils of the pierced window grilles, this ornament emphasizes the Persian reverence for vegetation and poetic passion for flowers, as well as the appeal for a continuance of abundant life. The pattern schemes for both the outer and inner dome, chains of repeating arabesques, although different in scale and elaboration, are essentially the same.

211

283. Masjid-i-Shah, Isfahan, 1612–1638. Recessed outer portal on maydan.
284. Masjid-i-Shah. View into a garden court.
285. Masjid-i-Shah. Quibla wall.

Following pages:
286. Masjid-i-Shah.Winter prayer hall, view toward the mihrab.
287. Masjid-i-Shah. Dome.
288. Masjid-i-Shah. Vault of sanctuary portal.
289. Masjid-i-Shah. Interior of dome.

284

285

XXIV

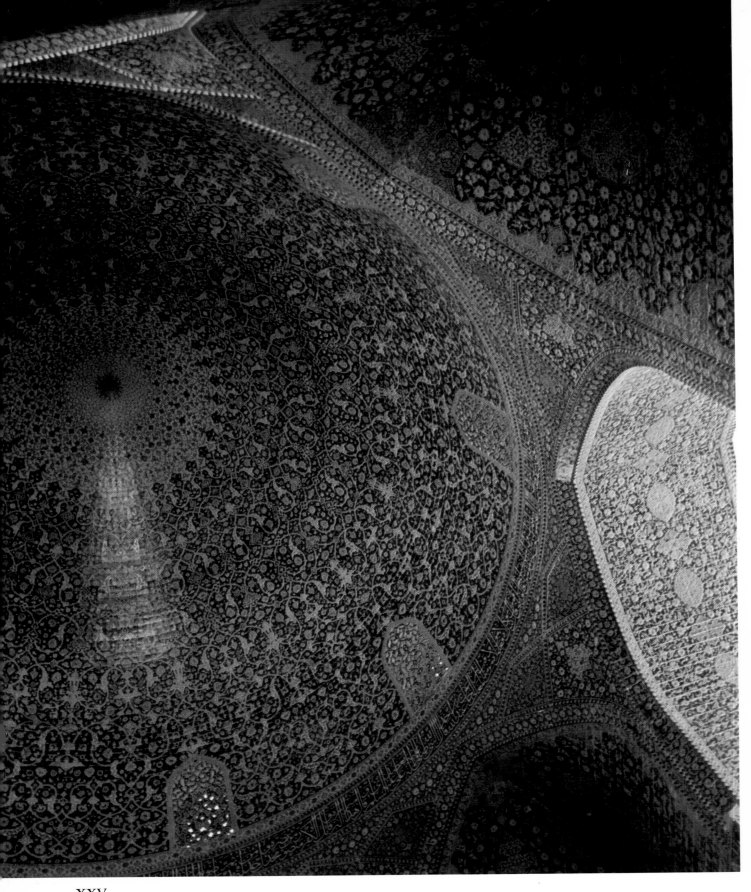

XXVII

XXVIII

XXXI

XXXII

XXXIII

Just as the medieval cathedral expounds pictorially the history and theology of Christianity and by its great forms conveys its mysteries and evokes a moving piety, so also the mosque by its plan and structure declares the Islamic way of life and by its many thousands of inscriptions reports the very words of the Prophet. In both, the major structural forms were created by a serious passion for beauty in the conviction that it furnishes in immediate experience, unimpeded by theory or argument, a valid approach to a transcendent reality, the ultimate goal of all worship. In both medieval cathedral and mosque, the deep and lofty vaults, so calm and majestic, are eloquent of spiritual certitudes and ultimate verities.

The seventeenth century was not the supreme period of Persian art, and in various details the Masjid-i-Shah is inferior to its model the mosque of Gawhar Shad, which preceded it by three hundred years. The enamel tile which covers the whole interior of the Masjid-i-Shah—so inferior to the mosaic faience of the preceding centuries or even to its own outer portal—is neither in design nor execution of more than routine interest. But in nobility of form, in serene strength and repose, in powerful affirmation and valid expression of the spirit of Islam, this building has few rivals.[179] Here is magnificence and power, happily expressed with the grace of harmonious proportions, rational and ample spaces, suave transitions.

The less ambitious mosque of Shaykh Lutf Allah (1601–28) is a contemporary work that, because of its modest size and simplified function, is more easily understood. The perennial form of a dome on a square chamber, inherited from Sasanian architecture, reappears in this beautiful little mosque which Shah Abbas built opposite the palace, in honor of his saintly father-in-law. It is an imposing single chamber, more of a private oratory than a mosque. Here, as in the Masjid-i-Shah, an adjustment was necessary to orient the quibla wall toward Mecca. This involved a diversion of forty-five degrees from the north-south axis of the maydan, which was effected by an ingenious and inconspicuous turn in the corridor. On entering the chamber, one is directly facing the mihrab. The reorientation is invisible on the exterior because only the dome appears above the wall that lines the whole maydan.

Figs. 290-293

Color Plates XXVI , XXVII

The low, single-shell dome, 42 feet in diameter, its excessive thrust taken up by massive walls (5 feet, 7 inches thick), gives the building a quiet repose. Midnight blue and white arabesques wheel majestically over a café-au-lait color ground, and a brilliant stalactite portal hints at splendor within. The chamber itself marks the final perfection of the dome-on-square plan, now simplified and suave as required by the growing refinement of the period. What was in ground plan just a square, and could have been a monotonous cube, has been developed into

217

290

291

a rich and highly dramatic paneled domed octagon, with contrasting treatment of the diagonal and cardinal elements. The abrupt little squinch of Parthian and Sasanian times, so obtrusively mechanical, has now been disguised and absorbed. Each corner arch, in reality a gigantic squinch, instead of being a small trumpetlike hollow, now reaches down to the floor. These have the same contour and dimensions as the four main arches, thus transforming the basically square chamber into an octagon. All eight arches are outlined by a thick cable molding of bright turquoise and framed with wide inscription bands of dazzling white on darkest opaque blue, the work of Ali Reza, the greatest calligrapher of the day. The flat panels of the arches on the main axis are broken by elaborate windows, grilles, and doors.

The ensemble, mostly faced with faience tile, is brilliant yet harmonious, and turquoise, cobalt, and milk-white are the dominant colors. The dado and the arches in the center of each wall are ornamented with satiny, almost soft-surfaced *haft-rangi* tiles, those in the arches containing large arabesques. The rest of the interior is faced with highly glazed mosaic faience that sends reflections dancing over the whole surface, sometimes with flashing sheets of light that momentarily blot out all color and design. These mirror-bright surfaces, most notably in the corner arches, consist of large interlocking cartouches sweeping over a café-au-lait ground. The mihrab is impressive by virtue of its clear, soft color as well as its harmonious composition and lines. From a golden sun medallion at the apex of the dome radiate expanding series of ogival cartouches filled with foliate forms, a textile pattern of which there are surviving examples. All these elements are bound by the wide inscription bands, the unifying dome above and the smaller dado that runs along the base.

The chamber is entirely empty. Any appurtenances would have been superfluous and quite overwhelmed by the powerful forms and commanding color. This is pure architecture, flawless and serene, and still as perfect as on the day of dedication three hundred years ago.

The lighting is a notable feature. The drum of the dome is pierced at regular intervals by windows. These are filled with a pair of grilles, an exterior and an interior grille, each composed of powerful arabesque patterns in an equal proportion of solids and voids, so that the light is doubly broken and filtered across the edges of cool blue faience. Thus softened and clarified, reflected on innumerable glittering facets of the wall and dome, light is shed over the shadowless interior like sparkling dew, revealing a perfection of unearthly beauty. No one in a receptive or contemplative mood can enter without a shock and the sense of being received into a Presence. For all its elegance and finish it has no weakness: the scale is too ample, the patterns too strong. Like the inspired architecture it is, it imposes its own mood.[180]

219

292

293

292. Masjid-i-Shaykh Lutf Allah, Isfahan, 1601–1628. Interior of dome.
293. Masjid-i-Shaykh Lutf Allah. Mihrab.

The urge to create perfect ensembles, royal cities, or little "Cities of God," which began in prehistoric times, finds a supreme expression in the sacred shrine of Imam Reza at Mashhad. Here Persia's greatest saint, a presumed martyr to royal jealousy, has long been the focus of piety and intense devotion. For Persians, it rivals Mecca and on this tomb has been lavished the patronage and wealth of kings and princes, not only from Persian but from Shi'ite communities in India and Central Asia as well. This shrine has had a tragic history, however, for since the ninth century it has been ravaged and almost destroyed many times—but reconstructions and additions have occurred even more frequently.[181] Shah Abbas I entered Mashhad in 1597 and ordered work begun on restoration in 1601. Without the Safavid contributions, this shrine would not reveal today the concentrated splendor that it does. Because it is the holiest site in Persia, and thus difficult to visit for non-religious purposes, it has not yet been thoroughly studied.

It consists of some thirty structures representing more than five centuries of building: mosques, oratories, colleges, libraries, sanctuaries, caravanserais—all connected by four huge courts, from 175 to 350 feet in length, which are surrounded with double-tiered arcades faced with enamel tile. A golden dome and two golden minarets, enriched with white inscriptions on ultramarine bands, are magically reflected in pools. A succession of courts punctuated by portals and twelve high ivans proclaim with dazzling opulence the Shi'ite veneration for the martyred Imam. From the entrance through the upper esplanade, through the old court to the farther end of the lower esplanade is well over a thousand feet (A, C, B on plan). Although the fifteenth century mosque of Gawhar Shad (AA on plan) is technically separate from the Shrine, it is physically contiguous to it and furnishes an impressive climax to the courts.

Figs. 294-298

Color Plates XXVIII

The court façades are not everywhere of the highest quality, with several of the modern ivans employing inferior painted tile or imitation faience mosaic painted on plaster. But the gold ivans, with their panels, arches and recesses, are dignified and sumptuous, and in their towering masses of softly shining gold framed in glowing blue faience mosaic they are not surpassed for sheer opulence in Islamic architecture.

In the old court, facing the gold ivan of Ali Shir Nawai (E on plan), is the blind ivan inscribed as the gift of Shah Abbas II and dated 1649 (F on plan). It is exceedingly tall and narrow and is faced with beautiful *haft-rangi* tile. Its deep blue-tinted depths make a perfect foil for the golden minaret rising behind it, and its collars of intense ultramarine bearing white inscriptions enhance all other colors.

Figs. 299, 300

221

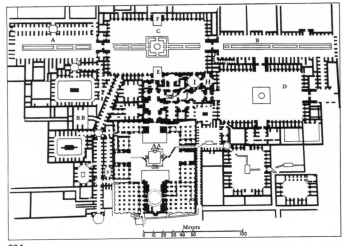

294

295

296

297

294. Shrine of Imam Reza, Mashhad. Plan: (A) Upper esplanade, (B) Lower esplanade, (C) Old court, (D) New court, (E) Gold ivan of Ali Shir Nawai, (F) Blind ivan of Shah Abbas II, (G) Tomb chamber of Imam Reza, (H) Hall of Hospitality, (I) Dome chamber of Allahvardi Khan, (J) Dome chamber of Hatim Khan, (AA) Mosque of Gawhar Shad, (BB) Madrassa Do-Dar.
295. Shrine of Imam Reza. Aerial view.
296. Shrine of Imam Reza. Entrance to old court.
297. Shrine of Imam Reza. Gold ivan of Ali Shir Nawai, late 15th century, with later restorations.
298. Shrine of Imam Reza. New Court.
299. Shrine of Imam Reza. Ivan of Shah Abbas II, 1649.

298

299

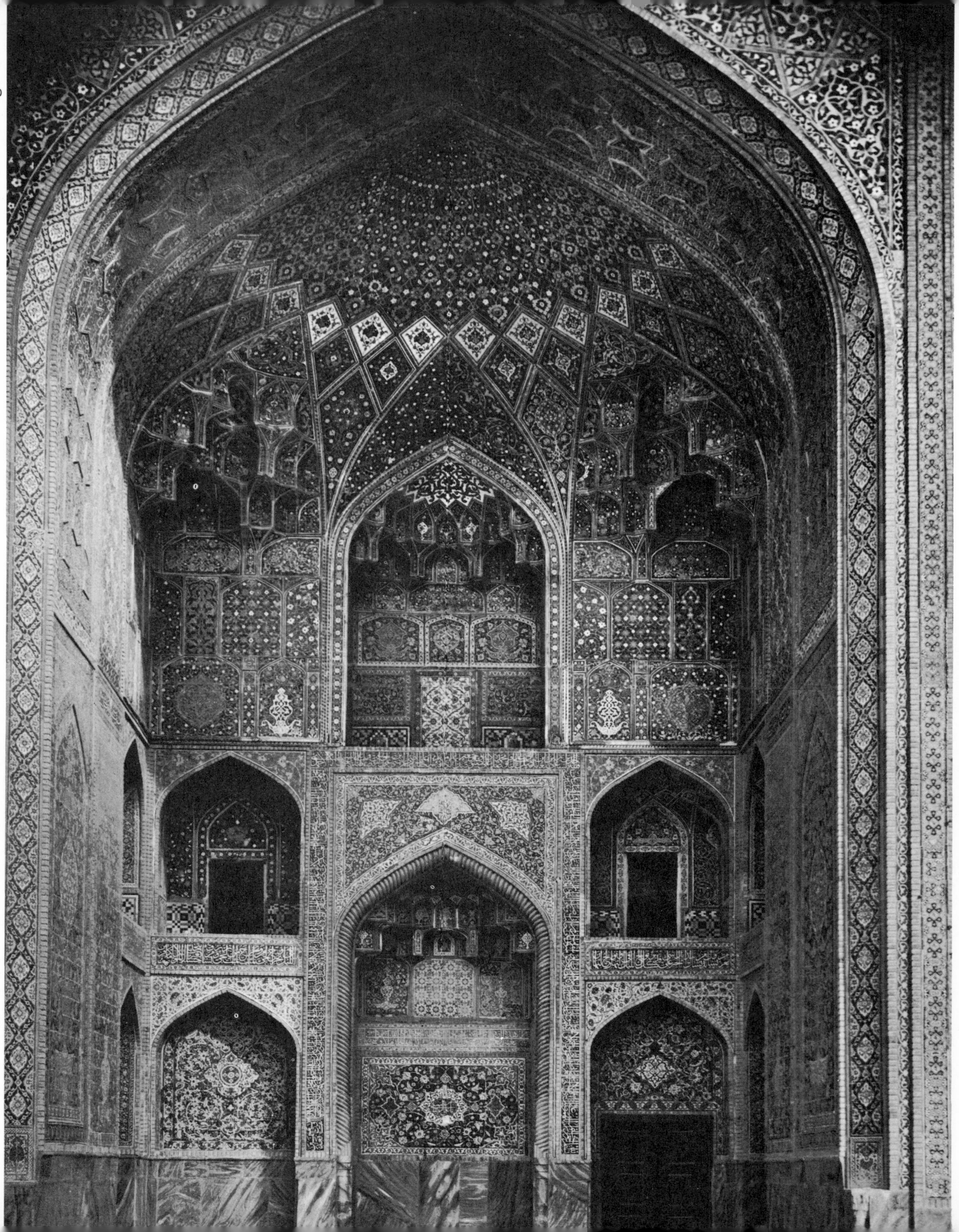

The interior structures are assembled around the sacred tomb chamber of Imam Reza (G on plan), which has been rebuilt and restored many times since the original structure of the ninth century. It is faced with gold and polychrome luster tiles, some of which date from the thirteenth century. There are special oratories in a variety of styles, from the faience-faced Hall of Hospitality (H on plan) with its cascading stalactite vaults, to a nineteenth century mirror-encrusted stalactite dome chamber, the Hall of Mirrors, which seems to enclose one within a vast diamond. The corridors and oratories are replete with magnificent panels, each a supreme decorative achievement of its time.

Figs. 301-303

Color Plate XXIX

The most perfect component of the shrine, however, is probably the domed chamber of Allahvardi Khan (I on plan), contemporary with the Shaykh Lutf Allah mosque in Isfahan. An octagonal interior structure, with no façade, the interior walls dissolve into arches, bays, and galleries, creating the air of a veritable holy of holies. The near blasphemous but almost convincing inscription of the designer proclaims that "this new building that equals in worth the Throne of God is the work of Amir the Architect." Judging by his style, Amir was from Isfahan, while the style of the adjoining domed chamber of Hatim Khan (J on plan) seems to be the craftsmanship of Tabriz. The dome of the sanctuary of Allahvardi Khan, 70 feet high and 36 feet in diameter, filled with a mass of stalactites, crowns the two storeys of sumptuously modeled recesses. The whole is faced with the finest mosaic faience of the period, each panel a serious work of art enlivened with subtle and unusual asymmetries. The 5-foot high dado of golden-toned marble sets off the deep blue tones of the revetments and a plain turquoise tile floor intensifies and enriches the ensemble.

Figs. 304-306

Here is space defined, densely compressed; space of expansive force, yet perfectly contained by its harmonious proportions and meticulous organization. Every angle and facet emphasizes location and concentrates on an irresistibly marked center which constrains every line of regard and every unconscious movement. One is enclosed in a world of glory that makes the world of common fact seem remote and curiously unreal.

The Isfahan palaces of Shah Abbas I, of which two have survived in good condition, are exceedingly modest in comparison to the royal residences and halls of the Sasanians or Mongols. The Chihil Sutan[182] continues the old *talar*, or columnar porch, a form used in every kind of structure—palace, temple, mosque or home—for centuries. At its simplest it is only a roof-high porch constituting the façade. When attached to a royal building, it provides a huge outdoor reception hall, and is susceptible to lavish embellishments which have included mirror-plated columns, panels and stalactites, and polychrome mosaic ceilings. The interior of this palace is covered with painted ornament of both figurative and abstract designs and capped with ceiling vaults of intense but harmonious color, such as azure, scarlet, light green and gold.

Figs. 307, 308

225

Fig. 309

Color Plates XXX

The Palace of the Ali Qapu,[183] on the maydan of Isfahan, was the principal residence palace and center of government. It is tall, square in plan, probably a northern type, with the *talar* as the second storey. The *talar* is here again a huge reception hall capable of holding two hundred or more courtiers and commands a fine view over the city with its mosques, domes and minarets, and particularly over the activities in the maydan below. The interior is covered with murals, all rendered in delicate polychrome relief. Many small rooms for private entertainment have fireplaces and are open on one side, evidencing again the Persian technique of bringing the out-of-doors into their houses.

Fig. 310

The intense building activity of the early seventeenth century, inspired and initiated by Shah Abbas I, included several beautiful domed mausolea. One of the most important of these, dedicated to Khwaja Rabi, a famous saint, was built in 1622 in a garden near Mashhad. Like the mausoleum of Oljeitu, it is octagonal in plan, but four of the sides have been added to its basically square mass simply by cutting off the corners. With second-storey galleries opening outward, it represents the midway development of a Persian type which culminated in the Taj Mahal. It is completely covered with tile of vigorous design and color in, perhaps, too great variety. Within, the effect is rich and harmonious, glowing in higher key than usual, but gracious and altogether charming; the applied ornament is painted, gilded, and polychromed with some delicate relief patterns. More important is the refined and subtle way in which the squinch is disposed and camouflaged, being carried to the ground in a variety of salient angles. The robust masculine Seljuk squinch is here concealed and distributed into a suave elegance of ample but undemonstrative strength. The dome thus rests on four arches whose heavy piers are diminished by the deep extension of the arch bays on either side and the multiplication of verticals which diffuse the function of support.

Figs. 311-313

The Shrine of Gadam Gar (1643), also a domed octagon with open galleries and gracious proportions, sits in a romantic garden up against a rocky pine-clad hill near Nishapur. Its plan, however, is more truly octagonal than the Khwaja Rabi, and the resulting structure seems more perfectly related to its dome. The shrine was built to enclose two fragments of rock which supposedly contain footprints of the Imam Reza. Although built in 1643, we know that it was thoroughly restored as early as 1680 during the reign of Shah Sulayman.

226

301

302

303

304

305

306

305. Shrine of Imam Reza, Mashhad. Chamber of Allahvardi Khan, 1612, detail.
306. Shrine of Imam Reza. Chamber of Allahvardi Khan, detail.
307. Peasant House, Mazandaran, 19th century. Drawing from Dieulafoy showing talar.
308. Chihil Sutan, Isfahan.

307

308

309

310

The little palace of the Hasht Behist in Isfahan, an extravagantly lovely pleasure dome placed in the vast Garden of Nightingales, was decreed by Shah Sulayman in 1669. The Hasht Behist or "Eight Paradises," so named because it is composed of four pavilions each with two storeys, is set on a marbled-faced foundation course. Identical wide half-octagon porches on the north and south sides have high roofs supported by exceedingly tall and slender columns (60 feet high) originally faced with mirrors. The spacious octagonal central hall, with pool and fountain originally silver lined, is crowned by a small but gorgeous dome, gleaming with polychrome stalactites. The hall is open on all sides so that the garden almost flows in. Now much ruined by Kajar redecoration, the interior was originally of bewildering magnificence: everywhere there was gold with azure, columns faced with mirrors, tile and multicolored glass, balustrades and soffits of the arches covered with gold. But the architectural importance of the building went beyond its almost hysterical splendor. It was the noble space relations which gave this cascade of opulence real dignity and power. The great central hall, open on all sides, is defined, but not confined by the four corner pavilions. On the other hand, this amplitude is counterbalanced by numerous smaller rooms and little cabinets in the corner pavilions. Such an emphatic contrast between imperial immensity and happy withdrawal into seclusion, here so skillfully accomplished, was an essential value in the rhythm of Persian life.

Architectural styles, so gradually developed in Persia, were also slow to deteriorate, and their momentum carried them for a while across periods of political and economic decline. Such a decline, of cultural vacancy and routine, set in with the death of Shah Abbas I in 1627 when, as Chardin said, "Persia ceased to live." But the madrassa Madir-i-Shah, a mosque and madrassa that Shah Sultan Husayn, the last of the Safavids, built in Isfahan (1706–14) is a noble and handsome building, a little perfunctory when compared to its great prototype the Masjid-i-Shah, but still outshining any comparable contemporary structure in Islam.

A monumental recessed portal covered with mosaic faience leads from the still beautiful garden, known as the Chahar Bagh, into a stately garden court.[185] The court façades consist of two-storeyed open arcades and the four usual vaulted ivans. The sanctuary, modeled after the Masjid-i-Shah, has a gracefully contoured dome covered with large arabesques in yellow and black that wheel majestically over the brilliant turquoise ground. The varied revetments of the building are for the most part of small scale panels created in mingled tonality of gold, green, and shades of blue. This is perhaps the last great building of Iran. Certain later structures, such as the Vakil mosque in Shiraz or the mosque of al-Hakim of Isfahan have charm, but the period of great Persian architecture had already ended.

The nineteenth century, under the Qajar dynasty, saw no important monuments, although there were some charming residences, a handsome caravanserai, and little Imamzada tombs with blue domes scattered throughout the country. The few large buildings of the period are without distinction. Some repairs, especially in Isfahan and Mashhad, are well done, thanks to the authority of the model, and tile-faced public structures are usually of acceptable quality.

Color Plates XXXI-XXXIII

Figs. 314-318

Fig. 319

231

311

312

311. Shrine of Gadam Gar, near Nishapur, 1643.
312. Shrine of Gadam Gar. Aerial view.
313. Shrine of Gadam Gar. Portal.
314. Madrassa Madir-i-Shah, Isfahan, 1706–1714. Sanctuary portal and dome.
315. Madrassa Madir-i-Shah. Sanctuary portal.

313

314

315

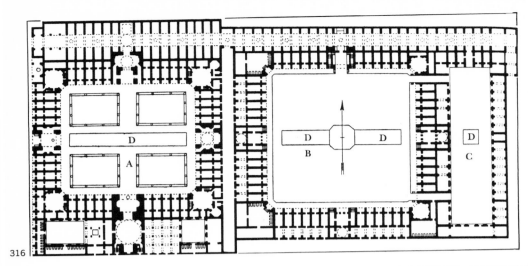

316

317

316. Madrassa Madir-i-Shah, Isfahan, 1706–1714.
Plan: (A) Madrassa, (B) Caravanserais, (C) Stables, (D) Canal.
317. Madrassa Madir-i-Shah. Dome.
318. Madrassa Madir-i-Shah. Outer portal.
319. Vakil Mosque, Shiraz, 18th century. Winter prayer hall.

318

319

IX. Summary of Forms and Structural Problems

Although the primary task, as well as the greatest achievements, of Persian architecture were in the service of religion, architectural activity was by no means confined to religious monuments and secular palaces. Other structures of considerable beauty and requiring equal skill and imagination were built throughout the land. Chief among these were bridges, bazaars, caravanserais, fortifications and gardens, in all but the last case dictated to a certain extent by necessity but given form by aesthetic imagination and practical needs. To discuss the various types of buildings separately, while convenient is unfortunately somewhat misleading for they are rarely totally separated and are usually built or meant to be viewed in relation to each other. For example, the finest caravanserai and bazaar in seventeenth century Persia adjoined a magnificent palace which, in its turn, was integrated with a superb garden. The complete plan was probably conceived as a unity and certainly it functioned as such. Similarly, an individual bridge often exists in conjunction with baths, caravanserais, even a mosque, and its function as a means of crossing water, purely as a bridge from one bank to another, is by no means the most important.

The life of the State depended on an efficient and secure system of communication without which Iran would have been but a congeries of separate and harassed communities instead of a great Asian power and potent factor in world civilization. The geography itself was a formidable challenge: an area as large as Western Europe, sparsely settled, divided by wide and ferocious deserts and mountains, the matrix of sudden destructive torrents and deep gorges. A practical conquest of these obstacles was indispensable for national life.

236

In the southwest, bridges, often combined with dams for much needed irrigation, were essential. Severely tasking the resources of the architect,[186] these dual purpose bridges must be open enough to let the dangerous floodwaters through. This difficult problem was often compounded by the necessity for abutments at different levels. Wheel and animal traffic constantly worked to break down the crown of a bridge, with sun and frost helping the process of disintegration, so that even the best bridges were doomed to short life or constant and expensive repair. Bold designing and first-class constructional techniques were indispensable; from Sasanian times they were highly developed. Roman prisoners, including masons captured at Shapur's defeat of Valerian, made important contributions: they laid out the mile long bridge and dam at Shushtar and were responsible for the crucial device of the pier tunnel with interior side vents that eased the pressure of suddenly backed up water, thus protecting the main channels and the piers themselves. The very fine ashlar masonry of some of the early bridges could Figs. 320-322 have been a continuation of Achaemenid practice revived by Roman skill. Stone blocks were fastened by iron and lead clamps, with iron and copper filings and cinders set in concrete.

The remains of the great Pul-i-Dukhtar near Sarvistan, 70 feet high and originally of huge span, confirm the contemporary descriptions of even more sensational structures: the bridge at Idhaj over the Karun river, according to the great geographer Yaqut, "spanned the river by a single arch rising 150 ells (approx. 225 feet) above water level,"[187] and the fourteenth century span over the Araxes river near Karkha was built entirely of stone "of utmost steadfastness, smoothness and beauty of construction,"[188] and included one arch 95 feet wide.

These bridges were more than means for crossing a river: they were often of notable beauty in proportions and contour, expressing power and grace. The later bridges were increasingly elaborate and were sometimes combined with mosques and caravanserais. They usually contained a toll or customs house as well as various amenities such as kitchens, baths, and, at frontiers, fortifications. Thus, two complex bridges over the Zayinda-rud at Isfahan are devoted to the skillful exploitation of the site of the river with its cool breezes and vital flow of water. These are the bridge of Allahvardi Khan, built by that favorite general of Shah Abbas I, Figs. 323, 324 and the Khaju bridge, built by Shah Abbas II to serve as both bridge and dam. Planned also for enjoyment, they are places for tarrying as much as for transit. The full length of each bridge consists of charming little open galleries along both sides, handsomely decorated with tile and mural ornament. Here people can still gather for sociability or contemplation. Several hundred people at the same time can find refreshment and entertainment on either of these bridges, both of which express the humane characteristic of Persian architecture.

320. Kaflan Kuh Bridge, 12th century, rebuilt early 17th century, repaired 18th century.
321. Kaflan Kuh Bridge. Pier tunnel, detail.
322. Pul-i-Kashgan, Sumaq, 9th or 10th century.

Caravanserais were quite as indispensable as bridges to the maintenance of commercial and economic prosperity. The great distance between commercial centers, the intervening natural perils of wilderness or desert, the dangers from too frequent civil wars and, in many periods, from a highly organized banditry, to say nothing of the constant threat of nomads and other marauders, all necessitated numerous secure sites for refreshment to ensure that caravans and other travelers would arrive safely at their destinations. Even in Achaemenid times, stations had been established (they must have been fortified, although we have little specific evidence on this matter) and the roads were patrolled. During the early Islamic period, fortified frontier posts, necessary defenses against hostile non-Muslim peoples, were established and known as *rabats*. They were often manned by volunteers who considered their defense a religious duty and no doubt they also served to shelter caravans operating in exposed territories. The name *rabat* later was applied to major fortifications large enough to protect the local populace.

Among early examples of caravanserais are the great caravanserai built by Harun ar-Rashid about 889 on the road to Tus and the tenth century caravanserai built by Adud ad-dawla which was amply supplied with sweet water and constructed of masonry coated with plaster.[189] In the midst of a formidable desert, between Samarkand and Bokhara, Sultan Sanjar sometime before

Fig. 148   1078 built an immense caravanserai, the magnificent Rabat-i-Malik. A main section of the long outer wall consists of engaged semi-circular piers joined at the top by little squinches—a building technique designed primarily for strength.[190] The total effect of this great wall is an imposing combination of severe simplicity with sheer power. In a few critical places it was ornamented with an unusual type of carved stucco.[191] At one time in the seventeenth century the caravanserais along the major routes were reputed to be only twenty miles apart, sometimes even closer. They were often quite large and intricate in plan and it is not surprising that a famous Seljuk caravanserai at Zabzavar contained 1,700 chambers.

These caravanserais constitute one of the triumphs of Persian architecture. Nowhere can we find a more complete accord of function and structure. The first requirement of security had to be met by special design since the ordinary layout of a fort or citadel with moat, barbicans, and machicolations would have been prohibitively expensive in the required quantity.

Figs. 326, 328, 329   The basic plan for later caravanserais is constant from structure to structure. They may be square, round or octagonal, often with towers at the angles; they may be small or covering several acres; but all are essentially concentric, with the outer wall quite blank, allowing access only through a single and easily defended portal. The central court is surrounded by open arcades, like a mosque or madrassa, the middle of each side sometimes being emphasized by a larger arch or even a vault—in effect the conventional four-ivan plan. These arcades, sometimes

238

320

321

322

323

324

325

323. Allahvardi Khan Bridge, Isfahan, *circa* 1600.
324. Khaju Bridge, Isfahan, 1642–1666. Lower side.
325. Caravanserai, Nishapur.

two rooms deep and often equipped with fireplaces for cooking or winter warmth, are not at ground level but are elevated several feet. In addition to the living quarters, there are provisions for special services: water, sometimes a commissary and quarters for guards and attendants and often larger quarters for special groups. Beyond and just within the solid peripheral wall, is the zone of the stable into which there is no external access. It is quite cut off from the court, except for a few easily controlled passages, thus minimizing any danger of stampede and making access to the animal quarters more difficult for marauders. In many of the isolated stations, theft of the animals would have meant almost certain death to their owners, and they had to protect them at any cost. All the requirements for defense and service, the primary considerations of these structures, are fully met.

The amenities are not neglected either for, in addition to baths and kitchens in the best stations, there is generally a mihrab and sometimes there are also fountains and special luxury rooms—often on the roof—for travelers of rank. Some of these interiors, which were usually of fired brick, sometimes combined with stone, were decorated with painted murals. The outer walls were frequently faced with enameled tiles and occasionally the portals were magnificently designed and ornamented, rivaling even the great mosque portals.[192] In the great seventeenth century caravanserai and bazaar at Kashan, serving thousands of Indian and European merchants, Chardin reported that the corridors were even lined with marble.

These caravanserai are often located near or contiguous to famous shrines or madrassas. In the large cities, they are also close to the bazaars or may be attached to one of the famous bridges. They were located not only in the commercial cities like Isfahan, which Chardin reported as having 1802 caravanserais,[193] but they also sprang up at convenient sites between major centers, so that a seventeenth century account describes the city of Deha as "a village where there are so many caravanserais that there is practically nothing else there."[194]

Figs. 325, 327

The system of the caravanserais logically leads to bazaars, those centers of commercial and civic activity. These were effective and economical, controlling varied but always intense activities in the minimum of space with maximum convenience and security. The standard plan, called the *chahar-su* (four rivers), consisted of two passageways intersecting each other at right angles, covered by a dome at the crossing. We know that this plan had a history of thousands of years, for the plan appears clearly on painted pottery of the fourth millennium B.C. Small apertures in the vaulted roof let in sufficient light yet kept out the intense heat of summer and retained warmth in winter. Here, public opinion was made and expressed and social intercourse flourished.

Bazaars were built and maintained by the government, by public-spirited donors, or by the merchants themselves. Often they were truly imposing and architecturally sophisticated

Figs. 330, 331

241

326. Bazaar and Bath of Hajji Sayyid Husayn, Kashan, 17th century.
Plan: (A) Bazaar, (B) Vestibule to the bath, (C) Main room of bath, (D) Hot room, (E) Summer pool.
327. Caravanserai, Qumm, 19th century.
328. Caravanserai, Chelesieh. Plan.
329. Caravanserai between Tabriz and Sultaniya. Plan.

structures. The handsomest bazaar of all was the Qaysariya of Isfahan, built by Shah Abbas I at the beginning of the seventeenth century. Its monumental portal opens on the great maydan opposite the Masjid-i-Shah, and is faced with handsome mosaic faience. The long, high vault, seemingly sustained by intersecting ribs, looks curiously like the nave of a European cathedral. The open domical vaults in each transverse vault provide light. Its great height permitted a second storey for offices and its proximity to the central square made access easy and convenient. It was an essential part of a perfect civic center in which government, religion and trade had their own conveniently located establishments.

Figs. 332-335 · There were, of course, many other types of public structures, among which is the important achievement represented by city walls which throughout Persian history were indispensable. Frequently these fortifications were of enormous extent, and it appears that the tenth century wall of Bokhara, which surrounded not only the city but gardens, orchards and suburbs as well, was over 100 miles long.[195] The walls of Isfahan and Balkh were triple and according to a frequent Persian practice, concentric. Qazvin had a double wall, the outer one with some 206 towers, while tenth century Herat had a double moat and a wall with 149 towers. City gates were usually double or triple, and the doors were of heavy iron plate, with the entrances not concentric or at least off the main axis, thus making entry slow. The twelfth to fourteenth century walls of Yazd, which are still standing, are perhaps the most interesting. Surrounded by a deep, dry moat, in places they are doubled, even tripled, and crowned with impressive machicolations. They are defended by towers, gates and by some formidable barbicans.

There are, however, almost no purely utilitarian structures in Persia. In addition to the decorative character of the machicolations, the walls at Yazd, and other places as well, bore elaborate, geometric ornamentation formed of raised brick. In other cities, such as Herat, the gates and towers were often covered with enameled faience. The eighteenth century fortress of Shiraz, intricately decorated and painstakingly designed, is nonetheless a building of strength.

Fig. 337 Similarly, less important structures, such as the curious pigeon towers around Isfahan, which were originally built to provide fertilizer, are by no means purely functional. Their complex forms were formerly coated with white plaster and often had a polychromed frieze and cupola.

In many periods, even Persian domestic architecture is quite worthy of note. The houses in Qazvin, Rayy and Tabriz were all complimented profusely by contemporary travelers[196] and every house of at least middle-class status has its own pool. For protection, most have traditionally had an off-axis entrance (as did the caravanserais). The intense heat of summer is allayed in a variety of ways and with skill. There are indoor as well as outdoor pools, and open water channels frequently run through the house. In the torrid sections like Kashan and Yazd, there

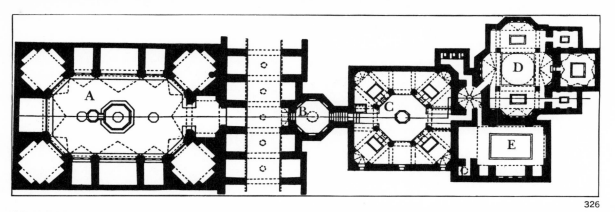

326

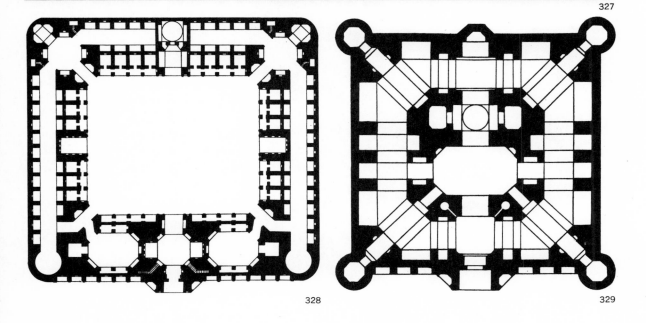

327

328

329

are sub-basement chambers aerated by the handsome *bad-girs,* tall square towers with open Fig. 336 vents on each side to catch any cooling breath of air and carry it down to the recesses of the house. In milder regions such as Mazandaran, the heat is kept at bay by wide porches and over-hanging eaves. On the south side, walls are often massively thick, absorbing heat without trans-mitting it to the interior and, in effect, storing up an insulating wall of heat against the short cold spells of winter. A few palaces were built with double walls, the space between being filled with ice. Other buildings, such as Adud ad-dawla's great library in Shiraz, were cooled with water circulating in pipes within the walls. From the tenth century on less expensive and equally effective devices were in common use. Fans and curtains of scented felt were saturated by a steady drip from overhead pipes, and each town had immense water tanks and deep cisterns as well as carefully constructed ice-houses and reservoirs.

The main rooms of the interiors, often with a whole wall of glass windows on the garden side, were (and still are) generally finished in white, frequently broken with charming little re-cesses and vaulted stalactite ceilings.

In contrast to these decorative structures, which also filled very specific and necessary func-tions, are the splendid Persian gardens which served more psychic and less measurable needs.[197] Since earliest times, the garden has been an essential part of Persian life and of its architecture, sharing and reinforcing the symbolic affirmation of the great temples. Just as the base of the mountain itself is "with verdure clad" (in plain evidence of its beneficent power) so as early as Sumer the garden surrounded the temple and palace of the king. Of course, the garden in such an arid climate had everything to commend it in the way of comfort and charm; but these con-siderations were secondary when the struggle for life itself was so much more important than individual pleasure. Since all things were believed to be managed by the gods, appeals to those gods were essential. It was thought that the surest way to gain their favor was by sympathetic magic: by displaying, as impressively as possible, a scene of what was most needed, thus stim-ulating the gods to imitate by producing similar—but more widespread—abundance. Hence the creation of a garden in connection with temple or palace might persuade the All Powerful to supplement man's puny effort to keep the earth fruitful.

Life in Persia depends upon water. It is almost the central factor of living—hence it be-comes the symbol of life and hope. The gift of water in this entire area works miracles, not merely because of its scarcity but because the soil is exceptionally fertile and once water is brought to it, the earth bursts into life. Alleviation of drought or flood and partial control of water sources were achieved by imagination and invention. If evaporation consumed too much of the exposed water surface, underground channels called *qanats,* sometimes over 100 feet deep

245

and extending for 50 or 100 miles, conserved water for irrigation. Dams for flooding flat areas, storage tanks, and deep wells strung along the desert routes made these difficult routes passable.

As early as 3500 B.C., the ornamentation of prehistoric pottery of Iran shows the intense concern with water and fertility. These ancient patterns realistically and symbolically depict all the water-bearing elements: mountains, clouds, pools, rushes, aquatic birds and trees, the mere display of which was intended to induce appropriate response from the powers of heaven. In the Samarra pottery (perhaps even earlier) we find the typical garden layout, based on the *chahar-su:* the crossing of two canals with birds and trees in each of the four corners. In the Luristan bronzes, about 1000 B.C., we again find the tree combined with flowing water—of all prospects the most pleasing in a dry land. Cyrus the Great told Lysander that he had himself planned the great park at Sardis and that he had planted trees with his own hands. We know that the gardens of the Achaemenid Empire were carefully designed with rectangles, alleys and symmetrical trees.

By the time of the great Sasanian Empire, gardens were of vast extent and parks, which were carefully laid out and attended, might cover nearly ten square miles. One example was the garden of the Imarat-i-Kusraw, the fabulous palace built by Chosroes II. Taking as long as seven years to create, it taxed the resources of the king and sometimes of the state itself but it was a bold and lovely modification of the environment.

In Islamic times, the more intensely cultivated gardens surrounding a palace were architecturally planned in accordance with the structure itself and regarded as an essential to it. These huge gardens were symmetrically laid out in relation to the main axis of the building. The terminal points were marked by pavilions. The palace was located at the intersection of two avenues and water courses at right angles to the main axis thus provided a long vista framed by parallel water channels. The whole area was further divided into rectangular beds defined by small water channels. Every kind of tree was planted, and we can be sure that the planting and the character of the shrubbery were harmoniously organized, repeating and accenting the plan and circulation of the ensemble. In the ninth and tenth centuries, the fabulous caliphs of Baghdad and Samarra built similar gardens, following their illustrious Persian predecessors.

In the garden—whether natural or man-made—man was at peace with his environment. The walled garden, which excluded wild beasts or other marauders and created a little enclosed and concentrated ideal kingdom, had from Achaemenid times been called *Paradaiza,* and paradise it was. Here man and nature were in perfect accord. Here the harsh and frustrated earth came to its own destined perfection, no longer man's enemy, indifferent to his needs, but instead providing peace, repose and joy. In twenty-two passages, the Koran describes the felicities of

246

332

333

334. Fortress, Shiraz, *circa* 1735.

Heaven, the joy and deep happiness of those who have been faithful to their lord and at last found peace, dignity, repose, dwelling forever in gardens with rivers flowing beneath, in shades cool and ever-deepening, resplendent with gushing fountains.[198]

The Persian garden is a place not merely for security and repose; it is the place for quiet meditation or thoughtful conversation. It is the place for contemplation, where one's tattered soul can be repaired and refreshed and new insights disclosed. Chardin noted that the Persians are quiet in their gardens, not rushing to and fro but rapturously inhaling the varied and intense perfumes from specially selected flowers. The garden, however, may occasionally be used for gay and charming evening processions, music, and dances, with soft lights or fireworks.

The garden ideal was so potent and enduring that, as prosperity waxed, wealth, ideas and disciplined judgement were lavished on gardens. Every great city and every palace had elaborate gardens—many of them public. All of them were opened for the New Year festivities to celebrate the spring. Clavigo reported that in Tabriz the fine roadways had open spaces, large squares connected by avenues with fountains for drinking and the central plaza was really a great park, framed by tall poplars evenly spaced, with garden pavilions buried in jasmine and roses. One park in Tabriz had 1,000 fountains, 1,000 rills and 1,000 rivulets.

Figs. 338-344

In Isfahan there were fabulous gardens, not merely the famous Chahar Bagh, which was really a mile long parklike promenade, but also numerous gardens which surrounded it on every side. These contained, or consisted of, rose hedges, open arcades framed in jasmine mingling with fountains and pools and exquisite, jewel-like pavilions. In Shiraz, the king's garden was 2,000 paces square with walls 14 feet high, and private gardens might well have been still larger. Even today one garden in Shiraz produces 12,000 pounds of roses each day—all of ravishingly intense color.

Of course the garden ideal completely penetrated nearly all the arts. The great sixteenth century carpets are all poetic, imaginative creations of the perfect verdure of paradise. The lotus throughout all periods in the entire breadth of Asia was a sacred symbol of the Divine. On the Persepolis sculptures, Artaxerxes holds it reverently in his hand and even Ahura Mazda, the Great God himself, is frequently depicted with a lotus blossom. The lotus is framed in a complex of silver lattice on the doors to the inner shrine at Ardabil. Modeled in massive scale in polychrome stucco, the lotus ornamented the palaces and temples of the Sasanians. The little desert mosque of Nayin is rich with flowing vines and immense rosettes, and architectural ornament throughout the Islamic period consists almost exclusively of elaborate organic vegetation. The gardener, the architect, and weaver as well, who performs his craft with poetic feeling, with rationality and imagination, seems to the Persian to bring the inherent potential of the earth to full bloom, aiding man in his long and perilous journey to perfection.

249

335. City gate, Yazd.
336. *Bad-gir,* or wind tower, Isfahan.
337. Pigeon tower, Buzan, 17th century.

Of less spiritual importance, but absolutely vital to the development of Persia's great architectural achievements, is that highly significant unit of construction: the vault. From Sasanian or even late Parthian times, the vault in its various forms was without doubt the most important element in Persian building. Its widespread adoption was necessitated by the lack of sufficient wood and timber in the region to continue the Achaemenid habit of post and lintel construction which was facilitated by wood. The Achaemenid kings not only probably had larger quantities of timber at hand than the later rulers were to have, but they also had the immense wealth to enable them to import the great cedars from Lebanon and teak from India, which records show were used in the great palaces at Susa and Persepolis. Because of the ever increasing importance played by the development of vault construction, a discussion of its principles and potentials is essential to an understanding of the greater part of Iranian architecture.[199]

Vault construction was not introduced merely as a substitute for the imposing trabeate architecture of the Achaemenids, however, for it was already in use from very early times. We know of the underground Egyptian vaults from the third millennium B.C. and, even more pertinently, of the Choga Zambil entrance vaults from about 1200 B.C. Of perhaps still greater significance are the Assyrian carvings of mountain towns, mostly in the Persian northwest, which show cities almost completely roofed by low saucer-shaped domes and occasionally a high dome of parabolic type. They seem to have been built of unfired brick and hence have long ago deteriorated leaving no physical evidence of their own.

Before following the complicated historical development of Persian vaults in preserved examples, it would be useful to be acquainted with some elementary but basic definitions. There are three major types of vaults and, theoretically, all are derived from a single elemental component: the arch. When an arch is prolonged in depth, a barrel or tunnel vault is created. When two tunnel vaults intersect each other, the diagonal vaults thus formed are called transverse vaults. And if the arch is rotated on itself to form a hemispherical vault, it is, of course, a dome. This last, in a more complex form, can become a vault over a square plan and is capable of innumerable variations.

The barrel or tunnel vault, the simplest of all, can be built relatively rapidly and cheaply. The Persian method required no centering, the timber framework on which such a vault usually rests until it is completely set. By slightly inclining each course against the already fixed fabric, the fast drying gypsum mortar generally used caused the inclined course to adhere in a matter of moments to each successive layer—including the peak, or what we would generally call the centerstone. Thus the vault itself marches forward from the fixed wall in steady and firm succession to the desired length.

250

335

336

337

338

339

Such a vault, however, although it can be almost limitless in length is restricted to a relatively narrow width. Also, since the weight and thrust of such a vault is carried by the walls, they cannot be pierced for windows without seriously, even fatally, weakening the structure. Hence these vaults are dark, with the only source of light emanating either from low apertures which are ineffective and disagreeable, or from the ends of the tunnels, which provide a harsh glare, intense but also productive of long, deep shadows. Despite these disadvantages, many great structures were built in this form. The single-ivan structure, such as the reception hall of the Taq-i-Kisra, is an example. Generally, such vaults are rather monotonous and structurally featureless on the interior, except when relieved by arched panels or recessed as at Firuzabad.

In a mosque, the poor illumination was not a serious disadvantage, for the light would always come from the back of the congregation, thus concentrating on the mihrab and the prayer leader. The earliest of the single barrel-vaulted ivan–mosques still survives, repaired and added to, at Nayriz. The fourteenth century Pir-i-Bakran is also a little Taq-i-Kisra, with some additions and embellishments. The most impressive of all, however, was the mosque Ali Shah built at Tabriz with the conscious intention of surpassing all other such structures.

The problems presented by the barrel vault were in principle solved in Sasanian times by one of the most important inventions in the history of architecture: the transverse arch and vault. The earliest known example is the ruined Ivan-i-Kharkha in southwest Persia, where a rectangular hall was covered by a brick vault with five transverse arches, apparently joined along their length by smaller tunnel vaults. This development concentrated the load directly onto piers so that the walls were relieved of their previously inhibiting weight-bearing function. Now thin and light, the vaults could safely be pierced for windows, thus providing ample and semi-indirect illumination. It is essentially the same scheme that later appeared in the church of St. Philibert at Tournus.[200] It was subsequently widely used in Persia for several centuries, in places where it was necessary to support a long vault. These vaults were often very long for a tunnel vault can be extended indefinitely, as in the great seventeenth century bazaars of Isfahan, Kashan and Shiraz where they stretched out for hundreds of feet.

With regard to the vault or dome placed over a square plan, the principal problem is how to manage the transition from square below to circle above. A dome cannot simply be placed upon a square base, for either it will project over the four sides of the square while it rests on the corners or it will rest on the sides but fall short of the corners. In either case a system of ugly bracketing or an inserted crude mass of mortar will have to be added to make do. For centuries this problem baffled the very competent Roman engineers, who did not provide an attractive or even certain solution.

253

340

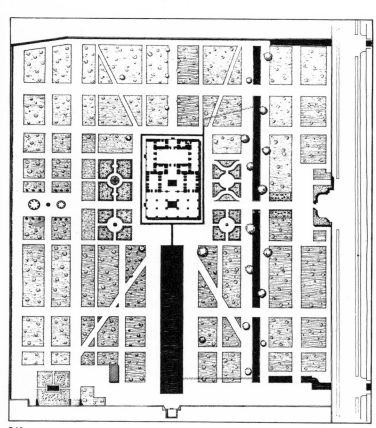

341

342

343

344

The earliest solution was reached by Persian engineers and masons who gradually realized that the question as posed was impossible. The answer required the development of a third section, a zone of transition, which involved building an arch across each corner thereby reducing the square to an octagon. If necessary, small arches could be built again to bridge the corners of the octagon thus producing a sixteen-sided figure which nearly approximated the ring of the dome. The slight corbelling necessary to smooth out the small discrepancies was not noticeable. In the earliest examples of this type of construction, the squinch or pendentive is rather crude and compressed, the arch creating a small trumpet shaped hollow in each corner or angle. The history of this device, the squinch, is essential to the story of Islamic architecture; the variety of solutions is the story of slow development, inventiveness and engineering skill.

The squinches are basically of two types: the hollow round-backed squinch of Sasanian times and later a simple groined squinch in which the bisecting line drawn up from the corner is carried to the back of the squinch arch itself. The problem that immediately followed the initial use of the squinch was how to fill its hollow space, whether to pierce it, to leave it empty, fill it with constructional forms, or suppress it in various ways by breaking it up or by dividing the corner angle into components to diminish the size of the squinch. The infinite number of ways in which the squinch is filled, divided, or multiplied are astonishing in their variety.

The problem of the small domical vaults is more complicated and offers an infinite variety of potential solutions. A full description of these solutions is largely a technical problem for the engineers, but brief descriptions are nevertheless possible. The vault can be solid and bell-like, as in the Roman Pantheon, but the result of setting the dome on circular walls, while eliminating the transition problem, limits the space below to circular forms only. In contrast, the small dome over a square chamber can be enlarged to create a building of any size, but raises new problems of transition and stability. It is also difficult to create from this engineering problem an aesthetically handsome edifice. The Persian solutions to the dome-on-square problem included groin vaults, cloister vaults, vaults on groin squinches, on articulated squinches, on systems of interlacing armatures, domical vaults, domical lantern vaults, saucer domes, and countless others,[201] as well as the dome, the half-dome and quarter-dome. In the Masjid-i-Jami of Isfahan there are about 470 vaults, and the general impression is that no two are identical. All of the types could be as varied in embellishment as in form and any one of them could be followed through a long history, although a few, such as the cloister vault, are rather rare.

The statics, the mechanical analysis of pressures and thrusts carried on various sections of these vaults, has still to be investigated; a detailed study has not yet been possible. The major question, still controversial, concerns the functional aspect of elements of the vaults. They are

345

346

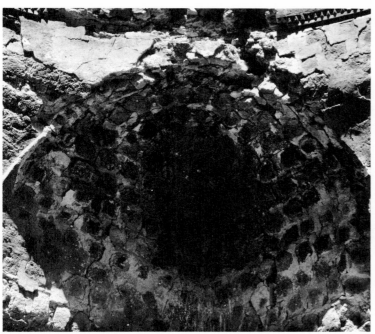

347

348

349

350

all decorative, true, but it has been too readily assumed that decoration was their chief purpose. It is a Persian characteristic to treat all structural functions decoratively if they are visible, and it is also commonplace in architectural history to find elements that have been abandoned as building techniques carried out as decoration. This was certainly true of many of the vaults and their once essential members. However, it is also common to find in other vaults an independent system of ribs incorporated into the fabric of the vault and almost concealed, but quite necessary to support the weight of the vault itself.[202]

Fig. 129 In great vaults like the half-domes of the large ivans, the intersecting ribs support the whole structure and the corner interstitial panels are principally for coverage rather than support. The scheme of intersecting arches, as in vault 60 of the Isfahan Jami, was applied on a large scale in the dome of the tomb of Sultan Sanjar, appeared earlier in the mosque at Cordova, and has major affiliations with techniques in Armenia. The origin of the scheme is as yet undetermined, but evidence points to Persia.[203] Some scholars deny that these ribs play a functional role, basing their arguments on the fact that current practice does not depend on the ribs for permanent stability.[204] This does not, however, apply to the powerful ribs of early structures where the ribs are composed of fired brick several courses deep and four or more wide at the base, ribs which are themselves heavier than the vault. Some of the ribs in the Isfahan vaults appear to be thin and possibly superficial—only one brick wide—but, when exposed by the collapse of interstitial panels, they are seen to be actually four or five courses deep, a real and powerful frame that supports the vault even after the structurally impotent panels have disintegrated and fallen out.

As the masons learned to build self-sustaining groin vaults, thanks to their increased skill and to the fast setting mortar that locked all elements in a tight and stable mass, the framework of independent ribs was given up. Even so, the masons or designers preserved the original line of the rib or armature which indicated its original function and the direction of its energies. This vestige of a non-functioning element might consist of a superficial rib only one brick thick, or perhaps only a plaster rib, cardboard strip, or even painted lines. Although no longer structural, these lines, by emphasizing the traditional directional energies, create the feeling of active, well co-ordinated and adequate support—all psychological necessities. Vaults and domes built up and supported by these wide interlocking arches, whether structural or merely as pictures of structural forces, continued almost to the present day.

Mastery in vault construction was by no means exhausted by the Seljuk masons or their immediate successors. The vault was the primary problem in every structure, from Sasanian times to the present. Its relentless challenge has evoked some surprising creations, all based on conventional forms but sometimes of astonishing skill and imagination which offered quite new effects, such as the vaults in the main hall of the caravanserai at Qumm, where a real genius transferred brick and plaster into an excited lyricism. In this case the practical function of roof Fig. 327 coverage, quite adequately met, has been made the occasion of a real *tour de force,* and the solid fabric is translated into a brilliant maze of luminous forms—almost ecstatic in their intensity. The basic structure is firm and powerful. The deep corner arches (each is actually a squinch complex reaching to the ground) sustain a bewildering play of intersecting arches, their salient outlines enclosing numerous subsidiary kite-shaped panels. These small square- and diamond-shaped segments diminish rapidly in size as they sweep up into the dome, speeded by the converging lines of the arches. Various sunken panels introduce a measure of retardation and enrichment, for they are alternately shadowed and illuminated, forming a quivering skein of light and dark. As a complex of harmoniously resolved and integrated energies it is convincing and satisfying; but in one sense it is only poetry, for the entire display physically adds nothing to the strength or stability of the basic structure, which is of plain brick following the conventional form of a dome (in this case two) on squinches. But psychologically it is compelling and very real: a simple mechanical form has been dematerialized and transformed into a vibrant celestial canopy. Ornamentation and basic form combine in the caravanserai of Qumm to provide an ample flood of light, let in from high windows and the open cupola of the two domes. This brightness, intense, palpable and buoyant, evenly distributed over a shadowless interior, has been a frequent triumph of Persian architects ever since the fourteenth century. The date of this building, however, is probably eighteenth or even early nineteenth century.

An additional type of vault is that built up by stalactites, or *muqarnas.* These clusters and tiers of cells that soften and enrich the broad masses and simple contours of buildings are a Figs. 353-359 delight to the eye. A touch of Persian fancy added to solemn and ponderous structures, they spread throughout the Islamic world. They are difficult to describe or record, and their planning is a baffling task. Briefly, they consist of rows of superimposed out-curving panels, generally miniature quarter-domes, the apexes apparently leaning on empty space, the point of each support being the dividing line of the row above. This is repeated as long as the general scheme requires, the sides forming a bracket that sustains the tier above. These cells can be quite varied and their relations can be subtly modified by an adroit mason.

Their first known use was in the little portal dome of the great funeral tower, the Gunbad-i-Qabus, where a rudimentary group of three fill the corner, humanizing the bleak mechanical juncture of dome and wall. Other early examples are made of brick and support, or actually are the cornice, as in the tower at Lajim, the Gunbad-i-Ali at Abarquh and the tower of

259

351

352

353

354

355

Toghrul at Rayy. It was a type of enrichment that was enthusiastically adopted in all regions for almost all purposes. Stalactites have been used for squinches, for the half- or quarter-domes of portals, the peaks of niches or deep recesses, for capitals and the support of minaret platforms and even—flattened out—for wall embellishment, as in the caravanserai of Khargird. Their decorative value was paramount, the constructive value completely dispensable, with the result that as early as the mid-twelfth century stalactites were made of plaster and applied directly to the brick surface, as at the Gunbad-i-Qabus. They were later cast separately and suspended from the interior of half domes by dowels or even ropes, as in the northeast ivan of the Isfahan Jami, where the suspension is now concealed under the recently restored shell.

For the most part the charm of stalactites lay in the multiplication of small but slightly varied units which broke and reflected the light in fascinating patterns. Several times the stalactite scheme was boldly used on a large scale and with immense energy setting the entire interior in apparent motion. The stalactite scheme has a high degree of individuality and is charged with endless possibilities of refinement and expansion. It was sometimes overdone, crowded and incoherent, as in the canopy of the otherwise impeccable Gawhar Shad, but even as late as the madrassa Madir-i-Shah in Isfahan it was used with beautiful effect and perfect taste.

The dome, which is only a special kind of vault, presents many problems and took many forms in Persia. As early as the twelfth century Persian builders had solved many questions of the variant thicknesses of the single-shell dome and the contours that provided maximum stability. Sasanian domes were round, ovoid, or parabolic. Later they assumed still other shapes: low saucerlike domes that require especially thick walls or buttresses to counter the excessive lateral thrust; or high domes set on tall cylindrical drums as in Timurid times; bulbous domes, expanding much or little beyond the cylindrical base. Both these latter types carried to excess can be distinctly unpleasant. But at its very best with only a modest extension beyond the base ring the bulbous dome can be quite beautiful and express power and vitality with perfect grace, as in the dome of the Masjid-i-Shah of Mashhad, or the Masjid-i-Shah and madrassa Madar-i-Shah of Isfahan. The onion-shaped dome, a convention of some of the miniature painters, was not beloved by architects because of structural problems involved and its feeling of restlessness, a fault particularly disliked by the Persians. Onion-shaped domes are uncommon in Persia until, in the eighteenth and nineteenth centuries, they appear on country shrines, on mausolea in the more important cemeteries, or occasionally on city mosques, like the Masjid-i-Chiragh in Shiraz, or the golden dome of the shrine of the Imam Reza at Mashhad. When seen in proximity to the older domes they are sadly diminished.

261

356. Sei Gunbad, Rezeieh, 1277. Interior stalactite squinch.
357. Shrine of the Imam Reza, Mashhad. Mosaic faience stalactite portal squinch.
358. Caravanserai, Khargird, early 15th century.
Carved stucco and faience brick stalactites developed for wall covering.
359. Masjid-i-Shah, Isfahan. Portal squinch, 1612.

Another type of dome in use from the twelfth century was adopted to crown circular or octagonal structures, such as tomb towers. These domes are either round and smooth, rising to a sharp peak and covered with blue tiles, or they may be polyhedral, generally octagonal. These from the earlier periods have nearly all collapsed, while the ovoid dome at Lajim has survived almost intact, although a bit shabby.

Double-shell domes were a necessity and were early achieved. One of the noblest structures in Islam, the Dome of the Rock in Jerusalem, had a double wooden dome, and several shrines in Iraq had double teakwood domes. But the wooden dome was too easily destroyed by fire, and the Seljuk masons preferred the single shell of brick, which in their capable hands attained a remarkable permanence. But the single shell, if large and high, was too empty to permit sufficient unity and concentration. The introduction of a lower ceiling provided more satisfactory and humane proportions. Early in the fourteenth century the double dome in brick was decisively achieved, and the little mosque at Ziaret shows it clearly. Although M. Godard saw in the mausoleum of Oljeitu only an outer shell made to supply a smooth ground for the tile coverage, others see there a true double dome with a definite, though small, space separating the two, with some difference in profile, the outer shell being more pointed than the inner. Perhaps the resolution of the controversy is a matter of definition, and two shells do not constitute a double dome unless there is a space between large enough for the entry of a man. But the advantages of such a separation were obvious and it was only a matter of time before almost contemporary structures, like the tomb at Tus, show widely separated shells.[205]

The ambitions, hopes and sometimes quite specific prescriptions of the patron were generally the immediate creative force behind the finest achievements of Persian architecture. This decisive influence under the Achaemenids was consistently renewed in later periods. Throughout Islamic history, the role of the patron was especially honorable and was of immense value to Persian culture as a result of both the individuals and the achievements they sponsored. Although ostentation or the need of public esteem was often a motive, the spirit of paternal encouragement was everywhere felt and an ethical responsibility was often the primary motive. Of all the noted patrons of talent, Ali Shir Nawai (1440–1501), living in the richly cultivated days of the Timurids, was outstanding for his discrimination and generosity. He was a poet, a musician and composer, patron of painters, including the great Bihzad, and an outstanding scholar and architect. He appears to have been directly connected with no fewer than 370 mosques, colleges and charitable institutions in Khurasan alone,[206] in addition to the lovely ivan-portal discussed in connection with the shrine of the Imam Reza in Mashhad.

262

The immense programs of the Ghaznavids, especially under Mahmud's personal impetus, have been established by contemporary documents and existing ruins. If anything, however, the importance of architecture grew successively under the Seljuks, especially the great vizier Nizam al-mulk, and under the Mongols, Ghazan Khan, Oljeitu and Ali Shah, until it became virtually obsessive under the Timurids. Shah Rukh, in the creation of many magnificent buildings, aimed at nothing less than perfection, and Shah Abbas I followed, albeit with monuments slightly less than ideal in detail yet of the highest conception.

The execution of the often extravagant visions of these monarchs and patrons—the specific designs and structural features—was the work of professionals, about whose training and operations we know all too little. In addition to a long apprenticeship which involved physical labor such as stone carving, masonry, tile cutting, carpentry, the architect during most eras had basic training in mathematics. He was also educated in literature and poetry, especially in that national epic, Firdawsi's *Shah Nama*.

Equally important as his formal training was his experience as an integrated member of a society united by a common faith and similar tastes. The architect indeed reflected national traits: quick intelligence, sensitive taste, inventiveness, a marked preference for the lucid and rational. His insistence on clarity—a Hellenic characteristic also—shows in all Persian planning and building. Because the eccentric and obscure are offensive to Persian taste, orientation and axiality, orderly and carefully proportioned relations of all parts endow individual buildings with a comprehensive simplicity that relieves the observer of distraction and uncertainty.

As yet we have found no record of the special training of the architect, but the historian, Ibn Khaldun, although writing in Tunis in the fourteenth century, when he discussed the role of the architect in some detail, seemed to speak for all Islam. His account is probably as valid for Persia as for North Africa, for he had a comprehensive and well informed knowledge of institutions in other lands.[207] Ibn Khaldun's account, after a brief discussion of the need for adequate shelter and the general building techniques and materials, then describes some of the talents the architect must have, and why. According to him, the architect, aside from the actual planning and supervision of construction, must be well versed in law, for, in the crowded conditions of cities there are many conflicts of interest due to mutual encroachments, rights of way, refuse disposal, the menace of faulty adjoining structures, or the division of a common courtyard. All such problems require the expert architect, who is familiar with all the structural details in the less obvious parts of buildings, and especially the complicated flow of conduits, which, if not properly designed and built, can cause great damage. These are technical problems which only the experienced architect can judge correctly.

264

Ibn Khaldun points out that the competence of the architect varies in accordance with the culture in which he lives. Nomadic people, even if they conquer additional lands, have not the traditions or skill in building, hence they have to call on architects of long established and wealthy urban centers to find experts who can build in accordance with their ambitions. Abd al-Malik had to seek help from the Byzantine Emperor for workers to construct the mosques in Medina and Jerusalem (the Dome of the Rock) and his own palace in Damascus (probably Ibn Khaldun meant the Great Mosque of Damascus).

With regard to the training of the architect, Ibn Khaldun stresses that he must know geometry, for example, the use of the plumb to keep walls strictly perpendicular. He must also be familiar with various kinds of mechanized apparatus, to raise water and control its flow. He must also be trained in the use of special machines, particularly pulleys for the lifting and placing of heavy loads which are beyond the strength of unaided manpower. Such problems can be solved only by geometrical and engineering techniques, and these make possible the creation of imposing and long enduring structures, which astonish the ignorant observer who thinks that they could have been constructed only by superhuman giants.

A fifteenth century document, presumably from Herat, contains a section devoted to "the calculation of areas and a diagram for the construction of a two-centered arch"—a delicate operation which made all the difference to the aesthetic value of the arch contour, which could be either inert and clumsy or graceful and alert.[208]

The achievement of Seljuk architecture was certainly neither by accident nor by any unconscious operation of social forces, but rather by individual talent. These builders were disciplined professionals, instructed in tradition and in current techniques reinforced by aesthetic enthusiasm gained from associated art forms and by contemporary study of mathematics. Additional support came from the study of models, both ancient and contemporary. They profited, moreover, not only from those that were successful but also from those that revealed defects, particularly cracked or distorted vaults and domes. Public approval and the enthusiasm of patrons created a personal prestige for these designers and builders who, especially after Mongol times, exhibited their confidence by incorporating their names into buildings or even parts of buildings. There was also a professional honor that induced individual architects to defy impatient monarchs whose eagerness for immediate results caused lesser artists to resort to unsound practices.

A certain degree of specialization characterized Persian cities beginning even in Sasanian times, a specialization that was economically sound and productive, and promoted communication and profitable cultural exchange. Jundi Shapur was for centuries the center of medical studies and supplied physicians to the Caliphate and its successors. Samarkand, Rayy and Kashan were the chief centers of artistic pottery making; the great *relieurs* and miniaturists came from Bokhara and Herat in the fifteenth century. Kufa had been the focal center where the great early Kufic script was formulated. Yazd has long been most famous for *qanat* builders and Natanz especially noted for its gardeners, who are still in demand in other cities. Similarly, Biyar, a pleasant little town east of Damghan, in the tenth century was known as the "architects' town," and builders from there were reported to have special skill and to be in great demand.

Muqaddasi, who had family reasons for knowing all about it, refers to Biyar three times as the "town of architects," where the "men have skill in building and planning." "I have never seen more graceful structures than those of Biyar, which (they) have fashioned so well." The talents of Biyar architects must have been appreciated everywhere, for there is another source telling that "a man from Biyar went to Bokhara and built there a fine castle. They carried him upon their shoulders until they set him down in the presence of the amir, Nasr ibn Ahmad (914–943) who was quite astonished and asked him to make a request."[209]

Even with the propulsive power of wealth and personal preferences, public opinion nonetheless played an important role. During Al Walid's time "architecture was what the people talked about, but in Sulayman's time it was women and cookery."[210] The non-professional but highly appreciative, and specific accounts by the geographers give some of the finest mosques, minarets, and bazaars as evidence of public pride and concern; and even a "world destroyer," like Timur, spared mosques and tombs from his frenetic devastations.

The architecture of Persia across the centuries displays great variety, both structural and aesthetic, developing gradually and coherently out of prior traditions and experience. Without sudden innovations, and despite the repeated trauma of invasions and cultural shocks, it has achieved an individuality distinct from that of other Muslim countries. Its paramount virtues are several: a marked feeling for form and scale; structural inventiveness, especially in vault and dome construction; a genius for decoration with a freedom and success not rivaled in any other architecture. While plan and layout, especially in later centuries, was of the highest order, construction was rarely equal in solidity and sophistication to European masonry. But the very survival of so many early monuments—especially the lofty minarets—in a country afflicted by devastating invasions and earthquakes, to say nothing of the damage inflicted by brick-hungry villagers, is proof that permanence was an effective ideal for many architects.

360

361

362

363

364

While decorative values are fully exploited, the primary function of these forms and patterns is to emphasize, suggest and correlate apparent constructive forces, and thus give the impression of continuous and harmoniously balanced energies. With the exception of the costly mosaic faience, the materials used in Persian building, and the methods employed permitted rapid and inexpensive construction, so that a relatively small country was able to create a disproportionately large number of important monuments.

There was a *humane* character to all of the arts of Persia. The agonizing scenes depicted in so much of Christian art were repulsive to the Persian, who had a lively appreciation of the charms of the present world. This humanity is evident in the architecture, which in the Islamic period especially, was for the general benefit, accessible and shared by all. The range of expressive effects varied from the solemn and austere, to grandeur, magnificence, or fairy-like charm. Mosques were places of beauty, conducive to joy, contemplation and religious fervor. As one inscription read: "The Mosques are the Gardens of Paradise"—and so the Persian builders and decorators made them, ornaments and valid expressions of Islam.

Finis

Historical Summary

B.C.

Pre-Achaemenid
4th and 3rd millennia: early settlements at Sialk, Susa, Tepe Hisar, Tepe Giyan, and elsewhere
ca. 2000–640: Elamite kingdom
ca. 1680: Kassites invade Babylon from Persia
ca. 1250: Choga Zambil, 1st major architectural site in Persia
825: rise of Medes near Lake Urmiya; Deioces establishes Medean empire in 728, Ecbatana ca. 722
640–559: Cyrus I, King of Fars, followed by his son Cambyses I who marries daughter of Medean King Astyages

Achaemenids (550–330 B.C.)
559–529: Cyrus II, "the Great," founds dynasty, captures Ecbatana and Babylon
529–521: Cambyses II extends empire to Egypt
521–486: Darius I, marries Cyrus' daughter, enlarges empire from Indus to Nile to Danube
486–330: Xerxes I, Greek wars; Artaxerxes I; Darius II loses Egypt; Artaxerxes II; Darius III, last Achaemenid
330: Macedonian occupation; Alexander takes and burns Persepolis

Seleucids and Parthians (ca. 312 B.C.–224 A.D.)
312–281: Seleucus I founds dynasty
250–174: foundation of Arsacid dynasty of Parthians in Khurasan followed by power struggle with Seleucids
174–127: Mithridates I, expands Arsacid empire, Phraates II, defeats Seleucids in 129
124–91: Mithridates II, height of Parthian power

A.D.

91 B.C.–110 A.D.: 23 kings, gradual decline of strength and rise of Roman influence in the east
114–224: fall of Artaban V, last Parthian king, to Ardashir I, ruler of Fars and Kirman

Sasanians (224–642 A.D.)
227–241: Ardashir I founds Sasanian dynasty, retakes Ctesiphon
241–272: Shapur I, captured by Roman emperor Valerian in 260
310–379: Shapur II, victories over Rome
461: relations established with China
531–579: Chosroes I, internal reforms, height of Sasanian empire
632–651: Yazdajird III, last Sasanian king, succumbs to Arab invasions sweeping from west; his heirs flee to China

Early Islam (651–ca. 1000)
660–750: Umayyad caliphate
744–749: Shi'ite revolt, led by Abu Muslim from Merv, to establish the Persian Abbasid caliphate
750–1258: Abbasid caliphate, Baghdad capital from 762
892–999: Samanids, former governors of the Oxus region, retake power and extend their dominions
935–1055: Buvayhids rise to power near Shiraz, also govern Kirman and Iraq
962–1040: Ghaznavids assume power in the east, taking territory from Samanids

Seljuks (ca. 1000–1157)
1000: invade Transoxiana
1031–1040: Toghrul Beq defeats Ghaznavids
1055: defeat Buvayhids
1063–1072: Alp Arslan, in 1071, captures Byzantine emperor 1072–1092: Malik Shah, height of the Seljuk empire which extends from China to Syria, from the Oxus river to Arabia
1118–1157: Sultan Sanjar, ruler of Khurasan only, last of the notable Seljuk rulers

Mongols (1218–1334)
1218–1220: first Mongol invasion under Genghis Khan
1231: second Mongol invasion
1256–1265: Hulagu, grandson of Genghis, founds the dynasty at Maragha
1295–1304: Ghazan Khan, final Mongol conversion to Islam
1304–1316: Oljeitu, international court
1334: Abu Said, end of Seljuk dynasty; division into four, and eventually more, provincial kingdoms

Timurids (1370–1502)
1370–1405: Timur conquers from the north, governing Khurasan, Herat, Azerbaijan, Iraq, Isfahan and Shiraz by 1392
1405–1447: Shah Rukh, governing from Herat, conquers Oxus region
1408–1453: rise of the Qara Qoyunlu Turkomans in the west, expanding to include Fars, Iraq and Isfahan
1461: Ottoman Turks enter northwest, pushing Timurids east

Safavids (1491–1722)
1491–1524: Shah Ismail, founds dynasty in 1502
1587–1628: Shah Abbas I, defeats Turks in north and Baghdad, transfers capital to Isfahan
1694–1722: Shah Hussein, last Safavid; his death is followed by general disorder

Modern Era (1737–present)
1736–1739: Nadir Shah, Afghan and Indian conquests
1750–1795: Zand dynasty, again followed by disorder
1796–1925: Qajar dynasty
1925–present: Pahlavi dynasty

Map of Persia

Notes

Certain indispensable works in the literature of Persian architecture have been cited very frequently: André Godard, *Athar-e-Iran,* 1936 to 1949, Annales du service archéologique de l'Iran; Arthur Upham Pope, ed., *The Survey of Persian Art,* London and New York, 1938–39, 6 volumes; Donald N. Wilber, *The Architecture of Islamic Persia, Il-Khanid Period,* Princeton, 1955; Ernst Cohn-Wiener, *Turan,* Berlin, 1930; and *Bulletin of the Iranian Institute,* New York, 1931–46. The titles of these works, therefore, have been shortened as follows: *Athar-e-Iran,* date; *Survey; Islamic; Turan;* and *Bulletin,* date.

1. The Persians were both conscious and boastful of their antiquity (*cf. Don Juan of Persia,* trans. and ed. by G. LeStrange, London, 1926, pp. 58–62), and there was a definite archaistic tendency throughout the Islamic period which echoed conscious encouragement by the Sasanians of earlier Persian forms; for example, Sasanian confrontation themes show up in Rayy 13th century pottery and themes of the Assyrian cosmological tree appear in 10th century pottery. This continuity in Islamic times was strengthened by the wide popularity of Firdawsi's epic poem, the *Book of Kings,* or *Shah Nama.*
2. See, for instance, the Masjid-al-Hakim, Isfalu and shrines at Qumm, Rayy, Arbela, and Kanzemain.
3. *Cf.* André Godard, *L'Art de l'Iran,* Paris, 1962, p. 226 ff.
4. *Cf.* Donald N. Wilber, *Persian Gardens and Pavilions,* Vermont, 1962.
5. Thus, even as late as the 16th century, we have the painted ornament of the maydan mosque at Sava (fig. 179) which is unsurpassed by anything earlier.
6. *Paradaiza,* or *Faradis,* is the origin of our word Paradise.
7. A garden layout with crossed canals was already a theme on painted bowls from Samarra, Mesopotamia, in the late fourth millennium B.C., and fragile garden delights were never absent in the ornamental arts of Persia, including various forms of architectural ornament.
8. The following tale illustrates a prevalent attitude: Shah Abbas once ordered a deputy to commence 1000 caravanserais throughout the empire. A year later he called the deputy to demand a progress report during the course of which it was revealed that 999 caravanserais were

well under way. In answer to the Shah's obvious question, the deputy is said to have replied: Because nine hundred and ninety-nine is a larger number than one thousand!"

9. Henri Frankfort, *The Art and Architecture of the Ancient Orient,* London, Penguin, 1958, p. 6.

10. For example, the crenelations crowning certain walls at Persepolis in fig. 18.

11. This portal to the sacred world proclaims both authority and protection. As Maqsud inscribed the carpet of the mosque at Ardabil: "I have no refuge in the world other than thy threshold. My head has no protection other than this porchway."

12. For an eloquent statement of the Persian evaluation of beauty, *cf.* A. J. Arberry, *Shiraz,* Oklahoma, 1960, pp. 165, 169–171.

13. R. C. Zaehner, *The Dawn and Twilight of Zoroastrianism,* New York, 1961, p. 134.

14. *Cf.* Braidwood, Howe, and Reed, "The Iranian Prehistoric Project," *Science,* 23, June 1961, and Braidwood in *Iranica Antiqua,* Leyden, 1961, vol. I.

15. This indicates that the plateau people had reached an advanced level of reflection, ordered speculation and planned action.

16. *Cf.* Roman Ghirshman, *Fouilles de Sialk,* 2 vols., Paris, 1933, 1939, and also his *The Art of Ancient Iran,* New York, 1964, chapter I.

17. *Cf.* Leonard C. Wooley, *The Art of the Middle East,* New York, 1961, p. 60 ff.

18. Roman Ghirshman, "The Ziggurat of Tchoga-Zambil," *Scientific American,* Jan. 1961, p. 69.

19. The Elamites seem to have been neither Semites nor Aryans. *Cf.* Ghirshman, *loc. cit.*

20. Ghirshman, *ibid.,* p. 71.

21. Some of these features of this monument—the brick vaults, a large interior court flanked by chambers, glazed brick, heraldic animals, emphasis on springtime renewal, extensive gardens —will recur in Persian architecture in varying degrees for nearly 3000 years.

22. Discovered recently (1960) by Roman Ghirshman, who was kind enough to inform me of his preliminary findings.

23. *Cf.* André Parrot, *Sumer,* New York, 1961, pp. 320–333, especially plate 406.

24. E. Herzfeld, *Archaeological History of Iran,* Oxford, 1935, p. 15. For excavations near Lake Van, *cf.* L. C. Wooley, *The Art of the Middle East,* New York, 1961, p. 137.

25. Richard N. Frye, *The Heritage of Persia,* New York, 1963, p. 64.

26. Naqsh-i-Rustam is now being excavated by a British expedition. *Cf.* E. Porada, *Iran ancien,* Paris, 1962, p. 140.

27. Godard, *L'Art de l'Iran,* p. 118.

28. *Ibid.,* pp. 118–119.

29. *Cf. ibid.,* p. 124 for arguments supporting the assumption that Xerxes, Darius' son, probably supervised construction at Persepolis in his father's absence.

30. Roman Ghirshman, *Iran, From the Earliest Times to the Islamic Conquest,* London, 1954, p. 167.

31. For the sake of clarity, I have taken some liberties with the elegant translation made by R. G. Kent, *Old Persian,* American Oriental Society, 1950, p. 144.

32. For characteristic examples of these beautiful ornaments *cf. Survey,* vol. IV, plates 115 A, C, 116 A, C, and 118, and Pope, *Masterpieces of Persian Art,* London, 1930, plate 37.

33. *Cf. Survey,* vol. I, p. 321 ff.

34. See A. U. Pope, "Persepolis as a Ritual City," *Archaeology,* X, 1957. In support of this view, Ernst Herzfeld (*Iran in the Ancient East,* London, 1941, p. 222) says, "On the whole Persepolis seems to have been a place that was founded and kept for historical and sentimental reasons . . . in the homeland of the dynasty, but used only for special occasions. . . . Compared to Susa, with its foreign ambassadors, special envoys, royal prisoners, large population and great commercial activity, Persepolis must have been relatively quiet."

35. *Cf.,* for example, an inscription of Shahameser III (859–824 B.C.): "A mighty image of my majesty I fashioned . . . my deeds of valor" quoted in Frankfort, *op. cit.,* p. 35.

36. Ezra, chapter IV. *Cf.* also A. T. E. Olmstead, *History of the Persian Empire,* Chicago, 1948, Chapters XII and XIII.

37. Ernst Herzfeld, *Iran in the Ancient East;* also J. M. Unvalla, *Survey,* I, pp. 336–345.

38. See notes 12 and 13 *supra.* Darius stated in one inscription: "I constructed it perfect and beautiful just as I intended." Xerxes declared that the great gateway "looks beautiful," and that "many other beautiful buildings were built in the land of Persia."

39. Herzfeld, *Iran in the Ancient East,* p. 227.

40. The magnificence of the structure is indicated by Darius' detailed inscription of the buildings of Susa (see note 30 *supra*), by the Persepolis

tablets (see George C. Cameron, *The Persepolis Treasury Tablets,* Chicago, 1948, p. 11 ff.), and by the booty captured by Alexander: vast amounts of gold and silver, both coined and uncoined, sumptuous fabrics, furniture and sundry appurtenances that, according to Plutarch, required 10,000 mules and 5,000 camels to carry away.

41. Godard, *L'Art de l'Iran,* pp. 127–128.

42. Discovered by André Godard and the Iranian Archaeological Services.

43. Godard, *L'Art de l'Iran,* pp. 123–124, and Herzfeld, *Iran in the Ancient East,* p. 255.

44. Herzfeld, *Iran in the Ancient East,* p. 236, says, "The masonry of the palaces goes to the extreme of highly polished stone, looking, when well preserved, like mirrors of black marble; but this unbelievable work was never finished in most of the buildings." This was accomplished by using three different grades of abrasive, a lengthy and laborious process.

45. See note 35 *supra* for an example. Also, it is interesting to note that only occasionally did real hunts take place; usually the hunts were well managed killings in an enclosed, closely guarded space.

46. This precious quality probably was introduced by carvers from Ionia (*cf.* Ernst Herzfeld, *Archaeological History of Iran,* London, 1935, plate LXXII and Frankfort, *op. cit.,* pp. 227–228 and note 82) who imported some of the Greek passion for sensitive and revealing surface. But, although some of the sculptors were Ionian, Herzfeld also points out (p. 237) that among the scores of mason's marks, none were Greek.

47. Cameron, *op. cit.,* p. 11, says, "There is no record of taxes secured from the many satrapies, no attestation of gifts which could be construed as taxes." Tribute was not just the personal exaction of a proud monarch; it was a form of taxation to a State that had immensely increased the prosperity of all its components. Religiously, it was an act of service and obedience to the monarch as surrogate of god, and by tradition, it also served as a kind of investment for security. In Sasanian times, all gifts to the king were recorded and if any donor thereof was subsequently in need, the gift would be returned a thousandfold.

48. This immense number has seemed to some modern critics to be excessive, and so it might if judged by strictly aesthetic canons. But the beauty of these columns, while essential, was only part of the purpose and meaning, which, possibly, was to present in imperishable material the vision and experience of a great forest, such as one would encounter in an ideal world.

49. Another interpretation is that the blood of the cosmic bull is essential for fertilization: slaying the bull transfers his life's force to the soil, increasing its fecundity. *Cf.* Zaehner, *op. cit.,* especially p. 128.

50. There may be some further significance in these structures of four equal sides, for we also note that the 550 columns are all arranged in multiples of four, that the column flutings are multiples of four, and we know that references to the four quarters of the universe are common throughout the East.

51. According to Godard, *L'Art de l'Iran,* p. 126 ff., the solids are 1/16 of the voids, whereas at Karnak the solids are about ½. The achievement of such clear space, ample and serene, was made technically possible by the use of enormous timbers from Lebanon which permitted the 30 foot span from column to column. But these timbers were only the means, not the creative cause, which is to be found in the Iranian devotion to light and to well ordered, rhythmical space, which characterized their sculptured friezes as well.

52. It has been said, however, that Persepolis and Susa were "the last creations of the Ancient Orient" and died without issue; *cf.* Herzfeld, *Iran in the Ancient East,* p. 247.

53. The early Indus Valley culture, in a number of ways the most developed at that time anywhere, was intrusive: in its initial stage it had come in from the west and, at least partially, from the northwest. Among shards in the Bombay Museum are examples that suggest Persian prototypes, or perhaps Mesopotamian, and recovery of Indus Valley seals in Mesopotamian sites shows that these two areas were in direct communication. Commerce certainly reached the Persian Gulf and the island of Bahrein, and the Iranian plateau was accessible most of the year; even the Oxus Valley could be reached overland, either via Khandar and Baluchistan or by the Khyber Pass.

54. *Cf.* Sir Mortimer Wheeler, *Early India and Pakistan,* New York, 1959, p. 24. Sir Mortimer was for many years Director General of Archaeology in India and has provided the most systematic

and experienced account of the still incomplete history of the early relations between India and Persia.

55. *Cf.* E. R. Bevan, *The House of Seleucus,* London, 1902.

56. For recently revised accounts of Parthian history and art *cf.* Roman Ghirshman, *Persian Art: The Parthian and Sassanian Dynasties,* New York, 1962, and Richard N. Frye, *op. cit.,* especially Chapter 5.

57. *Cf. Survey,* fig. 103.

58. Godard, *L'Art de l'Iran,* p. 155 ff.

59. *Ibid.,* p. 157.

60. *Cf.* Rudolph Naumann, "Ausgrabungen auf dem Takht-i-Suleiman," *Mitteilungen Institut für Auslandsbeziehungen,* July–Dec. 1960. Professor Sarre long ago suggested that the place represented the symbolic siege of a Zoroastrian castle presumably by Islamic forces. Now Lars Ivar Ringbom suggests that the fortress is really at Takht-i-Sulayman. The identity of the form of the foundation masonry would lend some support to the theory. *Cf.* Ringbom, "Die Burg der Magies in Beitrage zur Kunstgeschichte Asiens," *Diez Festschrift,* Istanbul, 1963, pp. 288–300, with full bibliography and illustration. See also Wilber in *Antiquity,* XII, 1938, pp. 389–410.

61. The building has been assigned to Sasanian builders of the third century by Ernst Diez, *Persien, Islamische Baukunst in Churasan,* Darmstadt, 1923; Ernst Herzfeld, *Reserbericht, Zeitschrift der deutschen Morgenlandeschen Gesellschaft,* 1926, pp. 274–276; and Godard, *Athar-e-Iran,* 1939, pp. 53–57, but for Dr. Wilber's argument *cf. Bulletin,* Dec. 1946, pp, 22, 28.

62. For an able exposition of Sasanian architecture, see Oscar Reuther, *Survey,* vol. I, pp. 493–578.

63. Due to contradictions in the earliest documents, opinions still differ as to the date of this monument.

64. This seems to be an adaptation from Hellenistic prototypes and also appears in Byzantine architecture, notably in Hagia Sophia.

65. For a severe criticism of the façade, *cf.* Herzfeld, *Archaeological History of Iran,* pp. 93–95.

66. Ghirshman, *Persian Art,* p. 140 ff.

67. *Ibid.,* p. 149.

68. *Survey,* vol. II, p. 505.

69. See Fiske-Kimball in *Survey,* vol. II, p. 579 ff. The Damghan site was excavated in 1931 by the joint expedition of the University Museum and the Philadelphia Museum of Art under the direction of Erich Schmidt. For the palaces at Kish, *cf. Survey,* p. 584 ff.

70. L. Vanden Berghe, *Archeologie de l'Iran ancien,* Leyden, 1959, p. 98, and Godard, *L'Art de l'Iran,* p. 224.

71. *Cf.* Reuther in *Survey,* vol. I, p. 519 ff.

72. This ribbon itself is always a symbol of royal or sacred power and is a normal attribute of great monuments. Similarly the arch of the royal palace at Damghan ends in a tassel no more structural than today's fluttering flag announcing that a king is in residence.

73. *Cf.* Baltrusaitis, *Survey,* vol. I, p. 588 ff.

74. *Cf.* Erdmann, *Die Kunst Irans zur Zeit der Sasaniden,* p. 83; Ghirshman, *Persian Art,* p. 200.

75. *Cf.* Ghirshman, *Persian Art,* for illustrations in color. His suggestion that some of these mosaics represent carpets is hardly probable in view of the long and almost continuous series of carpet designs from the 9th century threshold rug of Khorsabad through the Pazirik fragments and sample pieces recovered recently from the Amlash district. See also Herzfeld, *Archaeological History of Iran,* p. 294, and Pope, *Introduction to Persian Art,* London, 1930.

76. *Cf.* A. P. Hardy in *Athar-e-Iran,* 1938, p. 163 ff. and Godard, *ibid.,* p. 32 ff.

77. *Cf.* Monneret de Villard, "The Fire Temples," *Bulletin,* Dec. 1936, pp. 175–184; also Diez in *Survey,* vol. I, p. 794. For a convincing argument of westward diffusion *cf.* Ghirshman, *Persian Art,* especially p. 287 ff.; also Baltrusaitis, *L'église cloisonnée en Orient et Occident,* Paris, 1941, and Puig i Cadafalch, *Le Premier art roman,* Paris, 1928.

78. Variously called Shiz or Ganzaca in contemporary documents, it was an especially sacred spot and the site of a great fire temple (see note 60 *supra*) in which it was claimed that the holy fire from which all other sacred fires were replenished had burned uninterrupted for 700 years. The site has recently been studied by a joint German-Iranian expedition, *cf. Bulletin,* Dec. 1937.

79. Part of the True Cross was reputed to have been taken when the Sasanians captured Jerusalem in 618. It was taken first to Ctesiphon and then to Shiz. *Cf.* Pope, "Persia and the Holy Grail," the *Literary Review,* 1927; Phyllis Ackerman, "The Takht-i-Taqdis," *Bulletin,* 1937, and Lars Ivar Ringbom, *Graltempel und Paradies,* Stockholm, 1951.

80. *Cf.* Arthur Christensen, *L'Iran sous les Sasanides,* Copenhagen, 1944, p. 159.

81. According to Yakutand Qazvini, who has left the fullest account of the building. But a corruption of the Buddhist term New Vihara (new monastery) has been suggested by Sir Henry Rauham. Both, or either, could be true.

82. Just as the Caliph al-Mansur is said to have tried and failed, despite all warnings, to demolish the Taq-i-Kisra. The same story is assigned to several other buildings as well, but with less probability. For a description *cf.* Barbier de Maynard, *Dictionnaire Géographique de la Perse,* Paris, 1861, p. 569.

83. *Cf.* Pope, *Diez Festschrift,* and "Gothic and Armenian Contributions," *Armenian Revue,* 1944, and Ghirshman, *Persian Art,* Chapter v.

84. *Cf.* Thomas W. Arnold, *The Preaching of Islam,* London, 1913.

85. K. A. C. Creswell, *Early Muslim Architecture,* London and New York, 1932, vol. I, p. 7.

86. Within a few years, at Kufa in 663 and Basra in 665, Moslems were building costly mosques with stone columns fifty feet high, reminiscent of Persepolis; columnar mosques were built in many parts of Islam and contained sumptuous ornament. *Cf.* Creswell, *op. cit.,* vol. I.

87. *Cf. Survey,* vol. II, pp. 975–980; and Creswell, *op. cit.,* vol. I, chapter 8.

88. Actually, this is also a pre-Sasanian Iranian house plan.

89. Godard, "Les anciennes mosquées," *Athar-e-Iran,* 1936; *cf.* also Eric Schroeder, *Survey,* Vol. I, p. 933.
    The Tarik-Khana makes provision for the minbar, which was not included until 750—already into the Abbasid Caliphate—thus leading to the late 8th century suggested date.

90. *Cf.* Godard, *Gazette des Beaux Arts,* December 1934, vol. XII, p. 233.

91. *Cf.* Narshakhi, *The History of Bokhara,* (trans. Richard N. Frye), Cambridge, 1954, pp. 49, 50 and Creswell, *op. cit.,* vol I, pp. 215–219.

92. *Cf.* Pope, "Scientific Method and Cultural Studies," in *Aus der Welt der Islamischen Kunst: Festschrift für Ernst Kühnel,* Berlin, 1959, p. 386.

93. Abu Muslim was then young, only nineteen, and probably felt that an imposing building which correctly embodied the ancient magic formula might well give him more strength and a divinely sanctioned power. Almost a century earlier there had been a similar appeal to cosmic symbolism when a Turkish ruler, Bidum, built a castle in Bokhara which repeatedly collapsed; he then had it built on seven stone columns aligned with the major stars of Ursa Major, and it stood firm and solid. *Cf.* Narshakhi, *History of Bokhara,* p. 184.

94. Yaqut, the great geographer, quoted in Le-Strange, *Lands of the Eastern Caliphate,* Cambridge, 1930. *Cf.* also C. W. Wilkinson,. *Metropolitan Museum Bulletin,* XXXI, 1936, and XXXII, 1937.

95. See Chapter v for a more complete discussion of the functions and techniques of Persian ornamentation.

96. *Cf.* Narshakhi, *History of Bokhara.*

97. *Cf.* L. Rempel, *Bulletin,* Dec. 1936, and *Turan,* plates I–III.

98. Similar patterns were also common in irrigation constructions in the region.

99. For more on monuments of this area, see *Turan,* especially plates XII, XIV.

100. The arches of the Tarik-Khana and those of the tomb of Ismail are less than twice as high as they are wide.

101. These stuccoed piers recall the posts of a grape arbor, bound with richly loaded vines; energetic leaf ornaments of bursting vitality are set off by rich compound rosettes which recall the rosette bands of Persepolis; *cf.* plate 126 in Godard, *L'Art de l'Iran.* In sophistication and vigor these stuccos constitute an important chapter in the history of Persian ornament, worthy of the acute studies of Dr. Flury, *cf.* "Un monument des premiers siècles," *Syria,* II, 1921, pp. 304–316 and "La Mosque de Nayin," *Syria,* XI, 1930, pp. 43–58; *cf.* also *Survey,* p. 1270 ff.

102. The mosque of Nayin is not mentioned in the known literature, although both Nasir-i-Khusraw and Muqaddasi passed through—and the latter recorded his impressions of the citadel.

103. A small window in the roof opens to the east, thus permitting the morning sun to penetrate the empty interior which held only the glass coffin of Qabus. It would seem that this was again a deliberate attempt to bring man into contact with the primal forces of heaven.

104. For additional illustrations, *cf. Survey,* Vol. IV, plates 334–357; also Godard, "Les Monuments de Maragha," *Athar-e-Iran,* I, 1936, p. 133 ff.; also Myron Smith, *Athar-e-Iran,* 1939, pp. 318 ff., 361–363.

105. This was recently discovered; *cf.* André Marig and Gaston Wiet, *Le Minaret de Djam*, Paris, 1959, and Marig, "The Mystery of the Great Minaret," *Illustrated London News*, June 16, 1959.

106. Excavated and studied by Daniel Schlumberger; *cf.* his "Le Palais Ghaznevid de Lashkari Bazar," *Mémoires de la Delegation Archéologique en Afghanistan*, Cairo, 1957, and *Bulletin Monumental*, 1957.

107. Schlumberger points out that the palaces at Lashkari also featured the Royal Guard as at Persepolis. Their extensive murals recall the Sasanian-type paintings on some structures recently discovered in Central Asia, by a series of Russian expeditions in Sagdiama and Khwarazm, once populous areas west of Samarkand; *cf.* A. L. Mongait, *Archaeology in the U.S.S.R.*, Penguin, 1961.

108. Abu Nasr al Utibi, quoted in Muhammad Nazin, *Mahmud of Ghazna*, Cambridge, 1931.

109. Quoted in E. G. Browne, *A Literary History of Persia*, London, 1906, Vol. II, p. 120.

110. S. M. Afnan, *Avicenna*, London, 1958, p. 48; *cf.* also Browne, *A Literary History of Persia*.

111. The Sahib's library was probably much larger than all the libraries of Europe (except Spain) combined. For example, the Cathedral library at Constance had 356 volumes, the Cathedral of Bamberg had only 96, the library at Croyland (destroyed in 1091) contained 700 and the library at Peterborough, considered rich, had only 344 volumes by the end of the 14th century. Sahib ibn Abbad's library, while possibly the largest, was merely one of many; some were perhaps even more important. *Cf.* A. Mez, *The Renaissance of Islam*, especially chapter XII.

112. "Learning only unveils herself to him who wholeheartedly gives himself up to her; who approaches her with an unclouded mind and clear insight; who seeks God's help and focuses an undivided attention upon her; who girds up his robe and who, albeit weary, out of sheer ardour, passes sleepless nights in pursuit of his goal, rising, by steady ascent, to its topmost height, and not to him who seeks learning by aimless flights and thoughtless efforts or who, like a blind camel, gropes about in the dark. . . . He should discriminate *between the doubtful and certain, between genuine and spurious* and should always stand firm by the clear light of reason." Thus wrote Mutahhar in 966. (*Cf.* Mez, *op. cit.*, p. 171).

113. See Dorothy Shepherd, *Proceedings, IVth International Congress of Iranian Studies*, Tokyo, 1964; also Phyllis Ackerman, *Proceedings, IIIrd International Congress of Iranian Studies*.

114. For a more complete discussion of this epoch see G. F. Sarton, *Avicenna Memorial Lectures*, New York Academy of Medicine, 1956.

115. G. F. Sarton, *Introduction to the History of Science*, Baltimore, 1927.

116. For example, shortly after his investiture, Alp Arslan met a noted saint in the course of his travels. The worthy saint begged his ruler to pledge himself to responsible and enlightened government. With tears streaming down his face, Alp Arslan agreed, and henceforward, as a sign of his oath, he wore a terra cotta ring which the saint had broken off a jug's spout.

117. The strength of Persian theology fostered by the madrassas may explain the intellectual fortitude with which Persia (and Islam) was able to withstand the Crusades and the Mongol invasion. *Cf.* Godard, *L'Art de l'Iran*, p. 291.

118. The pre-Seljuk history of the Masjid-i-Jami is very complicated, due to the fragmentary and ambiguous nature of early documents, which sometimes contradict each other. Muqaddasi reported that it rested on round piers and had a minaret on the quibla side; Marfuki says that it was built (reconstructed?) by Ismail ibn Abbad; Yaqut that it was practically destroyed in 1066; while Nasir-i-Khorau (1067) says that it was a magnificent building. *Cf.* also Creswell, *op. cit.*, vol. II, p. 203 ff.

119. *Cf.* Pope, *Diez Festschrift, op. cit.;* for a different point of view compare Godard, *L'Art de l'Iran*, pp. 266–280.

120. *Cf.* Schroeder, *Survey*, vol. II, pp. 1004–1009, quoting E. B. Dennison on the mathematical theory of the dome.

121. The uninterrupted sweep, almost unique in Seljuk architecture, may be an Armenian contribution—exemplified in the cathedral of Ani, with its column clusters and vertical emphasis. This building was known to the Seljuks through Toghrul Beq's conquest and occupation. There were two mosques built in Ani, and it is significant that Dya al-mulk (son of the great Nizam) built a bridge and a domed building there; *cf.* Creswell, *op. cit.*, vol. I, p. 167.

122. For notes on the stucco ornament at Qazvin, see chapter V; *cf. Bulletin*, Dec. 1936, pp. 209–216.

123. *Cf.* Godard, "Les anciennes Mosquées," *Athar-e-Iran,* 1936, p. 83 ff.

124. See Turan, for other buildings of this region; also *Survey,* vol. IV, plates 271, 272.

125. For the Rabat-i-Sharaf, and the contemporary mosques at Zawzan and Faramad *cf.* Godard, "Khorasan," *Athar-e-Iran,* 1949.

126. For an illustration of the interior *cf. Survey,* vol. IV, plate 310.

127. *Cf.* Sir Thomas Arnold, *Painting in Islam,* Oxford, 1930.

128. There are none in Sunni mosques but, after the 16th century, representational forms make an appearance in Persia. *Cf.* Pope, "Use of Figures in Mosques," *Survey,* II, p. 1305.

129. For realistic panel illustrations *cf. Survey,* vol. IV, especially plates 514 A, B, and C.

130. *Cf.* Ehsan Yarshater, "Common Features in Persian Poetry, Music and Painting," *Proceedings of the IVth International Congress of Iranian Studies.*

131. *Cf.* Schroeder in *Survey,* vol. II.

132. *Cf.* Erdmann, *Proceedings of the IVth International Congress of Iranian Studies.*

133. See especially the corridors and two oratories of the Masjid-i-Jami of Yazd; the maydan and Masjid-i-Jami of Isfahan; the mausoleum of Abd as-Samad in Natanz; and the mihrab recess of the Masjid-i-Gawhar Shad in Mashhad.

134. The rather common name "Chihil Dukhtaran" means a "man of 40 daughters"—e.g., many tribulations, due to the difficulties of providing all with dowries and honorable marriages.

135. For an accurate and careful recording of the Isfahan minarets, *cf.* Myron B. Smith, "The Manors of Isfahan," *Athar-e-Iran,* 1936, pp. 313–358.

136. *Cf.* Godard, *Athar-e-Iran,* 1936.

137. Edwin Lutyen's "Persian Brickwork," *London Country Life,* February 1933, p. 118.

138. For a discussion of the relative position of stucco to other forms of ornamentation, *cf.* Herzfeld, *Archaeological History of Iran,* p. 74.

139. Examples of multi-layered stucco can be found at Nishapur, 10th century, Qazvin and Hamadan, 12th century, and Varamin, 15th century.

140. *Cf.* for instance, the fragments unearthed by Leyard at Warqa, reproduced in *Survey,* vol. I, p. 415.

141. *Cf.* Baltrusaitis in *Survey,* vol. I, pp. 601–630, with 35 illustrations, mostly from the excavated Sasanian palace at Kish.

142. See chapter II, *supra,* especially plates 59–67, 74–76.

143. *Cf.* Phyllis Ackerman, *Bulletin of Needle and Bobbin,* New York, March, 1953.

144. Other panels from nearby structures are carved in the conventional manner, with various figures like large-scaled six-lobed medallions, and accompanying designs, one of which in a ying-yang pattern was destined to be continued for several centuries. According to the excavators, both are 10th century work. *Cf.* C. K. Wilkinson, *Bulletin of the Metropolitan Museum,* vol. XXXII, 1936, and Second Section, 1937, and a thorough discussion by Mrs. C. K. Wilkinson to be published soon.

145. Herzfeld, *Oriental Studies Presented to Cambridge,* 1922, p. 191.

146. For a well illustrated account of other early Islamic stucco, *cf.* Franz, "Wesenzüge Omayydische Schmuckkunst. Beitrage zur Kunstgeschichte Asiens," in *Diez Festschrift, op. cit.,* pp. 69–87.

147. From about 1100 at Qazvin to 1422 at Varamin.

148. Important elements of this decoration subsequently appeared in manuscript illuminations from which, in turn, architectural ornament received fresh ideas and inspiration; some of these designs also influenced 16th century carpets of the Herat type.

149. *Cf. Survey,*

150. *Cf. Survey,* vol. II, p. 1258 ff. where some 150 motifs are illustrated in line drawings.

151. *Cf.* D. N. Wilber, *Islamic.*

152. An inscription on the Masjid-i-Ali specifies the designer as Shams ad-din Tabrizi and further contains the name of Shah Ismail and the date 1522.

153. Unfortunately, this technique is not very permanent, and large-scale restorations have been necessary in most interiors so decorated. *Cf.* Godard, *L'Art de l'Iran,* pp. 393–395.

154. See D. N. Wilber, *Islamic.*

155. The Masjid-i-Jami at Rezeieh, dated by the mihrab inscription 1277, replacing an older structure, was a costly building with new features characteristic of the Mongol period such as large windows in the dome. The stucco work and inscriptions are markedly richer and of finer detail than previous work. *Cf. Bulletin, op cit.,* June 1937.

156. *Cf. Bulletin, ibid.,* and Wilber, *Islamic,* pp. 124–126, pl. 31.

157. J. Morier, *Second Journey,* London, 1818, p. 23.

Of the Rashidiya, too, only a few ruins survive.

158. These galleries are relatively little known and unpublished because access to them is still difficult. *Cf. Survey*, vol. II, pp. 1103–1118, and vol. IV, pl. 381–385; also Wilber, *op. cit.*, figs. 72–95.

159. For discussion of the double dome development, *cf.* Creswell, *op. cit.*, and his "The Origin of the Persian Double Dome," *Burlington Magazine*, XXXIX, 1913–1914, and his "Persian Domes before 1400 A.D.," *ibid.*, XXVI, 1915. For contrasting opinions *cf.* Godard in *Survey*, vol. II, p. 1114 ff. and Wilber, *Islamic*, p. 62.

160. *Survey*, vol. II, p. 1115; and Wilber, *Islamic*, p. 154.

161. Ali Shah's role as chief architect of Oljeitu's tomb is indicated by the fact that his name appears three times in the painted ornament. (This reading, first noticed by Farajollah Bazl, has been confirmed by A. Beijean.)

162. See Wilber, *Islamic*, p. 162 and figs. 145–155.

163. *Cf.* Maxim Sirioux, "Le Masjid-i-Djuma de Yazd," *Athar-e-Iran*, 1946.

164. This monument is commonly, but wrongly, known as the Haruniya, or tomb of Harun ar-Rashid, who died in Tus and was temporarily buried there. It is not impossible that it was built for al-Ghazali, as both Yaqut and Ibn Battuta speak of al-Ghazali's tomb at Tus; *cf.* Creswell, *Early Muslim Architecture*, p. 389; also C. Defremery and B. R. Sanguinetti (trans.), *Voyages d'Ibn Batoutah*, vol. II, Paris, 1854.

165. *Cf.* Schroeder in *Proceedings III*.

166. Notably in the tomb of Kassim at Samarkand and the tomb of Bayan Kili Khan; *cf. Turan*, plates XLVI, XLIX–LI.

167. Clavigo, Guy G. de, *Embassy to Tamerlane* (trans. by G. LeStrange), London, 1928, pp. 207–208.

168. As Babur pointed out, it was then "incomparable," for the great vault in Tabriz had long since collapsed; *cf. Memoirs of Babur* (ed. Erskine-Beveridge), pp. 83, 85.

169. For a color plate of a contemporary panel, *cf. Survey*, vol. V, pl. 543.

170. The ruins of the Bibi Khanum have frequently been reproduced; *cf. Turan*, pls. LXIV–LXVII.

171. *Turan*, p. 23.

172. Robert Byron, in *Survey*, vol. II, p. 1138.

173. A. Godard, "Isfahan," *Athar-e-Iran*, 1937, pp. 47–57.

174. *Cf.* Godard, *Athar-e-Iran*, 1937, p. 51; also *Survey*, vol. II, p. 1130, n. 5.

175. For a 19th century description of this extraordinarily beautiful mosque, *cf.* Mme. Dieulafoy quoted in Godard, *L'Art de l'Iran*, pp. 387, 389.

176. See in this book chapter V, esp. p. 167 and figs. 154, 214–224 and color plates X, XIV.

177. Chardin quoted in Langles, ed., *Voyages en Perse*, Paris, 1811, vol. VIII, p. 134.

178. One of the reasons the Masjid-i-Shah took so long to build was that, after the basic structure had been erected, the architect disappeared. For two years, the building stood without a dome and when, at the end of that period, the architect reappeared it was to face a most wrathful Shah Abbas. The Shah, impatient though he was, was nevertheless more merciful than many of his predecessors and demanded an explanation. The architect's answer was that the massive building had to settle on its rather soft soil base before a dome could be added, otherwise the dome would have cracked badly. On measuring the walls, the Shah discovered that the building had indeed settled substantially and the designer's care—even in the face of an angry ruler—was amply rewarded.

179. According to Godard—and no one is better qualified—"the Masjid-i-Shah can hold its own with Chartres." *Cf. Athar-e-Iran*, 1936.

180. *Cf. Survey*, vol. II, p. 1191 ff.

181. For a summary of its various vicissitudes, *cf. Survey*, vol. II, pp. 1201–1211.

182. "Chihil Sutan," indicating forty, is also a phrase used to designate "many," in this case "many columns." This monument is commonly known as the Hall of the Forty Columns. It actually has only twenty columns, but the reflecting pool brings the total to forty.

183. "Ali Qapu" is Turkish for "high place" or the "sublime port," as in the Top Qapu near Istanbul.

184. Although Chardin (*op. cit.* vol. VIII, p. 40 ff.) and others who saw it in the moment of its perfection were literally gasping with astonishment and admiration, the Hasht Behist has largely escaped thoughtful attention by modern writers, because being private property it has been less accessible for serious study and also because much of its external beauty has been ruined by the insignificant Kajar redecoration which one sees there today. For plan and further illustrations see Pope, *Survey* II, p. 1195 ff. and Wilber, *Persian Gardens*, p. 107 ff.

185. The pool of this court, once converted into a

garden bed, has recently again been reconverted to its original function and filled with water.

186. *Cf. Survey*, vol. II, pp. 1226–1241.
187. For quotation of the original description see *Survey*, vol. II, pp. 1231–1232.
188. According to Ali Yazdi, who crossed the bridge with Timur in 1386. See *Survey*, vol. II, p. 1233.
189. Muqaddasi is quoted as saying that he "had seen no finer building of the kind in all of Persia," in Mez, *op. cit.*, p. 500.
190. This technique is probably of Turkish origin.
191. *Cf. Turan*, plate B.
192. "These (portals) are of colossal size, and reminded me of the grand structures of the ancient Romans," said Wilhelm von Freygang, *Letters from the Caucasus*, London, 1823, pp. 353–354. See especially the caravanserai at Kashan.
193. Chardin, *Voyages*, vol. VIII, p. 134.
194. Translated from J. Thevenot, *Suite du Voyage au Levant*, Amsterdam, 1727, vol. III, p. 260.
195. Creswell, *op. cit.*, p. 4611.
196. Yaqut wrote: "I have seen the famous Rayy, a town of extraordinary beauty, many houses built of fired bricks faced with blue tile and decorative calligraphic ornament brilliantly colored." And Ibn Hawqal said, "Except for Baghdad, it (Rayy) is the finest city in the whole East." In Kazerun, according to Muqaddasi, in the tenth century the houses "were like palaces," and in Siraf "the houses were the finest" he had ever seen, one house costing 30,000 dinars (not far from $100,000). These quotations are from LeStrange, *The Lands of the Eastern Caliphate*. For other accounts see also Creswell, *op. cit.*, pp. 279, 290.
197. For a more thorough and detailed discussion of Persian Gardens *cf.* Donald Wilber, *Persian Gardens and Pavilions*, and Pope, *Survey*, vol. II, pp. 1427–1445.
198. *"Eyes hot-seared by desert glare find healing*
    In its velvet shade. Splashing fountains and
        rippling pools
    In cool retreats sore-wearied limbs restore,
    And tired hearts awake with joy once more.
    The way was cruel.
    Baffled by monotony and mocked by phantoms
        delirious,
    Beset by stalking Death in guises manifold;
    The dreaded Jinns, the beasts ferocious,
    The flaming heat and the exploding storms;
    From all these perils here at last set free:
    In the Garden all find security."
    Taken from an anonymous Sufi poet's *Ode to a Garden Carpet*, written about 1500.
199. The vault problem has been seriously discussed in *Survey*, vol. I, by Eric Schroeder; by André Godard in *Athar-e-Iran*, IV, 2, 1949, and *L'Art de l'Iran*, pp. 226–278; by D. N. Wilber in *Islamic*, pp. 36–61; and by the author in *Diez Festschrift*. In addition to the illustrations grouped here, refer also to plates 115–131.
200. Dr. Roman Ghirshman agrees with me on this point, which is nevertheless emphatically denied by M. Godard.
201. *Cf.* D. N. Wilber, *Islamic*, p. 59.
202. In this opinion, still so controversial, I am supported by several engineers and historians, including Kurt Weil, Walter D. Binger, Eric Schroeder, Eduard Sekler, and the late M. de Villard.
203. *Cf.* Pope in *Diez Festshrift*, esp. pp. 16, 17.
204. *Cf.* particularly Godard, "Les Voutes Iraniennes," *Athar-e-Iran*, IV, 2, 1949.
205. A soundly constructed double dome was, obviously, of great importance to European architecture and the great Renaissance domes are all subsequent to early Persian treatments. Sultaniya had lively contacts with Venice and Genoa and there were sophisticated merchants who might well have been able to transmit ideas and even accounts of structural techniques.
206. *Cf.* Browne, *op. cit.*, vol. III, pp. 505–506.
207. Ibn Khaldun, 1322–1406 A.D., one of the great historians and social analysts of the period, was born in Tunis but his career carried him through North Africa, ranging from Granada to Cairo. His greatest work, *Muqadimmah* (English translation by Rosenthal, Pantheon, 3 vols., 1958), deals with the craft of architecture. The following summaries are taken from that edition, vol. II, pp. 357–363.
208. Quoted by D. N. Wilber in *Islamic*, p. 69.
209. I owe this reference and the translation to Miss Lisa Velow of the University of Michigan.
210. *Cf.* Schroeder, *op. cit.*, p. 203.

Selected Bibliography

In addition to the specific works listed below, articles of considerable value to the developing study of Persian architecture have appeared, and continue to appear, in numerous periodicals, especially: *Archaeology; Ars Islamica; Ars Orientalis; Artibus Asiaie; Arts Asiatiques; Bulletin Monumental; The Illustrated London News; Iranica Antiqua; Syria;* and bulletins of various museums. The *Proceedings* published after each International Congress of Iranian Art and Archaeology also contain important papers.

General: Architecture

Archaeologica Orientalia in Memoriam E. Herzfeld, Locust Valley, 1952.

Arnold, Sir Thomas, *Painting in Islam,* Oxford, 1928.

Ballif, Noel and Bourdelon, Georges, *La Perse millénaire,* Paris, 1958.

Burchard, John E., "Symbolism in Architecture," *Symbols and Society,* New York, 1955, especially pp. 371–408.

Cameron, George C., *Early History of Iran,* Chicago, 1936.

Choisy, A., *Histoire de l'architecture,* 2 vols., Paris, 1929.

Costa, A. and Lockhart, L., *Persia,* New York, 1957.

Dieulafoy, M., *L'Art antique de la Perse,* 5 vols., Paris, 1884–85.

———, *La Perse, la Chaldée et la Susiane,* Paris, 1887.

Diez, Ernst, *Iranische Kunst,* Vienna, 1944.

Diez Festschrift, Istanbul, 1963.

Ferguson, James, *History of Architecture,* 4 vols., London, 1873–74.

Frye, Richard N., *The Heritage of Persia,* New York, 1963.

Ghirshman, Roman, *L'Iran, des origines à l'Islam,* Paris, 1952 (English edition, Penguin, 1954).

Godard, André, *Athar-e-Iran,* Annales du service archéologique de l'Iran, Paris, 1936–49.

———, *L'Art de l'Iran,* Paris, 1962.

Grousset, René, *L'empire des steppes,* Paris, 1939.

Herzfeld, Ernst, *Archaeological History of Iran,* London, 1935.

———, *Archaeologische Mitteilungen aus Iran,* 9 vols., Berlin, 1929–37.

———, *Iran in the Ancient East,* London, 1941.

———, *Am Tor von Asien, Felsdenkmäler aus Iran Heldenzeit,* Berlin, 1920.

———, *Iranische Denkmäler, I. Vorgeschichtliche Denkmäler,* Berlin, 1932.

LeStrange, G., *The Lands of the Eastern Caliphate,* Cambridge, 1930.

Massé, Henri, Grousset, René and others, *La Civilisation iranienne,* Paris, 1952.

Mongait, Alexander L., *Archaeology in the U.S.S.R.,* Baltimore, Penguin, 1961.

Morgan, J. de, *Mission scientifique en Perse,* vol. IV, Paris, 1896.

Perrot, Georges and Chipiez, Charles, *History of Art in Persia,* English translation, London, 1892.

Pope, Arthur Upham, ed., *A Survey of Persian Art,* 6 vols., London and New York, 1938–39. Reissue, 1964.

———, *Introduction to Persian Art,* London, 1930.

Porada, Edith, *Iran ancien,* Paris, 1962.

Sarre, F., *Die Kunst des alten Persiens,* Berlin, 1922.

Sarre, F. and Herzfeld, E., *Archaeologische Reise im Euphrat und Tigris Gebiet,* 2 vols., Berlin, 1920.

Schmidt, Eric, *Flights over the Ancient Cities of Iran,* Chicago, 1940.

7000 Years of Iranian Art (exhibition catalog), Washington, 1964.

Stein, Sir Aurel, *Archaeological Reconnaissances,* London, 1937.

———, *Detailed Report of Explorations,* Oxford, 1928.

———, *Old Routes of Western Iran,* London, 1940.

Sykes, Sir Percy, *Ten Thousand Miles in Persia,* London, 1902.

Vanden Berghe, L., *Archéologie de l'Iran ancien,* Leyden, 1959.

Wilber, Donald N., *Persian Gardens and Pavilions,* Vermont, 1962.

Wooley, Leonard C., *The Art of the Middle East,* New York, 1961.

General: Background and Travels

Afnan, S. M., *Avicenna,* London, 1958.

Arberry, A. J., ed., *The Legacy of Persia,* Oxford, 1953.

———, Classical Persian Literature, London, 1958.

———, *Shiraz,* Norman, Oklahoma, 1960.

Arnold, Thomas W., *The Preaching of Islam,* London, 1913.

Browne, E. G., *A Literary History of Persia*, 4 vols., Cambridge, 1928.

Childe, V. Gordon, *New Light on the Most Ancient East*, New York, 1934.

Clavigo, Guy Gonzales de, *Embassy to Tamerlane* (trans. by G. LeStrange), London, 1928.

Defremery, C. and Sanguinetti, B. R., trans., *Voyages d'Ibn Batoutah*, vol. II, Paris, 1854.

Efendi, Evliya, *Narrative of Travels in Europe, Asia, and Africa in the Seventeenth Century* (trans. by J. von Hammer), vol. II, London, 1850.

Elgood, Cyril, *A Medical History of Persia*, Cambridge, 1952.

Flandin, E. and Coste, P., *Voyage en Perse*, 6 vols., Paris, 1843–54.

Freygang, Wilhelm von, *Letters from the Caucasus*, London, 1823.

Grey, C., *A Narrative of Italian Travels in Persia* (trans. by the Hakluyt Society), London, 1873.

Lammens, H., *L'Islam, croyances et institutions*, London, 1926.

Langles, L., ed., *Voyages du Chevalier Chardin*, Paris, 1811.

LeStrange, G., (The geographical part of the) *Nuzhat-al-Qulub of Hamd-Allah Mustawfi*, Leyden and London, 1919.

Lethaby, W. R., *Architecture, Nature & Magic*, New York, 1956.

Lewis, B., *The Arab History*, London, 1958.

Massignon, L., Massé, H. and others, *L'Ame de l'Iran*, Paris, 1954.

Mez, Adam, *The Renaissance of Islam*, London, 1937.

Monet, A., *Histoire de l'Orient*, 2 vols., Paris, 1929–36.

Morier, J., *A Journey through Persia, Armenia, and Asia Minor*, London, 1812.

Olearius, A., *Muskowitische und persische Reyse*, Schleswig, 1654.

Olmstead, A. T. E., *History of the Persian Empire*, Chicago, 1948.

Payne, Robert, *Journey to Persia*, New York, 1952.

———, *The Splendor of Persia*, New York, 1957.

Sarton, G. F., Introduction to the *History of Science*, Baltimore, 1927.

———, *Science and Learning in the 14th Century*, New York, 1947.

Schefer, C., (trans.) *Relation du voyage de Nassiri Khosrau*, Paris, 1881.

Schroeder, Eric, *Muhammad's People*, Portland, 1955.

Sykes, Sir Percy, *History of Persia*, 2 vols., London, 4th edition, 1958.

Tavernier, J. B., *Les six voyages*, Paris, 1681.

Texier, C., *Description de l'Arménie, la Perse et la Mésopotamie*, Paris, 1830–52.

Zaehner, R. C., *The Dawn and Twilight of Zoroastrianism*, in the Putnam History of Religion series, New York, 1961.

Prehistoric through Achaemenid

Braidwood, R. J., Howe, B. and Reed, C. A., "The Iranian Pre-historic Project," *Science*, 23, June 1961.

Cameron, George C., *The Persepolis Treasury Tablets*, Chicago, 1948.

Coon, Carlton S., *Cave Explorations in Iran, 1949*, Philadelphia, 1951.

Contenau, G., *L'Archéologie de la Perse des origines à l'époque d'Alexandre*, Paris, 1931.

———, *Manuel d'archéologie orientale*, 4 vols., Paris, 1927–47.

———, *L'Art de l'Asie occidentale ancienne*, Paris and Brussels, 1928.

Eliot, T. G. and Eliot, H. W., Jr., *Excavations in Mesopotamia and Western Iran*, Peabody Museum publication, 1950.

Erdmann, Kurt, "Grieckische und Achaemenidische Plastic," *Forschungen und Fortschritte*, XXVI, 1950.

———, "Die Palasterasse von Persepolis," *Mitteilungen, Institut für Auslandsbeziehungen*, July–Dec. 1960.

Frankfort, Henri, "Achaemenian Sculpture," *American Journal of Archaeology*, L, 1946.

———, *Art and Architecture of the Ancient Orient*, Baltimore, Penguin, 1955.

Ghirshman, Roman, *Fouilles de Sialk*, 2 vols., Paris, 1933, 1939.

———, *The Art of Ancient Persia*, Paris and New York, 1964.

Herzfeld, Ernst, *Zoroaster and His World*, 2 vols., Princeton, 1947.

Huart, C. and Delaporte, L., *L'Iran antique: Elam et Perse et la civilization iranienne*, Paris, 1952.

Kent, R. G., *Old Persian Grammar*, New Haven, 1953.

McCown, D. E., "The Comparative Stratigraphy of Early Iran," *Studies in Ancient Oriental Civilization*, No. 23, Chicago, 1942.

Mémoires de la délégation en Perse, 36 vols., Paris, 1900–54.

Moortgat, Autsn, *Helas und die Kunst der Achaemeniden,* Leipzig, 1926.

Pope, Arthur Upham, "Persepolis as a Ritual City," *Archaeology,* x, June 1957.

Reuther, Oskar, *Die Ausgraben der Deutschen Ktesiphon Expedition im Winter 1928/29,* Exhibition Catalog Staatliche Museen, Berlin, n.d.

Schmidt, Erich F., *The Treasury of Persepolis,* Chicago, 1939.

———, *Persepolis,* 2 vols., Chicago, 1953, 1957.

Speiser, E. A., *Excavations at Tepe Gawra, I,* Philadelphia, 1935.

Tobler, A. J., *Excavations at Tepe Gawra, II,* Philadelphia, 1950.

Seleucid, Parthian and Sasanian

Bevan, E. R., *The House of Seleucus,* London, 1902.

Bouché-Leclercq, *Histoire des Séleucides,* 2 vols., Paris, 1913.

Christensen, Arthur, *L'Iran sous les Sassanides,* second edition, Copenhagen, 1944 (first edition, 1936).

Debevoise, N. C., *A Political History of Parthia,* Chicago, 1938.

Erdmann, Kurt, *Das iranische Feuerheiligtum,* Leipzig, 1941.

———, *Die Kunst Irans zur Zeit der Sasaniden,* Berlin, 1943.

Filliozat, J., "Les Echanges de l'Inde et de l'empire romain," *Revue Historique,* 1949.

Ghirshman, Roman, *Persian Art—The Parthian and Sassanian Dynasties,* New York, 1962.

Godard, André, "Les Monuments du feu," *Athar-e-Iran,* 1938.

Naumann, Rudolf, "Ausgrabungen auf dem Takht-i-Suleiman," *Mitteilungen Institut für Auslandsbeziehungen* (Iran number), July–Dec., 1960, pp. 211–216.

———, with von der Osten, H. H., *Takht-i-Sulaiman,* Berlin, 1961.

Schroeder, Eric, "The Iranian Mosque Form as a Survival . . . ," *Iran Society Proceedings,* I, part 8, 1938.

Wilber, Donald N., "The Parthian Structures at Takht-i-Sulayman," *Antiquity,* XII, Dec. 1938.

Wolski, J., "L'Effondrement de la domination Seleucides," *Bulletin International de l'Acadèmie Polonaise,* supplementary issue no. 5, Cracow, 1947.

Islamic

Bahrami, M., *Récherches sur les carreaux de revêtment lustre dans la céramique persane du XIIIe au XVe siècle,* Paris, 1837.

Barbier de Meynard, C. (trans.), *Dictionnaire géographique . . . de la Perse,* extracts from Mo'djem el-Bouldan de Yakout, Paris, 1861.

Baltrusaitis, Jurgen, *Etudes sur l'Art medieval en Georgie et en Arménie,* Paris, 1929.

Cohn-Wiener, Ernst, *Turan,* Berlin, 1930.

Coste, P., *Monuments modernes de la Perse,* Paris, 1867.

Creswell, K. A. C., *Early Muslim Architecture,* 2 vols., London and New York, 1932–40.

Denike, B., "Quelques monuments de bois sculptés au Turkestan Occidental," *Ars Islamica,* II, 1935.

Dieulafoy, M., *L'Eglise et la mosquée,* Paris, 1909.

Diez, Ernst, *Churasanische Baudenkmäler,* Berlin, 1918.

——— and Gluck, H., *Die Kunst der Islam,* Berlin, 1925.

———, *Die Kunst der Islamischen Volker,* Berlin, 1915.

———, *Persien, Islamische Baukunst in Churasan,* Darmstadt, 1923.

Godard, André, "Les anciennes mosquées de l'Iran," *Athar-e-Iran,* 1936.

———, *L'art de l'Iran,* Paris, 1962.

———, *Les Monuments de Maragha,* Paris, 1934.

———, "Voutes iraniennes," *Athar-e-Iran,* 1949.

Hitti, Philip K., *History of the Arabs,* 6th edition, New York, 1937.

Howorth, H. H., *History of the Mongols,* 4 vols., London, 1888.

Pedersen, J., "Masjid," in *Encyclopaedia of Islam,* vol. III, 1927.

Lansdell, H., *Russian Central Asia,* vol. II, London, 1890.

Rice, Tamara T., *The Seljuks in Asia Minor,* London, 1961.

Richmond, E. T., *Moslem Architecture,* London, 1926.

Sarre, F., *Denkmäler persischer Baukunst,* Berlin, 1901–10.

Schwartz, P., *Iran im Mittelalter,* vol. II, Leipzig, 1910.

Wilber, Donald N., *The Architecture of Islamic Persia, the Il-Khanid Period,* Princeton, 1955.

Wustenfeld, F., ed., "Yakut, Mu'jam-al-Buldan," in *Geographical Dictionary,* Leipzig, 1866–73.

Yate, C. E., *Khurasan and Sistan,* London, 1900.

Index

Sources of Illustrations

*Figures not specifically acknowledged
are photographs taken by the author.*

Archaeological Commission of Uzbekistan: 148
Berlin Museum: 34a
Cleveland Museum of Art: 208
Robert Dyson, Jr.: 4
Roman Ghirshman: 1-3, 32, 33, 41, 45, 53
André Godard: 55, 56, 68, 70, 72, 80, 136, 144, 156, 272
Hermitage Museum: 35
Ernst Herzfeld: 22
Embassy of Iran: 26, 286, 309, 317, 319
Photos by Kermani, commissioned by the Secretariat of
     Fine Arts, Teheran, for the Asia Institute, New
        York: II, III, VII, XVI, XXI, XXII, XXVIII-XXX
Peter Marks: 20, 21, 30
Musée du Louvre: 12a, 12b, 48, 49
Messter, Berlin: 214
Metropolitan Museum of Art, Rogers Fund: 66, 67,
     174, 175, 177, 213
Noorai: 15
Nyman: 91
Oriental Institute of Chicago: 19, 24, 27, 28
Philadelphia Museum of Art: 57, 64, 65
Photo Researchers: 29, 58, 334, I, XXVII
Rashti: 374
Rostami: 6, 7, 11, 16, 17, 18, 23, 26, 44, 110, 218, 265, 295
Eric Schroeder: 252, 331
Hans C. and Sonia P. Seherr-Thoss: IV-VI, VIII-XV, XVII-
     XX, XXIII-XXVI, XXXI-XXXIII
Aurel Stein: 322
Survey of Persian Art: 5, 10, 51, 52, 132, 148
U. S. S. R.: 77, 79, 277, 278
Vanden Berghe: 13, 47, 69
Wide World Photos: 166, 184
Donald Wilber: 172, 316, 341
J. C. Wilson: 188, 356